P9-DTV-356

# Springer Series: Focus on Women

## Violet Franks, PhD, Series Co-Editor
## Carole A. Rayburn, Series Co-Editor

**Susan L. Simonds, PhD**, is a clinical psychologist whose interest in the psychology of women spans 20 years. She received a PhD in clinical psychology from the Fielding Institute in 1996, a master's degree in creative arts therapy from Hahnemann University in 1981, and a bachelor of arts with distinction in Chinese language and literature from the University of Wisconsin in 1973. She is a member of the Academy of Registered Dance Therapists. She currently works in private practice and part time on the faculty of Washington State University Counseling Services in Pullman, WA. Previously, she was director of a women's counseling center in the Philadelphia suburbs, was the cofounder of the Women Therapists' Network serving eastern Pennsylvania, and the cofounder of the Palouse Chapter of the Association for Women in Psychology. As a member of the founding Board of Directors of the Women's Therapy Center of Philadelphia (formerly the Feminist Therapy Collective), she helped to establish a community-based mental health center for women. She is also the author of the book, *Bridging the Silence: Nonverbal Modalities in the Treatment of Adult Survivors of Childhood Sexual Abuse*. Dr. Simonds hosts the show, *Wellness for Women*, on KUOI FM, the radio station of the University of Idaho.

# Depression and Women

## An Integrative Treatment Approach

## Susan L. Simonds

 *Springer Publishing Company*

Springer Publishing Company, Inc.
536 Broadway
New York, NY 10012-3955

Acquisitions Editor: Sheri W. Sussman
Production Editor: Sara H. Yoo
Cover design by Susan Hauley

01 02 03 04 05 / 5 4 3 2 1

**Library of Congress Cataloging-in-Publication Data**

Simonds, Susan L.
   Depression and women : an integrative treatment approach / Susan L. Simonds.
      p. cm.
   Includes bibliographical references and index.
   ISBN 0-8261-1445-8 (hbk.)
   1. Depression in women. 2. Depression, Mental—Treatment. 3. Depression, Mental—Adjuvant treatment. 4. Women—Mental health. I. Title.
RC537 .S545 2001
616.85'27'0082—dc21                                                                 2001032251
                                                                                    CIP

Printed in the United States of America by Maple-Vail.

To Leonard—
My life partner, colleague, and friend.

And to the memory of my mother, Miriam—
A feminist, writer, and wonderful person.

# Elements Of Therapy©

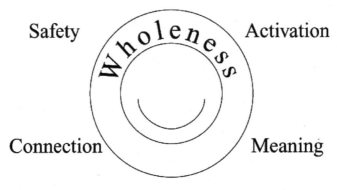

Assessment

Safety      Wholeness      Activation

Connection      Meaning

# Contents

# Acknowledgments

First and foremost, I want to thank the many clients who shared their stories and allowed me to use their struggles and successes in this book. I gratefully thank the following for their feedback on various drafts and early chapters: Nancy Corbin, Donna James, Shelly Kerr, and Cassie Nichols. The following people have been a great source of encouragement, many providing various kinds of help: Abby Cole, Linda Gallagher, Barbara Hammond, Cherie Kavanaugh, Dianne Phillips-Miller, Rosalyn Rivkin, Paula Seikel, David Simonds, Joel Simonds, Nina Simonds, Robert Simonds, Rita Sommers-Flanagan, John Sommers-Flanagan, Kathy Warren, and Jon Warren. I am especially indebted to the incredible women I have met through The Fielding Institute and want to give special mention to the Northwest Women's Retreat Group: Susan DeMattos, Donna James, Anne Leefeldt Kanters, B. J. Lyman, Benita Stiles-Smith, and Ava Stone; I want to particularly mention Donna James's many kindnesses in helping me through the final phase of this project. This book could not have been completed without the help of Suzanne Scheller, who became an efficient editorial assistant and friend. A special "thank you" goes out to Ken Clark, the master in the Washington State University Graphics Lab. My evolution as an integrative therapist owes much to the affirmative influence of Dianne Dulicai, Myra Levick, Laurie Pearlman, and Clara Sun. I greatly appreciate the support and enthusiasm of Violet Franks and Cyril Franks and want to acknowledge all the folks at Springer Publishing, particularly my wise editor, Sheri Sussman, and also Matt Fenton, Sara Yoo, and Liz Keech in the production department. Finally, I want to thank my husband, Len Burns, who helped in more ways than I can say.

# Introduction

This book was born in a moment of frustration during a meeting with a graduate student therapist whom I was supervising. We were talking about a client the trainee had just seen in therapy, a young woman who was depressed. The trainee was struggling to come up with a case conceptualization and treatment plan. She asked me the inevitable question that graduate students often ask in supervision: "Can you tell me if there is a book I can read?" After giving her a list of six books, I realized I had synthesized these readings into one comprehensive approach to psychotherapy with women who were suffering from depression. Knowing full well that most graduate students will not have the time to read six books, I decided to write one integrative book.

This book describes a model that I have been using for the past several years, which I call Integrative Relational Therapy (IRT). The model's integrationist, contextual, and relational perspective arose from my many years of viewing clients through the lens of trauma theory which, at its best, incorporates such an approach (Briere, 1989; Courtois, 1988, 1999; Herman, 1992; McCann & Pearlman, 1990; Pearlman & Saakvitne, 1995). In particular, I have been influenced by Constructivist Self-Development Theory (McCann & Pearlman, 1990; Pearlman & Saakvitne, 1995), the feminist relational writings from the Stone Center (Jordan, 1997; Jordan, Kaplan, Miller, Stiver, & Surrey, 1991; Miller, 1976; Miller & Stiver, 1997), silencing the self theory of women's depression (Jack, 1987, 1991, 1999), and research on women's adult development (Apter, 1995; Josselson, 1996).

This book builds on my previous work, *Bridging the Silence: Nonverbal Modalities in the Treatment of Adult Survivors of Childhood Sexual Abuse* (Simonds, 1994). In addition, my efforts here reflect a synthesis of 30 years of adult learning beginning with a Bachelor of Arts in Chinese language and literature, and extending to over 20 years of experience as a psychotherapist. During that time I have integrated my training in clinical psychology, dance/movement therapy and creative arts therapies, community activism, welfare rights advocacy, feminist activism, feminist therapy, and alternative therapies.

These many strands weave together the traditional/nontraditional, verbal/nonverbal, mainstream/feminist, monocultural/multicultural, and Eastern/Western therapies to form an integrative therapy approach. This model not only operationalizes a gender- and culture-aware, relational approach to psychotherapy but also integrates empirically supported therapy techniques in the treatment of depression. In short, I am presenting a truly integrative approach to psychotherapy with depressed women that has at its core the assumption that each individual holds the innate capacity for growth, healing, and self-actualization. While this idea is certainly not new for feminist therapists, multicultural therapists, and humanistic psychologists, it has only recently begun to be talked about in mainstream psychology (e.g., see Frederickson, 2000; Seligman & Csikscentmihalyi, 2000). The time is right for a truly integrative approach to psychotherapy, as a tidal wave of interest in integrative medicine is sweeping the country. In fact, the tidal wave has begun to lap at the feet of psychology as seen in the integration of Buddhist-derived practice in behavioral medicine (e.g., see Kabat-Zinn, 1990), in cognitive therapy which is incorporating mindfulness into time-limited treatment protocols (e.g., see Teasdale et al., 2000), and in the accessible work of psychotherapists writing for the so-called "popular press" (e.g., see Bennett-Goleman, 2000).

The idea of integrative healing is as old as the hills and was first passed down by the Chinese in what is believed to be the first book ever written, the *I Ching* (also called *Book of Changes*). The holistic concept of wellness as put forth in the *Book of Changes* is represented pictorially (the Chinese have a pictographic language) as the yin and yang symbol (see Figure 0.1).

**FIGURE 0.1   Yin/yang—symbol of wholeness.**

This pictogram provides an alternative paradigm for healing in contrast to psychiatry's model of psychopathology. According to the holistic paradigm, wellness is based on principles of harmony and balance. It is my hope that the growing influence of integrative medicine will bring these concepts closer to the mainstream of psychology over the next few years so that "integrative" therapy integrates east and west as well as various psychological theories. In this book, I am utilizing these concepts within the current language and framework of professional psychology. In fact, as the reader will see, the major principles of Buddhist-derived mindfulness are concordant with the major principles of a relational psychotherapy: non-judging (honoring the client's experience), attunement to the present moment (empathic attunement), patience (acceptance), beginner's mind (revisioning the self), compassion (empathy), trust (trust), non-striving (being present with one's experience), and letting go (letting go of dysfunctional schemas).

While I have made every effort to give credit to those responsible for particular ideas, I apologize if I inadvertently have failed to credit the author of a particular technique. There exists an oral history among psychotherapists, particularly among feminists, humanistic/existential therapists, wise women, and indigenous healers. This book attempts to present what has been known intuitively by those outside the mainstream within the larger framework of a scientifically driven field of clinical psychology. In other words, I am making a bridge between two worlds.

Many women clients validated my ideas through countless experiences of mutual resonance: As I listened to their stories about their lives and their depressions and what helped them get better, I heard confirmation for my approach. Simultaneously, time and time again, my clients let me know that my conceptualizations and suggestions supported their perspectives and their experiences. I have presented this material to mental health professionals as continuing education seminars in a number of forums (Simonds, 2000a, 2000b, 1999) and have found that other clinicians, from trainees to seasoned therapists, feel a deep affinity with my ideas.

One of the unique foundations of this book is the idea of creating what I call a *portable holding environment.* Psychotherapists have long been familiar with Winnicott's (1965) concept of therapy as a holding environment. Here I offer suggestions for ways that the therapist can assist the client in taking the holding environment out of the therapy office and into herself so that she has access to her own inner resources anytime, anywhere. The therapist may find it helpful to use these strategies for herself or himself, particularly in working with people in crisis.

These strategies are listed throughout the book. Some are reprinted from my previous book and some are new. Suggestions for their use will be found throughout the text, but it is left to each individual therapist to craft interventions based on the special needs of each person. I see psychotherapy as an artform and I am supplying some of the tools.

This book is organized from a user-friendly perspective, providing empirical, theoretical, and practical information. The first chapter of the book lays out the basic assumptions of Integrative Relational Therapy that flow directly from the research and theory presented in the next two literature review chapters. In an effort to organize the complexity and richness of factors and issues underlying each woman's depressive episode, I have developed a series of interlocking conceptual maps from which to understand the multiple factors contributing to a client's depression, to conceptualize the process of therapy, and to plan treatment interventions. These conceptual maps are introduced in chapter 1 and will be discussed throughout the book. Chapter 2 presents the research findings concerning gender differences in depression, epidemiology of depression, and causes of depression. Chapter 3 describes existing treatment outcome literature. Chapter 4 discusses the therapeutic relationship, focusing on special issues with women clients.

An important structural element of IRT is the conceptual map that organizes treatment themes into a nonlinear model which I call the five elements of therapy: Assessment, Safety, Activation, Connection, and Meaning. These five treatment elements are interrelated and will be addressed throughout the therapy. Chapters 5 through 11 present detailed descriptions of therapy interventions related to each of the elements of therapy. Chapter 12 describes strategies aimed at relapse prevention. Chapter 13 presents suggestions for addressing lack of client improvement. Chapter 14 discusses therapist self-care as a moral imperative. Appendix A provides integrative resources and recommended readings. Finally, the author's note at the end of the book explains the meaning of the elements of therapy "logo" which provides a visual representation of Integrative Relational Therapy.

Depression is merely a diagnostic category that describes a similarity of symptoms yet fails to explain the diversity and individuality of each client's personality, life circumstances, and life story. It is my hope that the information about women's depressions combined with the organizational structure of the five elements of therapy that I present in this book will allow each therapist and client to craft a course of recovery that weaves a common thread through the therapy while addressing the uniqueness of each client.

# CHAPTER ONE

# Integrative Relational Therapy with Depressed Women: Basic Assumptions

L ooking at the day's schedule ahead of me in my private practice, I see six unique women listed on my calendar. Two are in their 20s, three are in their 40s, and one is in her 50s. All came into therapy suffering from depression. They are from different cultural, religious, ethnic, and racial backgrounds. They are navigating different life paths and encountering different developmental markers of adulthood. One is a graduate student in her 20s, one is a graduate student in her 50s, two are professionals in human services, one is in retail sales, and one is an artist. Five are heterosexual and one is lesbian. Two are single, one is widowed, one is married, one is engaged, and one is going through a divorce. Three have children. Despite all their uniquenesses, I approach therapy with several unifying themes for the work we are doing together. This approach interweaves important assumptions from the vast knowledge about women and depression that will be discussed in the next two chapters. I call this approach Integrative Relational Therapy (IRT). The major assumptions of IRT are listed in Table 1.1. IRT offers the therapist a series of interlocking conceptual maps from which to understand the multiple factors contributing to a client's depression, to conceptualize the process of therapy, and to plan treatment interventions. This chapter discusses the theoretical foundations of IRT, while the rest of the book (with the exception of the two literature review chapters) will operationalize the theory, describing treatment interventions with case examples.

## AN INTEGRATIVE MODEL

IRT is a multimodal, integrative therapy in that it draws from interpersonal, relational, cognitive-behavioral, humanistic, psychodynamic, and

**TABLE 1.1   Integrative Relational Therapy for Depression**

Major assumptions
  An integrative model
  A relational perspective
  Identification of biopsychosocial risk factors
  Gender- and culture-awareness
  Developmental context of women's adult lives
  A model of the self
  Adaptational and relational view of symptoms
  Emphasis on strengths
  Mindfulness
  Relapse prevention
Five elements of therapy
  Assessment
  Safety
  Activation
  Connection
  Meaning
Phases of therapy
  Stabilization
  Transformation
  Future-orientation

postmodern therapy techniques. As will be discussed in chapter 3, which reviews treatment outcome studies, specific psychotherapy techniques are not capable of predicting outcome with depressed individuals (Asay & Lambert, 1999; Craighead, Craighead, & Ilardi, 1998; DeRubeis, Gelfand, Tang, & Simons, 1999; Karp & Frank, 1995; Nietzel, Russell, Hemmings, & Gretter, 1987; Robinson, Berman, & Neimeyer, 1990). Proponents of an integrationist model argue that

> Skilled therapists are constantly modifying their interventions in response to ongoing fluctuations in the patient's state. The most fruitful question to ask may thus not be "What treatment for what patient?" but rather "What specific intervention in what specific context?" (Safran & Inck, 1995, p. 427)

IRT is contextual in that the therapist chooses the treatment issues and therapy technique that most fit a given client at a given time. An integrative approach respects the individuality of each client. What works for one person may not necessarily work for another person. What works at one time in therapy with one individual may not necessarily work at another time with that person. After reviewing the range of treatment modalities for the treatment of depression, Karasu (1990) concluded,

> Instead of focusing on which single school of therapy is effective for the large universe of unipolar depression, ideally one should take a highly individualized approach to meet each depressed individual's needs, using a broad-based but selective shifting and sharing of therapeutic perspectives. (Karasu, 1990, p. 174)

IRT is a practical, contextual, integrative, and feminist model capable of addressing the needs of the wide range of diverse women who experience the heterogenous phenomenon known as unipolar depression. IRT simultaneously addresses the affective, cognitive, behavioral, and systemic issues related to depression and its recovery. In contrast to an eclectic model, IRT is based on the centrality of the therapeutic relationship and on a theoretically derived framework, which represent foundational principles of psychotherapy integration (Stricker, 1994).

## A RELATIONAL PERSPECTIVE

A relational perspective provides a guiding foundational philosophy in IRT. The primacy of relationships in women's lives has implications for personality development as well as for the therapeutic relationship.

### THE SELF DEVELOPS IN A RELATIONAL CONTEXT

Following the work of the Stone Center (Jordan, 1997; Jordan et al., 1991; Miller, 1976; Miller & Stiver, 1997), IRT holds the view that development occurs in a relational context, which has special implications for women. This perspective differs from traditional models of development that value autonomy and independence, pathologize the longing for relational connection as dependency, and fail to describe many women's normative experiences. Such traditional models were largely developed by men to describe male experiences. A relational model, which has been developed by women to describe women's experiences, values connection, interdependence, and collaboration. According to this perspective, the goal of healthy adulthood is to develop the capacity to maintain connection with others while simultaneously maintaining connection with self. Problems in living occur when there is an imbalance either through a loss of connection with others or a loss of connection with self. Depression, therefore, occurs in this relational context.

For women, the process of gender identity and sex role socialization leads to a sense of self organized around connections and relationships (Chodorow, 1978; Gilligan, 1982; Jack, 1987, 1991, 1999; Jordan, 1997; Jordan et al., 1991; Miller, 1976; Miller & Stiver, 1997). In our social structure, the primary caretakers of children are women, one of the more obvious sources of many women's attention to relationships. More subtle social influences reinforce particular sex roles, behaviors, and characteristics that are considered to be "masculine" or "feminine." Our families-of-origin combined with our sociocultural milieu provide templates of relational ways of being. For many women, these combined forces create rigid and limited relational images. Such images hold the larger culture's misogynistic values that simultaneously demean and idealize women. "Good girl," "good woman," "good mother," "good daughter," and "superwoman" are all schemas that oppress many women by limiting their relational repertoires to these moral injunctions of goodness while creating a sense of self that is hypervigilant, self-critical, and inauthentic (Jack, 1991). When relational repertoires are limited and a woman's sense of self is compromised, the result can be psychological symptoms.

## THE CLIENT-THERAPIST RELATIONSHIP IS AN IMPORTANT VEHICLE FOR CHANGE

The importance of the relational focus of women's experience extends to the process of therapy. The client-therapist relationship presents a vehicle for understanding current relational styles and learning new relational styles. Therapy provides an opportunity to examine beliefs and behaviors that women have about relationships, to examine the way others' expectations influence the client's sense of self, and to regain or strengthen connection with self.

A positive therapeutic relationship appears to mobilize change processes in therapy with depressed individuals (Ablon & Jones, 1999). Research in therapy outcome overwhelmingly supports the importance of the clinician-client relationship as related to positive outcome (Asay & Lambert, 1999; Blatt, Zuroff, Quinlan, & Pilkonis, 1996; Burns & Nolen-Hoeksema, 1992; Krupnick et al., 1996). IRT emphasizes the therapeutic relationship and the therapist qualities of acceptance and empathy, which are essential in establishing a good therapist-client relationship.

IRT stresses the importance of mutual attunement in the therapy relationship, through which the client not only experiences a positive attachment to the therapist but also experiences the therapist's empathy for her. Seeing herself through the therapist's eyes, the client has the opportunity to see herself differently, in a more accepting interpersonal context. It is through the experience of mutual empathy that the client has the opportunity to "re-vision the self" and experience her authentic self in relation, transforming negative meanings she has attributed to herself, and challenging limiting and rigid self-schemas. As will be discussed in chapters 4 and 9, processing here-and-now experience in the therapy session, a key part of the change processes in IRT, provides the client with an authentic experience of connection with herself while feeling in close connection with the therapist. Such experiences of authentic connection with self and therapist can give the client momentum to make changes that will counter depression (Ablon & Jones, 1999; Miller & Stiver, 1997).

## BIOPSYCHOSOCIAL RISK FACTORS

As will be discussed in the next chapter, research supports an interactive model of complex biopsychosocial risk factors involved in women's depressions. These risk factors are mutually influencing and reflexive. The model includes biological, life stress, sex role socialization, social, and developmental factors.

IRT stresses the complex interrelationships of biopsychosocial factors in women's lives that make each client uniquely vulnerable to depression. Hormonal and reproductive-related events alone do not appear to cause depression (McGrath, Keita, Strickland, & Russo, 1990; Sprock & Yoder, 1997; Wolk & Weissman, 1997). However, hormones and their interaction with other biochemical mechanisms, gender roles, differences in emotional expression and help-seeking behavior, cognitive styles, stress, poverty, and victimization must be considered for effective intervention (Sprock & Yoder, 1997).

A thorough assessment of a depressed woman includes asking about reproductive-related events and collaboratively unravelling the possible impact of these events on the client's current depressive symptoms. On the one hand, the clinician does not want to overpathologize the impact of events such as childbirth, premenstrual syndrome, perimenopause, and menopause. On the other hand, the therapist needs to acknowledge the potential for these events to be related to depressive symptoms, to provide the client with information about these events, to be aware of the psychosocial influences involved in such events, and to make a referral for medical or pharmacological intervention, if appropriate.

IRT recognizes that only through addressing risk factors can women decrease their vulnerability to recurrent depression. Identification of risk factors will assist client and therapist in having a realistic sense of issues and factors that impact depression, which, in turn, will lead to an understanding of the length of time that may be needed to decrease the client's vulnerability to depression, either for current or future episodes. For instance, underemployment, relationship difficulties, or poverty will need to be addressed through long-term goals that may extend the client's work on herself over several years, either with the therapist or other social supports. The therapist works with the client to find the resources she needs to address these issues over the long term. IRT does not merely focus on resolution of symptoms, but rather, on changes that increase resilience and minimize the likelihood of future episodes.

## GENDER- AND CULTURE-AWARENESS

Depression occurs within the familial, social, and cultural context of women's lives (Jack, 1991, 1999; McGrath et al., 1990; Worrell & Remer, 1992). We live in the sociocultural backdrop of women's victimization, misogyny, homophobia, ageism, and racism. Poverty, which has been called a "pathway to depression" (McGrath et al., 1990, p. xii), affects far more women than men. The conditions of a woman's life affects her moods as well as her sense of self. The therapist assists the client in examining her life situation and identifying familial, social, cultural, and economic realities that impact upon her well-being. Recognition of the realities of women's lives, including the direct and indirect results of sexism, racism, homophobia, ageism, and lower social status, help the woman client to understand that the source of her difficulties is not solely due to personal deficits, but rather, may be due, at least in part, to external realities. Using power analysis (described in chapter 6), the client and therapist will be able to identify ways that the client's self-efficacy is undermined by existing familial or sociocultural structures that place a woman in hierarchically diminished positions.

Race, ethnicity, culture, sexual orientation, socioeconomic class, or other sociocultural factors interact with gender to create a complex picture of identity issues. Core cognitive schemas interact with multicultural facets of identity, often leading to conflicts, ambivalences, and stresses. With an understanding of sociocultural issues, the therapist helps the client develop a more affirmative and integrated identity.

Gender- and culture-awareness extend to the therapy relationship. As will be discussed in more detail throughout the book, it is vital to acknowledge differences and similarities between client and therapist, particularly regarding gender and culture. Recognition of differences acknowledges the potential for power imbalances and disconnections while deepening the possibility for truly healing connections. Gender- and culture-aware therapists are constantly questioning their own assumptions about gender and culture, accepting that we are all vulnerable to the influence of the dominant culture and that being a therapist confers privilege, which in and of itself may create blind spots in our work.

## DEVELOPMENTAL CONTEXT OF WOMEN'S ADULTHOOD

Women's developmental pathway contains several key crossroads that have been called "danger points" (Apter, 1995, p. 30). At each of these crossroads girls and women face the struggle to conform to others' wishes, dreams, and roles for them while remaining true to themselves: outer pressures collide with inner visions. Each of these developmental crossroads has the potential to trigger depression. The first crossroad occurs during puberty when girls' sexual and social development thrust them into a struggle to please others as well as remain true to themselves. The second danger point occurs as girls pass into adulthood, fashioning a life away from school and family, often compromising their dreams for the sake of sustaining relationships with significant others and family. The third occurs between the ages of 25 and 40 when women are working against the ideals of marriage and motherhood to create a realistic life, often balancing needs for affiliation with needs for achievement. A fourth danger point begins when women become perimenopausal in their 40's and ends with the passage through menopause. A final crossroad occurs at around age 60 as women begin to face the loss of their own vitality and health as well as the loss of significant relationships. At this point, the losses of aging present a challenge to a woman's sense of self, as she must weather changes at multiple levels often occurring simultaneously, often taking away all that has been familiar—physically, familially, geographically, socially, and vocationally.

The therapist is a guide in navigating the vicissitudes of development. A woman must often jump outside of existing frameworks (Belenky, Clinchy, Goldberger, & Tarule, 1986) to honor her authenticity. Contemplating such a leap may elicit fear, anxiety, or immobility. A nonpathologizing model that envisions transformation as a normative lifespan development is particularly empowering and meaningful for women. Explaining the normalcy of a woman's struggle within the context of developmental crossroads can move a woman from feeling deficient or flawed to feeling hopeful and activated.

## A MODEL OF THE SELF

Recovery from depression entails reclaiming the self and often transforming aspects of the self (Jack, 1991, 1999; Lerner, 1988). The client's sense of self is one of the best predictors of outcome in therapy (Ablon & Jones, 1999; Asay & Lambert, 1999). Having a concrete model from which to understand the client's sense of self assists both client and therapist in the development of a realistic and individualized treatment plan. IRT adapts Pearlman and Saakvitne's (1995) model of aspects of the self, which draws from a number of psychological perspectives, including self psychology (Kohut, 1977), constructivism (Mahoney & Lyddon, 1988), and feminist relational theory (Jordan, 1991). "The self develops as a result of reflection, interactions with others, and reflection upon those interactions" (McCann & Pearlman, 1990, p. 17). There are three major aspects of the self (Pearlman & Saakvitne, 1995) that IRT uses in working with depressed women: frame of reference, self capacities, and core cognitive schemas. Frame of reference, which describes the client's view of herself and her world, consists of worldview, identity, and a larger sense of meaning. Self capacities are intrapersonal skills that have to do with the client's ability to manage her inner world and her emotions. Core cognitive schemas consist of basic assumptions the client has about herself, others, and the world. As mentioned previously, schemas related to "goodness" may contribute to depression. Schemas of goodness are influenced not only by family of origin but also by sex role socialization. Beliefs about being a "good" girl, woman, wife, mother, worker, and other salient roles may be discerned through core cognitive schemas. Taken together, aspects of the self and risk factors provide therapist and client with a nonpathologizing framework from which to identify strengths and areas for growth that impact the client's recovery and reliance against recurrence. The aspects of the self model is described in detail in chapter 6 and will be referred to frequently throughout the book.

## RELATIONAL AND ADAPTATIONAL VIEW OF SYMPTOMS

IRT views the client's depressive symptoms as adaptive strategies that were developed to manage feelings and thoughts. This view is particularly resonant with a feminist perspective of depression as women's response or resistance to oppressive interpersonal situations (Brown, 1994; Gilligan, 1982; Jack, 1987, 1991, 1999; Lerner, 1988). Depression may be a means to maintain important relationships at the cost of losing connection with self. The view of depression as an adaptive symptom has important implications for therapy and aids the client in withdrawing from a self-blaming or self-critical stance. Many clients have described depressive symptoms of sleeping, social withdrawal, and lethargy as escape from the stresses of their lives. In addition, sex role socialization teaches women to be passive, dependent, people-pleasing, and overly responsible for relationships, conspiring to make a woman vulnerable to depression. Examining the context in which depression became a coping strategy can be particularly fruitful with women who have recurrent depressive episodes. Viewing depression and its precursors from a perspective of adaptation paves the way for self-empathy and opens the door to new ways of coping.

## EMPHASIS ON STRENGTHS

IRT values the client's strengths and strives to identify, enhance, and increase the client's access to her strengths. By emphasizing the importance of authenticity, IRT appreciates the uniqueness of each individual person and undertakes to help each client recognize and respect the essence of who she is. The therapist helps bring forth efforts that each client has made, however small, to cope with her difficulties, highlighting the efficacy of the client's inner resources. The client is encouraged to listen to her own inner wisdom and to hear herself with greater confidence. It is the therapist's job to create an environment in which the client's strengths can shine and flourish.

## MINDFULNESS

Mindfulness, originally derived from Buddhist philosophy, is "basically a way of paying attention" (Kabat-Zinn, 1990, p. 12). The skill of mindfulness is a practical tool that will assist the individual in managing and reducing stress. Cultivating mindfulness will improve self-awareness, self-acceptance, and well-being. Mindfulness is embedded in many of the techniques and strategies described in this book.

## RELAPSE PREVENTION

The likelihood that a client will have a recurrence of depression is exceptionally high (Angst, 1986; Keller, 1985). IRT views treatment as encompassing relapse prevention as well as addressing the immediate distressing symptoms of depression. By viewing the whole person and her risk factors for depression, IRT helps the client develop resilience against future episodes. Each client will leave therapy with an individualized relapse prevention plan that will identify potential signs and symptoms of relapse and specific steps the client can take to address such symptoms. In addition, the client will be encouraged to continue to pursue life changes that will reduce risk factors that are changeable and minimize the impact of enduring risk factors.

## ELEMENTS OF THERAPY

Because each woman uniquely fashions a self and a life, the IRT approach weaves a common thread through the therapy while allowing for the individuality of each client. A map of treatment tasks incorporates pieces into a unified whole. There are five major treatment themes: Assessment, Safety, Activation, Connection, and Meaning. Because these treatment themes will not necessarily be addressed in a linear manner, and, in fact, will often be interconnected, I refer to them as *elements* of therapy rather than phases of therapy. This chapter presents a summary of the elements of therapy, which are then described in detail with specific treatment tasks and case examples in subsequent chapters.

Assessment refers to a nonpathologizing, contextual, culturally attuned, and collaborative understanding of the client and her world, which, in addition to being an important task for the therapist, will become an empowering tool for the client's own ongoing self-assessment. The treatment plan flows from assessment and is continually adjusted to address those needs revealed through ongoing assessment. Safety addresses the need to create a safe and containing environment in the therapy, for each woman to feel safe from self harm, and for each woman to strive toward safe and secure life circumstances. Activation embodies an attitude of commitment to personal empowerment and includes specific strategies to mobilize mind, body, and spirit leading to recovery and increased resilience. Connection concerns the authentic mutual connection between client and therapist in the therapy relationship, the client's connection with her own authentic self and her feelings, and authentic connection with others. Meaning refers to the transformation of meaning structures from rigid, socially prescribed, and disempowering to flexible, life-affirming, and empowering. Such meaning structures include core cognitive schemas, multiple aspects of identity, personal narratives, and the individual's larger sense of meaning.

Figure 1.1 shows the interconnectedness of the five elements of therapy and the multidimensional nature of their interrelationships.

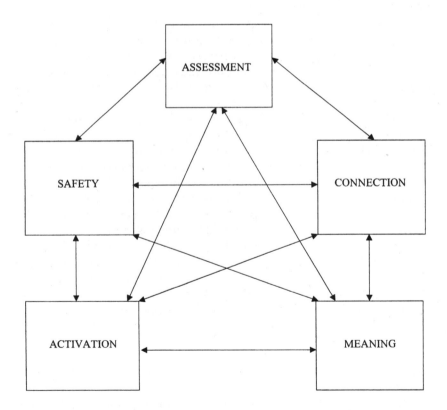

**FIGURE 1.1   Elements of therapy: A multidimensional model.**

## ASSESSMENT

Assessment gives us the information we need to understand the client and her world. The therapist is a cultural anthropologist discovering what makes each woman uniquely who she is in her own life. Assessment is the conceptual key to knowing the client, her strengths and weaknesses, the life path and experiences that have brought her to this place in her life, the developmental, familial, social, and cultural contexts of her life situation, and the people who make up her world. The more we can see the world through the client's eyes and know her language, the better we can connect with her to create a collaborative, healing relationship. In addition to leading to an understanding of who the client is and how she is, assessment leads to the development of a treatment plan, giving the therapy shape and direction.

Assessment is approached in a respectful and nonpathologizing manner. The client is viewed in terms of strengths and areas for growth. The major work of assessment is an ongoing collaborative endeavor gleaned from the client's verbal and nonverbal material. Because the therapist comes to the assessment process with a professionalized lens, the therapist is aware of the power imbalance inherent in the assessment process and strives to empower the client (DeBarona & Dutton, 1997). Some of the ways that the therapist can empower the client is through sharing information, explaining the reasons for particular types of questions, and including the client in the evaluative process.

From this aware and alert perspective the therapist evaluates whether the client is clinically depressed. The therapist recognizes that the diagnostic criteria for depressive disorders is only a description of symptoms and does not define who the client is. IRT does not treat symptoms, but rather, treats the whole person, working collaboratively with the client to define her goals for therapy. The therapist and client co-create a case conceptualization that makes sense to the client. The client develops the skills to engage in self-assessment not only to contribute to the ongoing therapy process, but also as a means to more effectively handle daily experiences and, in addition, as a tool to aid in relapse prevention. Chapters 5 and 6 give a comprehensive description of assessment in IRT that emphasizes strengths and competencies.

## SAFETY

Safety encompasses four areas: (a) a safe and facilitative therapeutic environment; (b) a safety plan for the high-risk client; (c) a zone of safety for the seriously depressed or low-functioning client; and (d) safe and secure life circumstances. The sense of safety is one that unfolds over time. As the client develops an increasing sense of feeling safe with the therapist, she feels freer to share more of herself, leading to a deeper sense of connection that may challenge long-held relational styles of keeping parts of herself out of a relationship or doubting her thoughts and feelings. When the therapist is from a more privileged background than the client (i.e., class, socioeconomics, gender, race, ethnicity, sexual orientation, and so forth), issues of safety and trust may be especially salient for the client. The therapist accepts the responsibility of establishing a facilitating and trusting relationship, recognizing that such differences may have powerful meanings for the client.

Safety is vital for the suicidal client. The therapist engages the client in a respectful and collaborative process to develop a safety plan, furthering the client's sense of comfort with the therapist and with the process of therapy.

A zone of safety for the seriously depressed or low-functioning client allows the client to take a break from the demands of daily life to focus on her recovery. Many women feel compelled to overfunction and such overfunctioning may contribute to depression. Devising a practical plan to take a temporary break from responsibilities gives the client permission to focus on herself and encourages her to take responsibility for her recovery.

IRT recognizes the need for women to live in physically safe environments, to have emotionally and physically safe relationships, and to have economic security and independence. Together client and therapist develop long-term goals that address risk factors related to safety and security, often including resources outside of therapy and extending into the future. Returning to school, moving, finding a better job, and learning money management are examples of the type of activities that may facilitate safe and secure life circumstances. Safety is discussed in chapter 7.

## ACTIVATION

Activation refers to an attitude that encompasses four areas: (a) state of mind (from passive acceptance to active commitment); (b) daily life (from uninvolved to actively engaged in daily life); (c) bodily state (from physically inert or immobilized to physically active); and (d) life goals (from passively allowing life to happen to proactively designing a life plan and solving life's problems). Activation represents empowerment for the depressed woman. As part of the assessment process, client and therapist determine to what extent the client embraced an active stance prior to her depression and if becoming activated will require skill acquisition. Restoring or developing self-efficacy is an important element in recovery from depression and in reducing risk for recurrence. In the early phase of therapy, the therapist will help the client become activated on a day-to-day basis, teaching the use of specific self care strategies that will increase self-mastery. As therapy progresses, the client will be encouraged to take an active and proactive approach to her life. The specific treatment tasks encompassing activation are discussed in chapter 8.

## CONNECTION

Connection refers to (a) a mutually empathic connection between client and therapist, (b) the client's connection with her own authentic, inner experience, and (c) healthy, authentic connections with others. An important principle of IRT is that depression results in and is caused by disconnections: a loss of connection with self or certain parts of the self and inauthentic connection with others (Jack, 1991; 1999). Efforts to maintain connection with others often result in disowning parts of the self. Familially and socioculturally influenced schemas of "goodness" reinforce the development of a false or inauthentic self who attempts to please others. The task of establishing balanced, authentic connections with self and others is one of the most important guiding principles of IRT. Through connection and reconnection the client will recover from depression and develop resilience against future recurrences. Chapters 9 and 10 describe connection and related treatment tasks and therapy interventions.

## MEANING

From the work of reconnection flows a transformation of meaning structures from negative, rigid, narrow, and fixated to positive, flexible, broadened, and receptive. As the client feels a deeper sense of connection with the therapist, she is able to bring into that relationship disowned parts of herself, thus challenging long-held relational schemas that promoted inauthenticity. As new images of relationship unfold between client and therapist, the client is activated to try out new ways of being with the significant people in her life outside of therapy. Such relational changes lead to shifts in defining meaning structures.

Together client and therapist deconstruct assumptions the client has made about herself, her roles, and her identities. The client actively chooses who she wants to be, rather than being limited by familially and/or culturally sanctioned roles and behaviors. She constructs a new narrative of her depression, one that no longer names her as the sole culprit in her life story, but one that incorporates the rich, multidimensional nature of the many factors related to her depression. "The client comes to rename experience, retell a narrative, in a way that no longer violates well-being, but rather, empowers and liberates" (Brown, 1994, p. 155). From this new narrative comes a relapse prevention plan that incorporates strategies for addressing the client's unique combination of strengths, competencies, and risk factors. To promote resilience against future depressions, IRT incorporates the concepts of positive psychology (Seligman & Csikscentmihalyi, 2000) which supports the cultivation of hope, spirituality, creativity, altruism, and other activities that broaden and build the individual's capacity for positive meaning (Frederickson, 2000). Chapter 11 describes the treatment tasks and intervention strategies related to the fifth element of therapy, meaning.

## PHASES OF THERAPY

The five elements of therapy and each of the related treatment tasks can be conceptualized to fall into three phases: (a) early phase—stabilization; (b) middle phase—transformation; and (c) late phase—future orientation.

In the stabilization phase, the emphasis is on improved functioning and decrease of distressing symptoms. In the transformation phase, the focus is on strengthening aspects of the self and reducing risk factors. In the future orientation phase, the goal is relapse prevention and planning for termination. Ongoing maintenance therapy is an option for clients with histories of recurrent or chronic depression or any client who wishes to maintain some kind of regular, ongoing therapeutic contact; maintenance may be as frequent as once a month or as infrequent as twice a year.

## HOW TO USE THIS MODEL

The elements of therapy serve as a guide to help client and therapist construct a therapy that addresses the uniqueness of each individual woman and her context while providing a common road to recovery from depression. For clients who are severely depressed, the process of therapy is likely to follow the elements of therapy in a somewhat linear fashion: from assessment, particularly of suicidal risk, to development of a safety plan, to activation, to a greater sense of connection with herself and others, to deconstructing and reconstructing the meaning of core assumptions and significant events. For many clients there will be an interweaving back and forth, with ongoing assessment, from safety (particularly in regard to feeling safe in the therapy relationship), activation, connection, and meaning, to the extent that the last four elements become intertwined in the middle and late stages of therapy and are continually mediated by assessment. The degree to which clients are interested and motivated to delve deeply into issues related to connection and meaning will be individualistic, with some clients briefly touching on these issues and others embracing the opportunity to explore their inner selves. The therapist, in listening carefully to each client, assesses the prominence of particular issues and presents the client with the choice to go down a certain road in the therapy, collaborating on the development and pursuit of particular treatment goals. In the chapters ahead, I will identify treatment goals related to each of the five elements of therapy and describe specific interventions that may be utilized to accomplish such goals. Not all treatment goals delineated within each element will be salient or relevant for each woman. The therapist acts as a guide, using professional knowledge to identify possible themes, patterns, key issues, and treatment strategies to address goals. It will be the therapist's task to attend to the client's verbal and nonverbal reactions in determining whether to pursue a certain issue, goal, or therapy intervention. The therapist takes her cues from the client and the material the client presents, empowering the client to co-create the treatment plan.

The length of treatment will be dependent on the strengths and vulnerabilities of each client in conjunction with the resources available for therapy, with length of treatment ranging from as few as 5 sessions to as many as 50 or more.

## FOR WHOM IS IRT APPROPRIATE?

As will be discussed in more detail in chapter 5, through assessment the therapist and client determine if unipolar depression is the primary diagnosis. IRT is appropriate for clients for whom unipolar depression or subsyndromal symptoms of depression is the primary diagnosis. It is also appropriate for those with comorbid symptoms of anxiety and so-called personality traits, labeled in IRT as vulnerabilities in self capacities, as described in chapter 6.

For individuals with comorbid eating disorders and substance abuse disorders, the therapist determines in the assessment process if specialized treatment for these problems should be the primary intervention, particularly when there is a health risk.

For trauma survivors who have already had trauma-based therapy and for whom depression, not posttraumatic stress disorder (PTSD), is the primary diagnosis, IRT may be appropriate owing to its emphasis on several key elements that are shared with trauma-based therapy, including safety, self-care, coping skills, and cognitive schemas. However, the therapist determines on a case-by-case basis if trauma-based therapy (Herman, 1992) is the most appropriate intervention. IRT may be especially useful for individuals who grew up in emotionally abusive family environments but did not experience discrete traumatic events.

## SUMMARY

This chapter presents an overview of IRT that is aimed at therapy with women experiencing unipolar depression or subsyndromal symptoms of depression as the primary diagnosis. IRT is based on a feminist, relational model of women's development (Gilligan, 1982; Jordan, 1997; Jordan et al., 1991; Miller, 1976; Miller & Stiver, 1997) and emphasizes the importance of a collaborative, mutually empathic therapeutic relationship. In order to meet the unique needs of each client, IRT takes an integrative approach to therapy, combining techniques from a variety of modalities. There are several interlocking conceptual maps in IRT from which therapist and client can co-create a case conceptualization. Taken together, these maps provide a multidimensional perspective on the causes of a woman's depression, encompassing biopsychosocial factors, developmental factors, personality factors, and incorporating the impact of gender, culture, and race. IRT addresses the recurrent nature of depression by developing long-term goals that reduce risk factors and increase resiliency. The course of psychotherapy interweaves five elements of therapy—assessment, safety, activation, connection, and meaning—fashioning a therapy based on the unique needs of each individual woman while sharing these common threads. The next two chapters present a review of the literature covering the epidemiology and causes of women's depressions (chapter 2) and depression treatment outcome research (chapter 3). These chapters provide the scientific context within which to understand how an integrative, relational approach to therapy makes sense for depressed women.

# CHAPTER TWO

# Why Are So Many Women Depressed?

"**I** want to know if I am depressed. I don't know why I'm feeling this way and I keep thinking I should just get a grip on myself, but nothing seems to help. I need a professional opinion. Can I make an appointment to talk to you?" Laura had gotten my name out of the Yellow Pages and had never before seen a therapist. A Caucasian woman in her late 20s who was married with three children and ran a daycare center out of her home, she was baffled by the tenacity of her symptoms during the past 6 months. As Laura and I unraveled her story, I tried to explain depression to her and to determine if she was, indeed, depressed.

What is depression? It is more than "the blues" or feeling down. Symptoms of depression fall into four areas: affective, cognitive, behavioral, and somatic—which are summarized in Table 2.1. My initial assessment of Laura revealed that she had a depressed mood, was having suicidal ideation on a daily basis, had lost interest in activities that normally gave her pleasure, was more irritable with her children, was forgetful, was exhausted all the time, and felt excessive feelings of guilt for being a bad mother. Laura met the criteria for a major depressive episode.

The treatment model presented in this book is relevant for women who are experiencing unipolar depression, including major depressive disorder (MDD), dysthymic disorder, depressive disorder not otherwise specified, and adjustment disorder. Individuals with subsyndromal symptoms of depression—that is, symptoms not numerous or severe enough to meet the criteria for a diagnosis of depression—are at risk for developing a major depressive episode and can benefit greatly from therapy. Major depressive disorder and dysthymic disorder are considered to be different subtypes of depression, but individuals with dysthymic disorder often can experience a "double depression," which is a major depressive episode superimposed on a long-standing dysthymia. Recent research suggests that dysthymia is similar to chronic major

*19*

**TABLE 2.1    Symptoms of Depression**

Affective
  Depressed mood
  Loss of interest
  Irritability
Cognitive
  Negative cognitions
  Concentration problems
  Difficulty making decisions
  Memory problems
Behavioral
  Social withdrawal
  Psychomotor retardation or agitation
Somatic
  Changes in sleep
  Changes in appetite
  Changes in energy

depression (Dunner et al., 1996). As will become evident throughout this book, depression is a very heterogeneous disorder and diagnostic labels provide limited information about a particular client and her depression.

In this chapter I will discuss the epidemiology and causes of women's depressions with particular emphasis on biopsychosocial risk factors. As I discuss clients such as Laura throughout the book, it will become clear how the therapist can integrate an understanding of risk factors into case conceptualization, treatment planning, and relapse prevention strategies. Laura is a composite of clients I have seen, as are all clients described in the book. Although I have changed identifying information to protect the confidentiality of clients, I have maintained the essence of key therapeutic encounters. Several clients have given me permission to write about specific therapy experiences that were particularly meaningful to them.

## GENDER DIFFERENCES

### INCIDENCE RATES OF DEPRESSION

Community studies of depression have consistently found that women have higher rates of depression than men, with a ratio of $2:1$ being the most frequent finding, although some studies have found ratios as high as 4 : 1 (Culbertson, 1997; McGrath et al., 1990; Wolk & Weissman, 1995). Studies consistently show no significant gender differences for prevalence rates of bipolar disorder. There is strong evidence that gender differences in rates of unipolar depression are real rather than artifactual (Wolk & Weissman, 1995).

Two major community studies provide the best estimates of rates of major depressive disorder in the United States (Wolk & Weissman, 1995), the National Institute of Mental Health (NIMH) Epidemiological Catchment Area Study (ECA) (Robins & Reiger, 1991) and the National Comorbidity Survey (Kessler et al., 1994). The ECA study was a multisite collaborative survey administered in the early 1980s to more than 18,000 participants in five urban areas in the United States. In this study, women's rates of depression were higher than men at all sites and in all age groups, with women five times as likely as men to have major depressive disorder in St. Louis and 1.9 times as likely as men in Los Angeles.

The National Comorbidity Survey was the first in the United States to use the DSM-III criteria for depression, surveying a nationally representative sample in the early 1990s (Kessler et al., 1994). This study, while still showing higher rates of depression for women, found a slightly lower sex ratio, with women 1.7 times more likely to report a lifetime episode of depression. Women's lifetime prevalence rates for a major depressive episode were 21.3%. This study concluded that homemakers had the highest prevalence rates of depression as compared with persons in other categories of employment. It also found that the approximate 2 : 1 sex ratio held for racial or ethnic groups but it appeared more prominent in African American and Hispanic women. African American males had one of the lowest prevalence rates. Other researchers, however, have questioned the accuracy of depression statistics for racial and ethnic minorities (LaFromboise, Berman, & Sohi, 1994; Sprock & Yoder, 1997; Zhang & Snowden, 1999) and elderly minorities (Iwamasa & Hilliard, 1999). One explanation for the sex ratio of 2.4 in the ECA study and 1.7 in the National Comorbidity Survey 10 years later is that men's depression rates may be increasing while women's are stabilizing (Sprock & Yoder, 1997; Wolk & Weissman, 1995).

One finding of the National Comorbidity Survey was that sex differences in depression rates emerged in early adolescence in all cohorts except the oldest cohort (those born before World War II), among whom the sex differences did not emerge until their mid-20s. "If this intercohort difference in age when the sex difference first emerges is genuine, it argues against the otherwise plausible interpretation that biological factors associated with puberty are somehow implicated in causing the sex difference to emerge" (Kessler et al., 1994, p. 23). As will be discussed below, there is great disagreement as to the role that reproductive hormones play in women's higher rates of depression.

In addition to the demographic risk factor of being female, epidemiological studies have found that those at higher risk for major depression are: (a) younger rather than older, (b) of lower socioeconomic status, (c) having a lower level of education, (d) separated or divorced, and (e) housewives (Blazer et al., 1985; Cross-National Collaborative Group, 1992; Myers et al., 1984; Sommerville, Leaf, Weissman, Blazer, & Bruce, 1989; Tennant, 1985; Weissman & Meyers, 1978).

While the major epidemiological surveys have concluded that those living in urban areas are more at risk for depression, two surveys of women in rural areas found that rural women have approximately a 40% incidence rate of major depression (Hauerstein & Boyd, 1994; Sears, Danda, & Evans, 1999), which is in sharp contrast to the typical urban prevalence rates of 13–20% (Mulder et al., 2000).

The above-listed risk factors do not represent a comprehensive list, but, rather, are based on the demographic factors that have been explored in epidemiological surveys. A broader look at the literature, as will be discussed further, shows that there are additional risk factors with complex interrelationships explaining women's high rates of depression.

Cross-national studies have found similar gender differences in developed countries including Australia, Canada, Denmark, England, France, Germany, Hong Kong, Israel, Italy, Lebanon, New Zealand, and Taiwan (Culbertson, 1997; McGrath et al., 1990; Wolk & Weissman, 1995). Gender differences in depression rates for developing countries are inconsistent. For example, studies in Africa show mixed gender depression ratios (Culbertson, 1997). One explanation for the mixed findings in developing countries is that some studies have evaluated only clinical populations that contain an overabundance of men who are more likely to be help-seeking outside friends and family than women. Another explanation is that symptoms of depression may vary according to culture. The findings are not yet conclusive in nonindustrialized countries.

In summary, women in developed countries are at high risk for depression with at least seven million women in the United States currently having a diagnosable depression (McGrath et al., 1990).

## COURSE OF DEPRESSION

The findings are mixed as to whether women have a more chronic course of depression (Kessler et al., 1994; Kornstein, 1997; Lewinsohn,

Zeiss, & Duncan, 1989). Women are more likely to have an earlier onset of depression than men (Sorenson, Rutter, & Aneshensel, 1991). During childhood, boys tend to have more depressive symptoms, but by age 13 or 14, girls are more likely than boys to be depressed (Nolen-Hoeksema & Gingus, 1994). Gender differences in depression may lessen in older age (Sprock & Yoder, 1997), although findings regarding prevalence in elderly women are contradictory (Fopma-Loy, 1988).

Although information about untreated depressions is not easy to obtain, generally, untreated episodes last six months or longer (APA, 1994) and episodes lasting more than two years are not unusual (Thornicroft & Sartorius, 1993). Depression tends to be a recurrent condition with the likelihood of a future episode increasing with each subsequent episode. Between 50 and 85% of those having a first episode will have a recurrence (Angst, 1986; Keller, 1985), with the risk of recurrence increasing with each episode and decreasing as the duration of recovery increases (Solomon et al., 2000). Those who do not fully recover from an episode and continue to experience residual subthreshold depressive symptoms may be more at risk for a more severe, relapsing, and chronic course (Judd et al., 2000). One study found that individuals currently in treatment for depression had an average of eight previous episodes (Coyne, Pepper, & Flynn, 1999).

Only recently have data begun to emerge that track depressed individuals over long periods of time. A unique 15-year follow-up study of patients who had pharmacologic treatment for depression found that 85% had a recurrence, including 58% of those who had been in remission for at least 5 years (Mueller et al., 1999). In this study, factors associated with greater recurrence included being female, having more prior episodes, never marrying, and having a longer duration of depression before intake. In another study, half of those initially diagnosed with dysthymia and 25% of those with subthreshold symptoms of depression had an episode of MDD within two years (McCullough, Klein, Shea, & Miller, 1992 as cited in Roth & Fonagy, 1996). Other factors found to be associated with relapse are: positive family history of affective disorder, poor health history, history of depression in first degree relatives, greater dissatisfaction with life roles, higher depression at entry into treatment, and younger age (Gonzalez, Lewinsohn, & Clarke, 1985). The answer to the question: "How critical is your spouse of you?" was the best predictor of relapse in a study of individuals hospitalized with unipolar depression (Hooley & Teasdale, 1989). Although the literature clearly shows that depression is a recurrent disorder, as will be discussed in chapter 3, the majority of treatment outcome studies fail to address this important issue.

## SYMPTOMS

There is some evidence that women may experience different symptoms than men. Silverstein (1999) found that female participants in the National Comorbidity Survey had more somatic symptoms, including fatigue, increased appetite, sleep disturbance, anxiety, and body aches. Increased appetite, weight gain, and hypersomnia are considered to be symptoms of atypical depression. Women have also been found to experience body dissatisfaction with a depressive disorder (Joiner, Wonderlich, Metalsky, & Schmidt, 1995). One study found that women with seasonal affective disorder (SAD), a variant of MDD, had more carbohydrate craving, greater weight increase, and greater increase in sleep as compared to men with SAD (Leibenluft, Hardin, & Rosenthal, 1995). Women are more likely to have SAD than men (Leibenluft et al., 1995; Sato, 1997). It has generally been believed that culture can influence symptoms (APA, 1994) and there is widespread belief that certain racial and ethnic groups have more somatic symptoms than psychological symptoms of depression. However, a recent review suggested that Whites and Blacks have just as many somatic complaints as Hispanic Americans and Asian Americans and assumptions about somaticization may be misleading when taken out of context (Zhang & Snowden, 1999).

Individuals experiencing depression may also concurrently have another psychiatric disorder. In the National Comorbidity Survey, 56% of those with depression had another disorder (Blazer, Kessler, McGonagle, & Swartz, 1994), with anxiety disorders, substance abuse, alcoholism, and eating disorders most commonly being comorbid with depression (Hammen, 1997). Between 5 and 6% of those individuals who have a depressive episode develop mania as a manifestation of recurrence, leading to a diagnosis of bipolar disorder (Mueller et al., 1999).

Approximately 10 to 15% of those with MDD will commit suicide (Canetto, 1995). Men are more likely to kill themselves and women are more likely to make attempts. In women, suicidal behavior is more common among young adults from economically and educationally disadvantaged backgrounds with a history of emotional and physical abuse (Canetto, 1995).

## CAUSES OF DEPRESSION

"No one theory or single theory explains gender differences in depression" (McGrath et al., 1990, p. 5), concluded the American Psychological

**TABLE 2.2   Course of Depression**

Untreated episodes of MDD typically last from 6 to 18 months.
The prevalence rate for lifetime MDD is 17% in developed countries.
Depression is a recurrent disorder.
The probability of relapse increases with each episode.
The role of stress may be less prominent in later episodes.
20% having MDD will have only one episode.
25% with subthreshold symptoms go on to have MDD.
50% of those with dysthymia go on to have MDD.
Individuals born after World War II are at higher risk.
10–15% of those with MDD commit suicide.
Over 50% with MDD have comorbid diagnoses.
5–6% of those with a first depressive episode will develop bipolar disorder.

Association's Task Force on Women and Depression. Differential rates of depression are due to multidimensional and interactive issues that are dependent on idiographic factors (Sprock & Yoder, 1997). Integrative biopsychosocial theories of depression have been espoused by a number of theorists (for example, see Staats, 1996). As Figure 2.1 shows, there are complex interrelationships among five major categories of risk factors: biological, life stress, sex role socialization, societal, and developmental. This interactive model of risk factors was adapted and expanded from Worrell and Remer (1992). For the sake of conceptual clarity, each of the five risk factors is discussed below in discrete sections. In reality, however, most factors are interrelated and involve more than one factor at a given time. For this reason, some factors will be discussed in more than one section.

## BIOLOGICAL FACTORS

In the past, it was assumed that there were two subtypes of depressions, endogenous and neurotic. Endogenous depressions were thought to be purely biologically driven, whereas neurotic depressions were thought to be related to intrapersonal and interpersonal factors. It is now believed that very few depressions are purely biological and there is general agreement that most depressions have a biopsychosocial basis (Hammen, 1997; Sullivan, Neale, & Kendler, 2000). While genetics play a role in unipolar depression, heredity is not as important a factor as it is in bipolar depression nor is it thought to explain gender differences

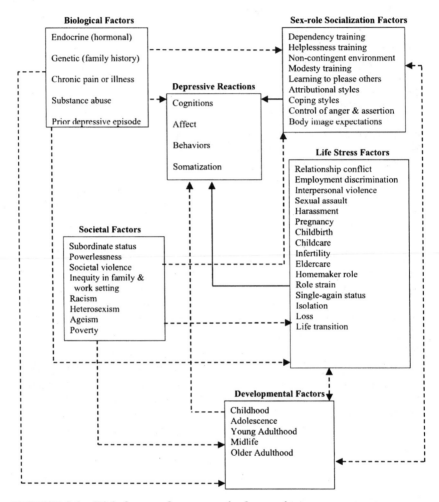

**FIGURE 2.1   Risk factors for women's depressions.**

*Note:* Adapted from Worrell & Remer, 1992.

in unipolar depression (Hammen, 1997; Sprock & Yoder, 1997; Wolk & Weissman, 1995). The authors of a recent meta-analysis of data from primary studies of the genetic epidemiology of major depression concluded: "We cannot now state with confidence that a particular person's major depression is or is not genetic in origin, much less that some percentage of the disorder is 'due to genes' " (Sullivan et al., 2000, p. 1559).

## Female Reproductive Hormones

Although hormonal differences between women and men would seem an obvious explanation for women's higher rates of depression, which begin in adolescence and decrease in older age (with the exception of the cohort born before World War II whose rates of depression do not increase until the mid-20s), the evidence is inconclusive. Reproductive-related depressions do not account for the high rate of depression in women and there is widespread disagreement as to what extent psychosocial factors contribute to most reproductive-related depressions, including premenstrual syndrome (PMS)—which is a controversial diagnosis—and postpartum depression. Recent findings suggest that some hormonal factors contribute to vulnerability or function as stressors that precipitate depression rather than directly causing depression in women (Seeman, 1997; Sprock & Yoder, 1997). It should be noted that depression experts vary in the importance they place on hormonal factors to explain gender differences in depression rates, and careful reading of the literature does not provide clear answers. All agree that a number of factors and their interaction contribute to women's higher rates of depression.

Research findings, although inconclusive, suggest that the female reproductive hormones, estradiol and progesterone, appear to influence the synthesis, metabolism, and turnover of those neurotransmitters implicated in depression, particularly norephinephrine, serotonin, dopamine, their metabolites, and precursors (Halbreich & Lumley, 1993; Hamilton, Grant, & Jensvold, 1996; Sprock & Yoder, 1997; Stewart, 1998; Wolk & Weissman, 1995; Yonkers & Bradshaw, 1999; Young & Korszun, 1998). Pharmacologic research is beginning to conclude that reproductive hormones interact with medication, resulting in gender differences in clinical responses to antidepressant medication and differential responses to medication at different points in the menstrual cycle (Hamilton & Jensvold, 1995; Jensvold, 1996; Kornstein, 1997; Raskin, 1997; Stewart, 1998). However, findings are still tentative and inconsistent.

A review of the literature concerning reproductive-related events and depression reveals a shocking lack of systematic investigation. Here I will briefly describe what is known about the depressions associated with reproductive events.

*Postpartum Depression.* The postpartum period is associated with a higher vulnerability for depression. Studies have estimated that within a few days of childbirth between 26 and 85% of new mothers experience the maternity "blues," a relatively mild syndrome that usually remits within a few days (Swendsen & Mazure, 2000). However, between 7 and 22% of new mothers develop postpartum depression with serious symptoms that meet the diagnostic criteria for a depressive episode (Llewellyn, Stowe, & Nemeroff, 1997; Swendsen & Mazure, 2000).

To date, studies have not been able to identify specific neurotransmitter irregularities that differentiate postpartum women with and without depression. The research suggests that psychosocial risk factors, including social support, stressful or adverse life events, marital instability, health problems in infants, and unwanted pregnancy, contribute to increased vulnerability for postpartum depression (Llewellyn et al., 1997; Swendsen & Mazure, 2000).

*Premenstrual Syndrome.* While at least 75% of women report minor premenstrual mood changes, studies show that only between 2 and 5% of women actually experience serious depressive symptoms similar to a major depressive episode during the late luteal phase of the menstrual cycle (APA, 1994). PMS is not an official diagnosis and the DSM–IV has listed premenstrual dysphoric disorder (formerly called late luteal phase dysphoric disorder) in Appendix A among those diagnoses proposed for further study and inclusion in the next edition of the manual. The criteria include significant affective symptoms and functional impairment during most cycles in the past year. It has been argued that there is insufficient evidence to support naming a disorder and such a diagnosis remains controversial (Caplan, McCurdy-Meyers, & Gans, 1992; Figert, 1996; Hamilton & Gallant, 1990; Parlee, 1992).

Some research has found that women with histories of recurrent major depressive disorder, bipolar I or II disorder, or a family history of these disorders may be at higher risk for premenstrual depression (APA, 1994). Studies have also found an association among premenstrual syndrome (PMS), postpartum depression, and non-reproductive-related depressive episodes (Bancroft, Rennie, & Warner, 1994; Parry, 1992; Pearlstein et al., 1990). Women with SAD have been found to have more premenstrual mood changes (Parry, 1992). However, some research suggests that different mechanisms exist for PMS and major depression (Kendler, Karkowski, Corey, & Neale, 1998).

Although biological theories abound as to the etiology of PMS, thus far, studies have failed to identify specific neurotransmitter or hormonal changes that differentiate women who have severe premenstrual symptoms from those who do not (Davis & Yonkers, 1997).

*Perimenopause and Menopause.* Menopause, which is defined as the cessation of menses for 12 consecutive months, occurs at the median age of 51. The term, "perimenopause," while not having a standardized definition, refers to the time of transition to menopause, usually 5 to 7 years with a median onset at age 47.5, during which time menses are irregular and levels of follicle-stimulating hormone are elevated on the 2nd to 4th day of the cycle (Burt, Altshuler, & Rasgon, 1998; Yonkers & Bradshaw, 1999).

Women appear to be more at risk for depressive symptoms during perimenopause than menopause (Yonkers & Bradshaw, 1999). There is some evidence to support a relationship between perimenopause-related hormonal changes and depression, but this remains controversial. Misri and Kostaras (2000) identified risk factors for perimenopausal depression:

1. A history of postpartum depression
2. A history of premenstrual dysphoric disorder
3. A history of other depressive illnesses
4. A perimenopausal period of at least 27 months
5. Surgical menopause
6. Thyroid dysfunction

Sociocultural factors are also considered to play a role in exacerbating perimenopausal symptoms (Misri & Kostaras, 2000).

There is little evidence that depressions associated with menopause (formerly called involutional melancholia) are responsible for increased rates of depression in women (Sprock & Yoder, 1997) and, in fact, the incidence of major depression in women decreases beginning in the mid-40s (Weissman et al., 1988). Some assert that while menopause may cause depressive symptoms, they are subsyndromal (Sheehy, 1998). Overall, findings are contradictory as to whether perimenopause and menopause are associated with major depression (Burt et al., 1998).

*Other Reproductive-Related Influences on Mood.* Pregnant women experience depression at the same rate as nonpregnant women. Thus, pregnancy does not increase per se the risk of depression (Klein & Essex, 1995). However, symptoms of depression and pregnancy may overlap, making depression in pregnant women sometimes challenging to diagnose.

Although infertility does not in and of itself cause depression, women who are struggling with infertility may be vulnerable to depression, and depression may play a role in infertility (Domar & Dreher, 1997). Some studies show a relationship between depressive symptoms prior to attempting to conceive and infertility. However, an inability to conceive may result in depression, affecting success in conceiving (Cooper-Hilbert, 1998; Llewellyn et al., 1997). In addition, fertility medications such as Clomid, Pergonal, and Motrodin are known to cause significant mood and anxiety symptoms (Sichel & Driscoll, 1999).

Oral contraceptives (OC) may induce mood symptoms in some women, although the findings appear mixed. While a review of empirical studies found limited support for OC-induced mood deterioration (Yonkers & Bradshaw, 1999), prescribing practitioners who specialize in women's mood disorders reported a link between depression and OCs for some women (Raskin, 1997; Sichel & Driscoll, 1999).

Overall, women having abortions are not at higher risk for depression (Russo & Dabul, 1997) and psychological responses to the event depend on a number of factors, including mental health history, the reason for the abortion, pressure to have an abortion, the developmental stage of a woman, the stage of pregnancy, and social support for the decision (McGrath et al., 1990).

In regard to the impact on mood of hormone replacement therapy (HRT) prescribed to alleviate the symptoms of perimenopause and menopause, the findings appear to be somewhat contradictory. Yonkers and Bradshaw's (1999) review of empirical studies concluded that progestins, one of the two hormones used in HRT, do not cause mood worsening. However, a report by the National Women's Health Network (2000) concluded that progesterone can cause depression, a conclusion shared by Raskin (1997) and Sichel and Driscoll (1999) who cautioned:

> In post-menopausal women, HRT can induce PMS-type symptoms that may be mistaken for depression. Estrogen and progesterone use can worsen the mood states of bipolar women to the extent that their condition may become impossible to stabilize. . . . If you have any mood history, bipolar or otherwise, you need to exercise caution in introducing HRT. (1999, pp. 25, 28)

The study of mood and menopause is a relatively new area and clearly more research is needed to understand the impact of HRT on women, particularly those who have a history of unipolar and bipolar depressions.

## Other Biological Factors

Another biological explanation for women's high rates of depression is dysregulation in the hypothalamic-pituitary-adrenal (HPA) axis (Sprock & Yoder, 1997). However, it remains unclear to what extent reproductive hormones interact and influence the HPA and stress hormones, particularly cortisol. Thyroid dysfunction is associated with depression and changes associated with the HPA during pregnancy and the postpartum may be related to thyroid problems. Other biological hypotheses for women's high rates of depression concern sex differences in several biological markers, including gender differences in sleep EEGs, cerebrospinal fluid proteins, and levels of natural killer cells (Sprock & Yoder, 1995). However, findings are inconclusive.

Several medical conditions can cause symptoms of depression including Addison's disease, AIDS, anemia, asthma, Cushing's disease, cancer, diabetes, hyperthyroidism, hypothyroidism, infectious hepatitis, influenza, mononucleosis, multiple sclerosis, rheumatoid arthritis, systemic lupus, and ulcerative colitis (Yapko, 2000). In addition, medical conditions such as heart disease, hypoglycemia, and asthma can cause anxiety-like symptoms. Thus, the responsible psychotherapist should refer all depressed individuals for a medical clearance. Of particular note is the relationship between depression and coronary heart disease (CHD) in women. CHD is the leading cause of death in women in the United States (Kuhn & Rackley, 1993). Depression is known to occur with a high rate after CHD, and recent research shows that depression is a risk factor for CHD and a predictor of poor outcome (Schwartzman & Glaus, 2000). Furthermore, those with a history of MDD have an increased risk of becoming depressed post-myocardial infarction, which increases risk of morbidity and mortality:

> Ideally, psychotherapy for depressed women should incorporate interventions designed either to reduce risk factors for CHD, such as obesity, smoking, and alcohol abuse, or to enhance health-maintenance behaviors, such as exercise and adherence to a low-fat diet, which are associated with cardiovascular health. (Schwartzman & Glaus, 2000, p. 48)

## LIFE STRESS FACTORS

The role of stress has long been suggested as a key to understanding depression for both sexes as well as explaining gender differences in depression. Those with a genetic loading for depression have a heightened susceptibility to the depressive effects of stressful life events, although heredity does not explain women's high rates of depression and stress can precipitate depressions in the absence of heritability (Kendler et al., 1995). Certain types of stressful life events have predicted onset of major depression with an odds ratio greater than 10, and the depression-inducing impact of stressful life events tends to occur quickly (Kendler et al., 1995).

One explanation for the recurrent nature of depression is the kindling hypothesis. According to the kindling hypothesis, the strength of the association between stressful life events and depressive onsets declines with increasing number of episodes. It is unspecified changes that occur during depressive episodes—either learning or brain changes—rather than stressful life events that kindle future episodes (Kendler, Thornton, & Gardner, 2000). One study found that in individuals with recurrent depressions, the association between stress and depression progressively declines through approximately nine episodes but then remains stable through future episodes (Kendler et al., 2000).

Stress-diathesis theories of depression explain depression as resulting from the individual's interpretation of stressful life events. Hopelessness depression is a stress-diathesis theory of depression whereby an attributional style interacts with negative life events to produce a particular subtype of depression with symptoms of loss of motivation, sadness, and suicidal ideation (Abramson, Metalsky, & Alloy, 1988). According to this model, internal factors (an attributional style) interact with external factors (negative life events). "While the hopelessness model does not purport to explain gender differences in depression, the increased importance women place on interpersonal relationships suggests that they may be especially vulnerable to negative life events" (Sprock & Yoder, 1997, p. 282).

The impact of stress in women's lives, therefore, has important implications for depression. It has been suggested that women's lives are more stressful than men's for several reasons:

1. more women live in poverty than men;
2. women are more likely to have lower-status jobs;
3. women experience more role strain;
4. women are more affected by other people's stress;
5. women are more often victims of violence; and
6. women are primarily the caretakers of children and the elderly (Hammen, 1997; Kendler, Kessler, Neale, Heath, & Eaves, 1993; McGrath et al., 1990; Sprock & Yoder, 1997).

As this list suggests, life stress factors combine with biological, sex role socialization, social, and developmental factors to put women at higher risk for depression. Next, I discuss several other key contributing factors related to stress and women's depression.

## The Stress of Parenting, Caretaking, and Interpersonal Relationships

Parenting and caretaking demands on women may confer an increased risk for depression. Women with young children are at high risk for depression, particularly women who do not work outside the home (Blazer et al., 1994). "The more children in the house, the more depression is reported" (McGrath et al., 1990, p. xii). The responsibility of caring for aging parents often falls to adult daughters, increasing vulnerability to depression (McGrath et al., 1990).

Women seem to be more vulnerable to the negative effects from interpersonal relationships (Sprock & Yoder, 1997). Women in unhappy marriages are three times more likely than men or single women to be depressed (McGrath et al., 1990) and the quality of marriage affects depressive symptoms more strongly for women than for men (Earle, Smith, Harris, & Longino, 1998). Some studies have found that marital difficulty is the single most common stressor in the six months prior to the onset of depression in women (Paykel et al., 1969; Sprock & Yoder, 1997).

### Victimization

Women are more likely to be victims of interpersonal violence than men, and depression has long been recognized as one of the aftereffects of interpersonal violence. Depression may be the result of neurobiological and psychological changes caused by interpersonal traumas. There is some evidence that individuals with histories of childhood physical and sexual abuse have a particular symptom picture of reversed neurovegetative depressive symptoms, including increased appetite, weight gain, and hypersomnia, suggesting unique biological processes in trauma-related depressions (Levitan et al., 1998). Depression may also be related to the biological effects of brain injury in battered women (McGrath et al., 1990).

In addition to causing particular neurobiological changes, chronic trauma or childhood victimization also impacts the individual's worldview and sense of self, increasing risk for depression, personality disorders, and other comorbid psychological symptoms. One theory that is repeatedly mentioned as linking interpersonal violence with women's depression is learned helplessness (Seligman, 1975). For example, Walker (1984) proposed a learned helplessness model as an explanation for battered women's difficulty in leaving violent partners.

In trauma survivors, depression and posttraumatic stress disorder (PTSD) have been found to be independent sequelae that interact to increase distress and dysfunction (Shalev et al., 1998). A recent study found that women who were victims of interpersonal violence had an increased risk for unemployment, reduced income, and divorce. These factors, which also happen to be risk factors for depression, increase vulnerability for future victimization, indicating the cyclical nature of victimization and associated socioeconomic factors (Byrne, Resnick, Kilpatrick, Best, & Saunders, 1999). The research suggests that having one risk factor for depression may also act as a vulnerability to produce additional risk factors.

## Gender and Stress

A review of the research of life stressors as risk factors in depression concluded that the data are limited as to whether women experience more stressors than men and the evidence is inconclusive as to whether women experience stress differently than men as a function of role expectations (Mazure, 1998). However, while inconclusive, the research highlights the likelihood of an interaction of stressors by gender in the etiology of depressive episodes.

> Recent conceptualizations on the study of gender, stress, and depression emphasize the complexity of this potential relationship due to the interaction of gender with variables such as role and the different defining developmental and socio-cultural experiences for women versus men. (Mazure, 1998, p. 299)

## SEX ROLE SOCIALIZATION FACTORS

As suggested by Mazure (1998), it is impossible to discuss the impact of life stress factors without including the influence of gender roles and sex role socialization. Certain types of stereotypically female personality traits as well as gender role socialization contribute to women's greater vulnerability to depression (Helgeson & Fritz, 1998; Jack, 1991, 1999; McGrath et al., 1990). Some studies have shown that women who have stereotypic beliefs about women's gender roles and higher scores on femininity measures have increased depression (Sayers, Baucom, & Tierney, 1993; Sanfilipo, 1994). There is some evidence that gender-related personality traits such as instrumentality are related to depression (Bromberger & Matthews, 1996a) and socially influenced stereotypical female personality traits such as passivity and dependency are conceptualized as mild manifestation of depression (McGrath et al., 1990).

Helgeson and Fritz (1998) proposed a personality theory of women's depression whereby gender socialization leads to development of the gender-related traits of communion and unmitigated communion. Communion accounts for women's superior interpersonal skills and closer relationships as compared with men and is characterized by balanced relationships that include providing support, receiving support, and having satisfying relationships. Unmitigated communion is related to psychological distress, including depressive symptoms, and is characterized by an excessive concern with others and placing others' needs before one's own. It is associated with a negative view of the self, low self-esteem, overinvolvement with others, including caretaking, imbalanced relationships, relationships as a source of self-esteem, and neglect of the self. The authors believe that unmitigated communion is likely to be rooted in environmental events and that this style of interacting can be changed. Thus, women's sex role socialization appears to be responsible for a number of risk factors, including personality style, coping style, cognitive style, attributional style, relational style, and victimization. Traditional feminine socialization conditions women to be passive and wait for fulfillment, rather than to be independent and action oriented, which are traditionally masculine attitudes (Ritter, 1993). As will be discussed further, being action-oriented may be a buffer against depression and may reduce the severity of depressive symptoms (Nolen-Hoeksema, 1987, 1990).

Certainly not all women develop a vulnerable personality style. However, the process of sex role socialization produces particularly stress-inducing beliefs for many women, such as:

I must be loved and approved of by every significant person in my life.

Other people's needs count more than my own.

It is easier to avoid than to face life's difficulties.

I need a strong person to lean on or provide for me.

I don't have control over my emotions. (Fodor, 1988; Lewis, 1994; Wolfe & Fodor, 1975).

Many women are socialized to value the ethics of care and responsibility (Gilligan, 1982), resulting in cognitive and attributional styles that are overly self-blaming and ruminative. The negative impact of a ruminative cognitive style is discussed next.

## Response Styles

According to response styles theory (Nolen-Hoeksema, 1987; Nolen-Hoeksema, Larson, & Grayson, 1999), the way a person responds to depressive symptoms will affect the duration and severity of depressive episodes. Persons with a ruminative response style tend to have longer and more severe episodes of depression, and women appear to be more likely than men to have a ruminative response style. A ruminative response style consists of cognitions and behaviors that repeatedly focus the depressed person's attention on symptoms and possible causes and consequences of symptoms. Typical ruminative response style activities are writing in a journal or repeatedly telling others about one's bad feelings. Distracting response styles consist of cognitions and behaviors that draw a person's attention away from symptoms of depression, such as engaging in activities with friends or working on a hobby that takes concentration. Distracting response styles do not include activities that are maladaptive, dangerous, or violent and are also distinct from a repressive defense style (Nolen-Hoeksema, 1990). Rumination has been found to mediate gender differences in depression rates (Butler & Nolen-Hoeksema, 1994; Nolen-Hoeksema et al., 1999; Roberts, Gilboa, & Gotlib, 1998). In other words, while women are more likely to have a ruminative coping style, men who ruminate are also at risk for longer and more severe depressions. A recent study found that rumination, chronic strain, and low mastery were more common in women and that rumination amplified the effects of low mastery and chronic strain on depressive symptoms (Nolen-Hoeksema et al., 1999).

## Relational Theories of Women's Depression

Several theories of women's depression are based on the primacy of caretaking and relationships in women's lives, which are the result of socially prescribed gender roles. Kaplan (1991b) described women's depression as due to the devaluation of the capacity to connect with others, a core principle of women's sense of self. Simultaneously, gender-based socialization leads to inhibition of anger, action, or assertiveness, and feelings of low self-esteem, including feelings of responsibility and "badness" for relational difficulties.

Lerner (1987, 1988) explained women's depression as due to self-sacrifice or "de-selfing" (Lerner, 1987, p. 201) in relationships and the concomitant loss of self-esteem. Such de-selfing is the result of familial, social, and cultural influences. De-selfing leads to difficulties with anger, either through inhibition of anger or constant anger (Lerner, 1988).

Jack (1987, 1991, 1999) developed a theory of women's depression called silencing the self theory (STST). In a study of depressed married women, she found that women experienced a loss of self or self-silencing as a result of efforts to alter the self to meet the needs of the men they love. In contrast to stress-diathesis theories of depression, which view predisposition to depression as due to stable, enduring personality traits, STST views depression as based on a reflexive model of depressive vulnerability, whereby images of relatedness are socially constructed and interact with an individual's life history, situational variables, and sociocultural contexts. Women's internalized images of relatedness are hypothesized to relate to depressive symptoms through the specific dynamics of self-silencing, loss of self, inner division, anger, and self-condemnation:

> The problem is not considered to lie in a deficit (such as ruminative coping style) or in a favored personality style (dependency-autonomy) that interacts with environmental events to create depression. Rather, the problem is considered to lie in specific forms of unequal, negative, intimate relationships as well as larger social structures that demean an individual's sense of social worth. Such specific conditions are assumed to be internalized differently (depending on personal history and social contexts) and to manifest in images of relatedness that contain moral standards, which then affect the individual's behaviors, self-evaluation, and self-esteem. (Jack, 1999, p. 232)

Expanding on Kaplan's (1991b) and Jack's (1987, 1991) theories, Stiver and Miller (1997) viewed many women's depressions as the result of disappointment in the important relationships in their lives and their inability to act in ways that will improve such relationships:

> [M]any women . . . often feel unable to act to change the situation because the important people and the whole surrounding culture do not provide the framework of thoughts and words with which they can even begin to formulate—let alone express—what they are feeling and seeking. They cannot become empowered. It is the very experience of being disempowered that contributes to lack of self-worth, a deep sense of failure and self-blame and an inability to identify and feel entitled to those things which really matter—i.e., connections in the way women are seeking them. This is, of course, the set of conditions which will inevitably lead to further immobilization and depression. (Stiver & Miller, 1997, p. 232)

The practical application of the previously discussed relational theories (Jack, 1987, 1991, 1999; Kaplan, 1991b; Lerner, 1987, 1988; Stiver &

Miller, 1997) and response style theory (Nolen-Hoeksema, 1990) are described in later chapters.

## Social Support

Although social support can be a buffer against depression (Hammen, 1997), it can also exacerbate distress for some women, particularly homemakers and low-income women (Sprock & Yoder, 1997). For example, in a sample of low income women, Belle (1982) found that social support reinforced negative behaviors such as substance abuse. For women who do not work outside the home, the emotional demands and expectations to care for others may lead to depressive symptoms. In one study of homemakers who were discharged from the hospital and recovered from an episode of major depression, the likelihood of relapse increased as the network of supportive relatives increased (Veiel, 1993). The researcher in this study theorized that upon discharge these recovered women probably appeared not to need help from supportive others and that their availability as homemakers left them no means to escape their families' demands.

While role diversification seems to be a buffer against depression, role conflicts and role transitions exacerbate stress, which can lead to depressive symptoms. Research also suggests that social ties may be detrimental for women in demanding training environments, such as medical and dental school, because relationships compete with academic and occupational pressures (McGrath et al., 1990).

## SOCIAL FACTORS

While it is often difficult to isolate social factors from life stress and sex role socialization factors, several specific social factors have important implications for women's depressions.

## Social Status

Women are likely to face lowered social status in family roles, community roles, and work roles. Despite the many gains women have made socially and economically, inequality between the sexes continues to be prevalent in our society. Worrell and Remer (1992) described a social status hypothesis of women's depression based on reinforcement deficit theory

(Lewinsohn, Youngren, & Grosscup, 1979). According to the theory, depression is related to an unfavorable ratio between positive and negative person-environment outcomes. "The low rate of positive outcomes is assumed to result in increasingly passive behavior and dysphoric mood, as the individual feels incapable of reaching personal goals and reacts with withdrawal and despair" (Worrell & Remer, 1992, p. 184).

## Family Roles

Family roles have an impact on women's risk for depression. Despite the gains of the women's movement, 80 to 90% of married women have primary responsibility for cooking, cleaning, and shopping (Galinsky & Bond, 1996). One study found that men's lower contributions to household labor were related to higher rates of depression in employed and unemployed women (Bird, 1999). Inequity in family decision making and in access to family financial resources can cause women to feel unimportant and powerless, precursors to depression.

## Work Roles

A high percentage of women report that job stress is their number one problem (Reich & Nussbaum, 1994). However, the relationship between depression and work roles for women is complex. Economic status, job satisfaction, work salience, role conflicts, and family relationships all play a role in vulnerability to depression. Women who are homemakers are at higher risk for depression, and the preponderance of the research suggests that multiple roles may insulate women from depression by moderating family stress (Sprock & Yoder, 1997). Negative job quality appears to have less impact for partnered women and women with children as compared with single women and women without children (Barnett, Marshall, & Singer, 1992). However, when women lack sufficient childcare and household help from spouses and work in psychologically demanding jobs, their health and well-being suffer (Swanson, 2000).

It has been estimated that between 40 and 90% of all women will experience sexual harassment on the job (Fitzgerald, 1993; Hamilton, Alagna, King, & Lloyd, 1987; Piotrkowski, 1998). Sexual harassment has been found to be related to physical and psychological symptoms, including depression (Piotrkowski, 1998; van Roosmalen & McDaniel,

1998). Specific gender-related job stressors such as sex discrimination and difficulties combining work and family have only recently been studied (Swanson, 2000).

Women are often subject to subtle forms of sex discrimination that do not constitute sexual harassment per se, but nevertheless, are based on gender bias or gender role stereotyping. This may include working in a predominantly male-oriented culture that does not support the demands of parenting, penalizes women for using work time to meet family demands, and fails to promote women because they are on the "mommy track." Furthermore, the existence of a gender-bound "glass ceiling" limits women's opportunities for advancement in the upper echelons, which may lead to frustration, anger, despair, and low self-worth. One study found that 60% of women had little or no opportunity for advancement (Reich & Nussbaum, 1994). Most workplaces reward competitiveness and independence, yet ignore collaboration and team-orientation, devaluing those who tend to function this way (Fletcher, 1999). The result can be that women find their contributions in the workplace ignored and undervalued, which may then lead to suppressed anger, low self-worth, or distress. The stresses of employment interact with female gender socialization, resulting in self-doubt about competence, disavowal of skills, fear of success, difficulty in resolving conflicts between family and work roles, and avoidance of competition (Stiver, 1994).

Silverstein and colleagues (Silverstein & Blumenthal, 1997; Silverstein & Lynch, 1998; Silverstein & Perlick, 1995) developed a theory of women's depression whereby limitations placed on women's achievements result in a particular subtype of depression, anxious somatic depression, which is characterized by somatic symptomatology such as appetite or sleep disturbance and fatigue. In contrast, the pure depression subtype does not include these somatic symptoms and is hypothesized to be more related to genetic factors. These researchers found that more women than men showed symptoms of anxious somatic depression, while a subtype the researchers called pure depression was equal between men and women (Silverstein, 1999). Women with anxious somatic depression had fathers who reported attitudes of male superiority and had mothers who reported emphasizing the importance of professional success but feeling that the jobs they held were not respected by others (Silverstein & Lynch, 1998).

Some research has concluded that professional women, particularly those in traditionally male-dominated professions, are at higher risk for suicide and depression (Craig & Pitts, 1968; Lloyd, 1988, as cited in McGrath et al., 1990; Walrath, Li, Hoar, Mead, & Fraumeni, 1985).

However, findings appear to be mixed. A recent study of women physicians found that depression was as common as in the general population of women and suicide attempts may be fewer (Frank & Dingle, 1999) in contrast to an earlier study which found higher rates of depression and suicide (Craig & Pitts, 1968). Another study found that 76% of women mental health practitioners had suffered from some form of depression, which is much higher than the incidence among the general population of women (Gilroy, Carroll, & Murra, 1998, cited in Carroll, Gilroy, & Murra, 1999). Yet another study of successful women professionals and managers did not find increased levels of depression and hypothesized that the impact of stress is lower under conditions of high control (Beatty, 1996).

The APA Task Force on Women and Depression (McGrath et al., 1990) concluded that the relationship between women's depression, women's education, work roles, work status, and family variables is complex and requires further research. This conclusion continues to be true 10 years later.

## Poverty

"Poverty is a pathway to depression" (McGrath, 1990, p. xii). Seventy-five percent of those living in poverty in the United States are women and children. One study found that 10% of new cases of major depression were the result of poverty (Bruce, Takeuchi, & Leaf, 1991). Other studies have found that depression is related to poverty and financial hardship (Belle, 1982; Kaplan, Roberts, Camacho, & Coyne, 1987). Some researchers have proposed an indirect path model whereby lower income is related to depression indirectly via effects on stress level and social supports; thus, it is the resulting increased subjective stress level that directly predicts depression (McGrath et al., 1990). Other demographic factors can contribute to increased risk of depression for low-income women. For example, one study found that single mothers were twice as likely than married mothers to be in financial hardship despite full-time employment and their risk of an onset of depression was double that of married mothers (Brown & Moran, 1997).

## Special Populations

Although gender differences in depression rates generally do not differ by culture, ethnic minority women, lesbians, and older women are at increased risk owing to the complexity and number of risk factors they may face. Furthermore, an understanding of the special issues of oppressed or minority groups is essential for effective case conceptualization and treatment planning.

*Ethnic Minority Women.* "Ethnic minority women are more likely than Anglo women to share a number of socioeconomic risk factors for depression, including racial/ethnic discrimination, lower educational and income levels, segregation into low-status and high stress jobs, unemployment, poor health, larger family sizes, marital dissolution, and single parenthood" (McGrath et al., 1990, p. 76). Being the member of a nondominant group can also lead to experiences of oppression and discrimination, which are risk factors (Ritter, 1993). Colonized individuals experience cultural disruption, alienation, exploitation, and victimization, placing them at risk for depression and other mental health problems (Comas-Diaz, 1994). Further, intergroup and intragroup racism can be conceptualized as stressors that contribute to poor health and psychological distress (Clark, Anderson, Clark, & Williams, 1999).

Cultural role prescriptions for some ethnic minority women may be related to depression. For example, for Asian and American Indian women, cultural norms of passivity, deference, and courtesy may lead to difficulties in self-assertion, particularly concerning issues of power, which may then lead to depression. For Hispanic and Latina women, traditional cultural expectations of passivity, manipulation, seduction, and obligation may predispose women to depression (McGrath et al., 1990). Experiences of migration for any ethnic minority group may lead to lack of social support, diminished social status, cultural conflicts, cultural adjustments, lowered self-esteem, identity confusion, and feelings of powerlessness. In understanding ethnic minority women, it is important to consider a variety of variables rather than simply identifying acculturation or cultural norms as the problem (McGrath et al., 1990).

There is some evidence that diagnostic bias may be associated with minority group status and some reviews have suggested that depressive disorders may be underdiagnosed in African Americans (Sprock & Yoder, 1997) and in American Indians (LaFromboise et al., 1994). A careful analysis of the rates of mental disorders concluded that ethnic differences in rates of depression are related to the influence of sociocultural environment, suggesting that generalizations cannot be made on the basis of racial or ethnic identity alone (Zhang & Snowden, 1999). In particular, race and ethnicity are often confounded by socioeconomic status (Sprock & Yoder, 1997).

*Lesbians.* At this time, research exploring lesbians' risk for depression is limited. The National Lesbian Health Care Survey, the most comprehensive study on U.S. lesbians to date, surveyed 1,925 lesbians in all 50 states (Bradford, Ryan, & Rothblum, 1994). Over half of the sample had thoughts about suicide at some time and 18% had attempted suicide. Eleven percent reported being currently depressed and 37% reported past depression, although the criteria used in this study was less rigorous than that used in the National Comorbidity Survey. Lesbians are considered to be at risk for alcoholism, which has been related to depression (Rothblum, 1990). In a recent review of the literature on lesbians and depression, Kerr and Emerson (in press) concluded

> It is clear that few, if any, definitive conclusions can be drawn from the literature pertaining to depression, stress, and lesbians. It seems safe to say that these mental health problems are problematic for lesbians, but one cannot say that they are more, or less, problematic than for women in general. (Kerr & Emerson, in press, p. 18)

These authors identified several risk factors and mediating variables including social support, hate crime victimization, self-esteem, relationship status, and satisfaction with relationship status. In their review, internalized homophobia and self-disclosure on sexual orientation were not as directly linked to depression, but research is quite limited regarding these factors and is particularly lacking regarding internalized homophobia.

Ethnic minority lesbians may be at risk due to additional stressors and the influence of other cultural factors (Greene, 1994; Sprock & Yoder, 1997). Depression among older women, another special population, is discussed in the next section.

## DEVELOPMENTAL FACTORS

### PRIOR DEVELOPMENTAL EXPERIENCES

There is much support for the influence of prior developmental experiences on susceptibility to adult depression, particularly for those with a childhood history of abuse, neglect, and parental loss (Bifulco & Moran, 1998; Kendler et al., 1993), as well as for those who grew up with a depressed mother (Hammen, 1997). In addition to pre-existing childhood developmental risk factors, subsequent developmental transitions and their accompanying stressors contribute to vulnerability for depression.

## ADULT DEVELOPMENTAL TRANSITIONS

Traditionally, the study of adult development has focused on men and there is a lack of systematic and integrated theory about women's adult development, particularly encompassing women of diverse sociocultural identities (Lippert, 1997). While developmental transitions vary according to individual differences and sociocultural influences, there are some general conclusions that have been made about women's identity development.

Women's developmental pathway contains five key change points beginning when girls show increased rates of depression in adolescence, and continuing to transitions at young adulthood, midlife, and older adulthood. Each of these transitions presents challenges and stresses. Depending on the unique personality, familial and social supports, life circumstances, and sociocultural contexts of each woman, failure to successfully navigate and resolve the particular issues related to a developmental transition may lead to a depressive episode or other psychological difficulties.

### Adolescence

One interactive model of women's depression theorizes that girls arrive at adolescence with more pre-existing risk factors than boys and that these risk factors interact with the biological and social changes of adolescence which then extend into adulthood (Nolen-Hoeksema & Gingus, 1994).

Another theory is that adolescence is a particular time of stress for girls due to the pressures to adopt increasingly inflexible gender roles that emphasize appearance, dependency, and passivity (Gilligan, 1982; Kaschak, 1992; Miller, 1991b). Pleasing others becomes the source of dangerous templates of perfectionism and control that may lead to increasing conflicts and tensions. At adolescence, girls undergo a kind of "psychological footbinding" (Brown & Gilligan, 1992, p. 218), as they are forced to lose connection with themselves to maintain connection with others, particularly with boys (Miller, 1991b). "Women's psychological development within patriarchal societies and male-voiced cultures is inherently traumatic" (Brown & Gilligan, 1992, p. 216).

Empirical support for the negative influence of sex role socialization on adolescent girls is beginning to emerge. For example, one study found that girls who felt overly responsible for the welfare of others and experienced difficulties being assertive in their relationships had higher levels of depressive symptomatology (Aube, Fichman, Saltaris, & Koestner, 2000). Another indicator of the negative impact of sex role socialization is body image dissatisfaction and eating disturbances, which begin to appear in girls in adolescence. Body dissatisfaction has been found to predict later major depression (Stice, Hayward, Cameron, Killen, & Taylor, 2000) and there is high comorbidity between eating disorders and depression (Lewinsohn, Striegel-Moore, & Seeley, 2000). Girls who have their first onset of depression in adolescence are at risk for recurrence in young adulthood (Rao, Hammen, & Daley, 1999).

### Young Adulthood

Young adulthood is a time of potential stress and strain for young women. It is a time when women must make significant vocational and interpersonal life choices, including decisions related to marriage and motherhood. Young mothers with children at home are at risk for depression (McGrath et al., 1990).

Epidemiological data shows that the mid to late 20s is the age of most frequent onset of depression (Mueller et al., 1999; Robins & Reiger, 1991). In the transition to adulthood, women who have had exposure to childhood adversity are more likely to become depressed following less total stress than women without such adversity (Hammen, Risha, & Daley, 2000).

The mid-20s are often the first time that a woman must face the realities of her life in comparison with the dreams and visions she mapped out in adolescence. The discovery that adulthood is not what she expected it to be can thrust a woman into confusion and despair. Facing the challenges and stresses of adulthood for the first time, she may feel unprepared and overwhelmed by the demands of adult life. These stresses make the young adult woman vulnerable to psychological distress, particularly depression.

### Midlife

In her study of 80 diverse women at midlife, Apter (1995) concluded that for women in the current midlife cohort, a midlife crisis is a normal developmental experience. While women in their 20s and 30s believed that they would not need to compromise and that with more energy and organization they would be able to fulfill their entire array of needs, aims, and obligations, this view changed in their 40s:

> As they took note of their new—really grown up—phase, they felt the panic of self-responsibility, and sought means of gaining greater control over their compromises. But to gain this, they had to see what they had compromised and what it had cost them or those they cared for most. Regrets and doubts are violent feelings, and this was often a violent time. (Apter, 1995, p. 20)

Women are vulnerable to depression not only in the initial phase of this transition, but also if they ultimately are unable to resolve their dissatisfactions. Although this crisis appears to resolve for most women as they reach their 50s (Apter, 1995) and complete the passage through menopause (Northrup, 2001), women who fall short of career goals at midlife have been found to have higher levels of depression (Carr, 1997). At midlife the incidence of major depression among women decreases (Weissman et al., 1988) and midlife depression is not related to menopause (Bromberger & Matthews, 1996b; Woods & Mitchell, 1996). At midlife, however, the incidence of dysthymia increases (Weissman et al., 1988) and little information is available to explain this phenomenon.

## Older Age

It does not appear that aging in and of itself increases the risk for depression, but, rather, it is the accompanying physical health problems, disabilities, and losses that precipitate depression (Roberts, Kaplan, Shema, & Strawbridge, 1997; Turvey, Carney, Arndt, Wallace, & Herzog, 1999). Depression during old age has been overestimated and underrecognized (Gatz, 2000). According to one review, the percentage of older adults with depression is 15% in community samples, 20% in medical outpatients, 33% in hospitalized inpatients, and 40% in nursing home residents (Blazer, 1994).

A woman's adjustment to retirement or to her partner's retirement may impact vulnerability to depression (Kim & Moen, 2000). Because women outlive men, married women often face sudden changes because of the loss of a spouse, including loss of social support, lowered economic status, and change of residence. Lesbians and cohabitating heterosexual women often face stress and discrimination due to being ineligible for a partner's medical or retirement benefits (McGrath et al., 1990). However, it should be noted that loss factors that function as risk factors in younger adults are not as strongly associated with depression in old age and the one stressor that seems to result in depression in older adults is caring for an impaired family member (Gatz, 2000).

Older women may be susceptible to two different types of depression. Those with a history of depression may be vulnerable to relapse due to stressful life events that accompany aging. Older women may also be susceptible to late onset depression, which appears to be related to brain changes and more likely to be associated with a family history of dementia rather than depression (Gatz, 2000).

Developmental phase may interact with other risk factors to influence the meaning of a particular stressful life event. For example, divorce in young adulthood may be less catastrophic than divorce in older age, particularly when the woman is not the initiator of the divorce and has limited financial resources. In addition, women who hold more stereotypically feminine views, behaviors, and personality traits may experience more negative attitudes about the physical effects of aging, making them more vulnerable to depression. On the other hand, an older woman may have more social support, maturity, and internal resources with which to handle life stresses.

## SUMMARY

In addition to having a higher incidence rate of depression, many features of depression differ for women as compared with men, including likelihood of recurrence, symptoms, and risk factors. Table 2.3 summarizes important facts about women and depression.

The literature overwhelmingly supports a multidimensional model of risk factors for women's depression with complex relationships between biological, life stress, sex role socialization, social, and developmental factors. At this time, the exact neurophysiological mechanisms underlying depression have not been pinpointed, but stress appears to play a key role in onset of depressive episodes, particularly in earlier episodes. While the traditional view of depression has supported a biopsychosocial model of risk factors, more recent research and conceptualizations have emphasized the impact of sex role socialization:

> Gender expectations clearly influence how depression is dealt with; women who adopt more stereotyped female roles experience more depres-

**TABLE 2.3   Women and Depression**

Women are twice as likely than men to have MDD.

Women are twice as likely than men to have dysthymia.

Women's lifetime prevalence rate for MDD is 21.3%.

Gender differences begin in adolescence.

Women are at higher risk for recurrences.

Women have more body image dissatisfaction and somatic symptoms.

Multiple roles act as a buffer against women's depression.

Reproductive-related depressions do not explain women's high rate of depression.

The exact role of reproductive hormones is not known.

Women's depressions are most likely due to complex interrelationships of biological, life stress, sex role socialization, social, and developmental factors.

sion. . . . Women are also likely to make more complex inferences and to engage in more ruminative self-focus which may maintain or exacerbate depression. . . . While there are a number of societal factors that contribute to women's greater risk for depression, ways of thinking and responding to the social milieu must be considered within the context of an individual's respective roles. (Sprock & Yoder, 1997, p. 283)

As will be discussed later in this book, each woman is unique in her history and predisposing risk factors. Many clients want to know why they are depressed and conceptualizing possible contributing risk factors may provide pathways to potential therapeutic strategies and approaches. By having a clear grasp of the five categories of risk factors—biological, life stress, sex role socialization, social, and developmental—the therapist can assist the depressed woman client in identifying the multiple factors that may have contributed to her current symptoms. While "the causation of depression is probabilistic, not deterministic" (Sullivan et al., 2000, p. 1559), constructing a story about the causes of a woman's depression reduces self-blame, increases self-efficacy, and facilitates solutions to life problems.

This book is based on a comprehensive, gender- and culture-sensitive, biopsychosocial model that is supported by the previously discussed literature. The five categories of risk factors contribute in a significant way to the integrative treatment model described in this book. The next chapter presents of a review of the treatment literature.

## CHAPTER THREE

# What Can We Learn from Treatment Outcome Studies?

Psychotherapists today are working within the context of a culture that aggrandizes antidepressants as the treatment of choice for depression (Antonuccio, Danton, & DeNelsky, 1995). Prozac has become such a part of our popular culture that most people, even those who should know better, take for granted that antidepressants are the best treatment for depression. The result is that myths abound concerning effective treatments. This chapter presents an overview of the treatment outcome literature not only to lay the groundwork for an integrative therapy approach, but also to provide solid information about the efficacy of psychotherapy.

Almost weekly I hear misinformation about treatment for depression from physicians, psychiatrists, psychologists, graduate students, clients, and managed care representatives. The most prevalent of these myths follow.

1. Medication is the most effective treatment for depression, particularly severe depression.
2. Cognitive behavioral therapy is the best psychotherapy approach for treating depression.
3. Short-term treatment—such as 5 to 10 sessions—should be sufficient.

As I will show in my review of treatment outcome studies, the findings not only fail to support these popular myths but there is scant research available that truly replicates real life clinical situations or that addresses the particular issues of depressed women. Nevertheless, the treatment outcome studies do provide some helpful gems of information. In this chapter, I will discuss depression treatment studies that compare various modalities of psychotherapy, psychotherapy versus pharmacotherapy, and monotherapy (psychotherapy alone or pharmacotherapy alone) versus combined therapy. I will also describe other factors besides type of therapy that have been found to be related to improvement in depressed individuals.

## COMPARISON OF THERAPY MODALITIES

A wide range of therapy modalities for treating depression have been described in the literature, and there are a number of studies reporting outcome and comparing the efficacy of various modalities. Therapies for treating depression include aerobic exercise, assertiveness training, behavioral therapy (BT), cognitive therapy (CT), cognitive behavioral therapy (CBT), electroconvulsive therapy (ECT), feminist therapy, group therapy, interpersonal therapy (IPT), marital therapy, pharmacotherapy, problem-solving therapy, psychodynamic therapy (PDT), and self-control therapy. The most studied and most mentioned are CBT and IPT, a turn of events that has been attributed to the "sociology of science" (Craighead et al., 1998, p. 228). The politics of funding favors research studies of treatment approaches that are supported by mon-eyed organizations such as the National Institute of Mental Health and drug companies. The most studied treatment approaches then become the most well known.

The most well-known depression treatment outcome study is the NIMH Treatment of Depression Collaborative Research Program (TDCRP) (Elkin et al., 1989) which played a significant role (Craighead et al., 1998) in the development of treatment guidelines for out-patients suffering from major depressive disorder (MDD; Agency for Health Care Policy and Research, 1993b). This study compared four treatment conditions during 16 weeks: CBT, IPT, pharmacotherapy using imiprimine hydrochloride (a tricyclic antidepressant) plus clinical management, and a placebo pill plus clinical management. Clinical management was a weekly 20-minute meeting to discuss medication, side effects, and the patient's clinical status. Thus, the medication condi-tion in this study actually contained psychotherapeutic elements and did not replicate medication treatment as it is typically administered in real-life situations.

Initial findings of the study were that there were no significant differ-ences among the four treatment groups (Elkin et al., 1989). A later reanalysis based on level of depression at intake found that participants with severe depression showed the most improvement in the imiprimine plus clinical management condition; when the severity criterion was based solely on depressive symptomatology, the imiprimine condition was not superior to IPT (Elkin et al., 1995). In other words, CBT was not as effective for severe depression. This study has been described as controversial due to its treatment-by-site interactions for more severely depressed and functionally impaired patients and its small number of severely depressed participants (Craighead et al., 1998). Furthermore, meta-analytic reviews and the majority of comparative studies have consistently found little to no difference in the efficacy of pharmacological treatments over psychological treatments and no difference among types of psychological treatments (for example, see Asay & Lambert, 1999; Blackburn & Moore, 1997; Craighead et al., 1998; DeRubeis et al., 1999; Karp & Frank, 1995; Nietzel et al., 1987; Robinson et al., 1990; Schulberg, Pilkonis, & Houck, 1998). In fact, a reanalysis of the NIMH study data found that CBT was just as effective as medication for severe depression (DeRubeis et al., 1999) and a subsequent study found IPT just as effective as medication for severe depression (Schulberg et al., 1998).

Although some reviews suggest that behavioral and cognitive therapies are superior to other psychotherapies (Roth & Fonagy, 1996), these exceptions have often been explained as methodological artifacts (Asay & Lambert, 1999; Lambert & Bergin, 1994). It appears that findings can be influenced by the type of statistical analysis chosen (DeRubeis et al., 1999) or by the allegiance of the researchers to a particular modality (Robinson et al., 1990).

There is currently a battle raging in the American Psychological Association between researchers who advocate manualized treatments (therapies such as CBT and IPT in step-by-step, session-by-session formats) and practitioners who advocate more flexible approaches emphasizing the therapeutic relationship (for example, see Addis, Wade, & Hatgis, 1999; Abrahamson, 1999; Godfried, 1999; Norcross, 1999). The question of how strongly to rely on manualized types of treatments or treatments supported by outcome studies is currently under debate with no hope of any immediate consensus. Complicating the matter is pressure from managed care companies for clinicians to utilize the briefest treatments, adding suspicion to treatments that may appear to collude with the managed care companies.

As a proponent of psychotherapy integration, a view supported by many who have reviewed the outcome studies (Asay & Lambert, 1999; Brems, 1995; Karasu, 1990; Nezu, Nezu, Trunzo, & McClure, 1998; Roth & Fonagy, 1996; Yapko, 2000) including the APA's Task Force on Women and Depression (McGrath et al., 1990), I take the position that not everyone can be helped by the same approach, that women and minorities have particular issues that require special attention, and that research findings can give us valuable information that we can *adapt* for use with our clients as we deem appropriate. As will become apparent in the remaining chapters, this book presents a wide range of treatment techniques, many of which are based on empirically supported therapies.

Treatment outcome studies, while providing valuable insights, cannot provide us with the magic bullet as to what works in therapy. Typically, studies exclude many people, including pregnant and postpartum women, ethnic minorities, and people with comorbid diagnoses and medical problems. Studies seldom replicate the complexity of problems and the conditions of real life clinical practice. "Efficacy of [randomized clinical trials] under research conditions does not necessarily imply effectiveness in general practice" (Biggs & Rush, 1999, p. 158). NIMH has recently recognized the shortcomings of efficacy research and is supposedly making changes in research methodologies that will be more reflective of actual practice in the community (Norquist, Lebowitz, & Hyman, 1999). For the moment, I believe we can look to treatment outcome studies to *enrich* our knowledge about what works in therapy.

## DURATION OF TREATMENT AND RECURRENCE PREVENTION

An important issue in the treatment outcome literature is the duration of treatment. Typically, treatment outcome studies of depression are short term (12 to 20 sessions) and it has been suggested that longer-term or maintenance therapy is needed to prevent recurrences. In the TDCRP, approximately 33% were considered recovered at the end of 16 weeks of treatment with no significant differences among treatment groups. Of those who recovered, approximately 20% remained recovered after 18 months with no significant differences among treatment groups (Shea et al., 1992). "The major finding of this study is that 16 weeks of these specific forms of treatment is insufficient for most patients to receive full recovery and lasting remission" (Shea et al., 1992, p. 782). Clearly, managed care companies have no interest in this outcome data!

Other studies have found that those who have residual symptoms at the end of short-term treatment are at higher risk for relapse (Thase et al., 1992) and longer psychotherapy treatment durations tend to be associated with better outcomes overall (Orlinsky, Grawe, & Parks, 1994).

Despite the findings that depression appears to be a recurrent disorder, treatment outcome research has seldom been designed to address this aspect of the disorder. In one of the few studies of maintenance psychotherapy, Frank and colleagues (1990) found that in a randomized 3-year maintenance trial of remitted individuals, the length of time before relapse increased dramatically from an average of 25 weeks between episodes to an average of 92 weeks for those treated with a monthly maintenance form of IPT (IPT-M) plus imiprimine (IMI), 83 weeks for those treated with medication clinic and IMI, and 61 weeks for those treated with IPT-M alone. Continued study of this group for 5-year outcome with maintenance medication therapy found that active IMI treatment was an effective means of preventing recurrence beyond 3 years. The effect of maintenance psychotherapy on this group was not studied (Kupfer et al., 1992).

Blackburn and Moore (1997) found that CT was just as effective as medication in acute and 2-year maintenance treatment of outpatients with recurrent depression. In another maintenance therapy study, patients over age 59 with a history of recurrent MDD who received combined treatment of nortriptyline and IPT had the lowest recurrence rate over 3 years as compared with those who received nortriptyline and medication clinic, IPT alone, placebo and IPT, and placebo and medication clinic (Reynolds et al., 1999). More research is needed to study maintenance therapies given the recurrent nature of depression.

> Nonmedication alternatives directed to prevent or minimize the probability of recurrent depression are particularly crucial given the current thinking pharmacologically is to maintain fully remitted patients up to 5 years on dosages similar to that prescribed during the acute phase. However, the long-term effects of continued medication are not well known, regarding both iatrogenic physical complications and various psychosocial consequences. (Nezu et al., 1998, p. 502)

Because many individuals are reluctant to continue medication for long periods of time and the long-term effects of taking the currently popular antidepressants, selective serotonin reuptake inhibitors (SSRIs), are not yet known, more research on maintenance psychotherapy is clearly needed.

## PSYCHOTHERAPY VERSUS PHARMACOTHERAPY

As described above, several studies have found little to no difference between psychotherapy and medication (Blackburn & Moore, 1986,

1997; DeRubeis et al., 1999; Elkin et al., 1989; Robinson et al., 1990; Schulberg et al., 1998; Simons, Murphy, Levine, & Wetzel, 1986). These studies compared psychotherapy to tricyclic antidepressants. To date, there are few published studies for the treatment of MDD comparing psychotherapy and treatment with an SSRI, the new and popular class of antidepressants. One study of individuals with chronic depression found no difference in efficacy between psychotherapy and nefazodone (Serzone) (Keller et al., 2000). This study, as discussed in more detail in the next section, did find that combined therapy was more effective than monotherapy. Another study of patients with dysthymic disorder found that there were no significant differences in efficacy between cognitive therapy and fluoxetine (Prozac) (Dunner et al., 1996). Obviously, more research is needed concerning SSRIs, particularly concerning long-term effects (Mulrow et al., 1999).

Given the current popularity of SSRIs, the question arises: Are the newer antidepressants—SSRIs—any more effective than the tricyclics? A review of more than 80 studies of newer antidepressants (SSRIs) by the Agency for Health Care Policy and Research (AHCPR) of the U.S. Department of Health and Human Services found that response rates were 50% for active treatment compared with 32% for placebo for adults with major depression (Mulrow et al., 1999). However, their efficacy and drop-out rates were similar to older antidepressants. While the 50% rate found in this study is higher than the efficacy rate in the NIMH study, it still fails to justify the popular belief that antidepressants are the solution to treating depression. AHCPR (1993a) reviewed 48 trials of psychotherapy, including cognitive therapy, behavioral therapy, interpersonal therapy, brief psychodynamic therapy, and marital therapy and estimated that the overall efficacy rate was also 50%.

A critical look at the existing research comparing psychotherapy with pharmacotherapy reveals that there are actually two kinds of outcomes, although they are rarely reported from this perspective. The first outcome is measured immediately or soon after the end of time-limited treatment conditions. In these studies, medication and psychotherapy, overall, have equal outcomes. However, when outcome is measured several months after the end of treatment (with medication tapered off at the end of the treatment condition), findings suggest that psychotherapy may have more long-term effects as compared with medication (Blackburn, Eunson, & Bishop, 1986; Fava, Grandi, Zielezny, Rafanelli, & Canestari, 1996; Simons et al., 1986). Because drug companies fund outcome studies for medication and psychotherapy lacks similarly generous funding sources, drug treatment outcome studies far outnumber psychotherapy treatment outcome studies.

## MONOTHERAPY VERSUS COMBINED THERAPY

The literature is confusing as to the efficacy of monotherapy (medication or psychotherapy alone) over combination therapy. Karp and Frank (1995) reviewed the literature on combination therapy for depression to determine if this would be of special value to women. They theorized that combination therapy would be advantageous due to women's greater psychosocial stress and increased cognitive distortions. However, they concluded that the research generally failed to find benefit for combination therapy over monotherapy. In contrast, Roth and Fonagy (1996) in a review of depression treatment outcome studies concluded that

> There is little evidence of an advantage to treatments combining pharmacotherapy and psychotherapy, though the adequacy of implementation of medications in studies examined is questionable and the study designs tend not to be comparable. . . . Nevertheless, there seems to be a consistent value added by psychotherapy to the medical regimen, although the magnitude is hard to estimate. (p. 84)

A review article by Conte, Plutchik, Wild, and Karasu (1986) found that among 17 studies, combined therapy was more effective than psychotherapy alone, pharmacotherapy alone, psychotherapy plus placebo, or pharmacotherapy plus minimal contact, but the effect was not strong.

The AHCPR report of antidepressant efficacy described previously concluded: "Data are insufficient to determine whether the combination of newer antidepressants with psychosocial therapies is more effective than antidepressants alone" (Mulrow et al., 1999, p. 59).

Since the previously described reviews appeared, there has been only one published study that compared combination therapy using an SSRI to psychotherapy alone and to pharmacotherapy alone. Keller and colleagues' (2000) large, multisite study compared nefazodone (Serzone), psychotherapy, and combined therapy for treatment of chronic depression. The psychotherapy treatment is called the cognitive behavioral analysis system of psychotherapy (McCullough, 2000), which draws on many behavioral, cognitive, and interpersonal techniques used in other forms of psychotherapy with special attention to the psychotherapeutic relationship. This study found that combined therapy was the most effective, with nefazodone producing more rapid effects than psychotherapy in the first 4 weeks of treatment, and psychotherapy showing a greater effect during the second half of the treatment trial.

> The fact that the efficacy of combined treatment and nefazodone was similar during the first four weeks of the study but that combined treatment was more efficacious later in the study suggests that when medication and psychotherapy are administered together, they continue to have independent rather than synergistic mechanisms of action. (Keller et al., 2000)

It should be noted that this study has been criticized for its researchers' affiliations with drug companies and for methodological flaws (Duncan, Miller, & Sparks, 2000b). Clearly more research is needed concerning the efficacy of combination therapy, particularly given its widespread use in clinical practice.

## COMMON FACTORS

Another direction in which researchers have gone in order to understand effective treatments is to identify so-called curative factors or common factors in psychotherapy. "Different therapies embody common factors that are curative, though not emphasized by the theory of change central to any one school" (Asay & Lambert, 1999, p. 29). The common therapeutic factors can be divided into four areas, each comprising a percentage of the total factors that influence positive outcome in therapy: client factors and extratherapeutic events (40%), relationship factors (30%), expectancy and placebo effects (15%), and technique and model factors (19%) (Lambert, 1992). I will discuss some important findings related to client factors and relationship factors extrapolated from the depression outcome research.

### CLIENT AND EXTRATHERAPEUTIC FACTORS

In psychotherapy outcome research, particular client factors have been linked with positive outcome, including length or severity of symptoms, personality, ego strength, psychological mindedness, motivation, the ability to identify a focal problem, and childhood history (Asay & Lambert, 1999). In addition, positive outcome has been linked to extratherapeutic factors including support network, marital relationship, and experiences outside of therapy. As discussed above, the emphasis in depression treatment outcome research has been on identifying the most effective treatment modality. There is some research that investigates client variables.

## Type of Symptoms

As stated, findings have been mixed as to whether a particular therapy modality is effective based on symptom severity. There is little research concerning the efficacy of particular therapy modality as related to types of depressive symptoms. One study found that individuals with atypical depression characterized by reversed neurovegetative symptoms such as hypersomnia and weight gain, did better with CBT and IPT than IMI (Sotsky, 1997, as cited in Weissman & Markowitz, 1998). This may be an important finding given that women may have more reversed neurovegetative symptoms of depression (Silverstein, 1999).

## Emotional Involvement

The degree to which a client is emotionally involved in the therapy experience was positively related to improvement in one study of CBT (Castonguay, Goldfried, Wiser, Raue, & Hayes, 1996). The authors of this study asserted that their findings support the importance of affective processes in cognitive-behavioral treatment and that emotional experiencing in cognitive therapy may facilitate change by helping clients access and modify basic meaning structures.

> It is also possible that the experience of "primary feelings" (e.g., sadness) provides information to clients about their needs (e.g., desire to be close to others) and thereby facilitates behavioral change (e.g., motivating clients to increase social contacts). (Castonguay et al., 1996, p. 497)

## Sense of Self

In one of the few process studies of depression treatment outcome research, Ablon and Jones (1999) investigated process elements of CBT and IPT in the TDCRP study. They concluded that positive outcome was not linked to modality-specific characteristics but, rather, was linked to client characteristics in both therapy modalities. Based on a Q-sort method, those items associated with positive outcome were a positive sense of self and an idealized view of the therapist.

> Patients' experiences of a sense of adequacy, effectiveness, self-assurance, trust, security, and relaxation were related to positive outcome. Improvement was also associated with patients being compliant, admiring or approving of

their therapists, desiring greater closeness with them, and accepting interventions without ambivalence or suspiciousness. This process was observed to
happen rather quickly—by the fourth session—because the process was quite
stable over the course of treatment. (Ablon & Jones, 1999, p. 72)

These researchers concluded that the process of change occurs
through a positive, dependent attachment to the therapist and that it
is this type of therapeutic relationship that can mobilize certain change
processes. More process and follow-up research is needed to identify
particular client, therapist, and therapy characteristics that are related
to a positive outcome.

## THERAPEUTIC RELATIONSHIP FACTORS

A positive therapeutic alliance has been consistently demonstrated to
be a central contributor to therapeutic progress and has been shown
to be an interaction between client and therapist, and not just a therapist
quality (Beutler, Machado, & Neufeldt, 1994). In the TDCRP, the therapeutic alliance was related to a positive outcome for both psychotherapies and active and placebo pharmacotherapy (Krupnick et al., 1996).

Blatt, Zuroff, and colleagues (1996), demonstrating how client characteristics can interact with therapeutic relationship characteristics in
the TDCRP, found that clients who, early in treatment, experienced
the therapeutic relationship as positive were more likely to complete
treatment and to show greater improvement. Therapy modality was not
related to remaining in treatment. Clients with higher pretreatment
levels of perfectionism were more likely to complete treatment but
to have less of an improvement. For those clients with low levels of
perfectionism, the therapeutic outcome was only marginally related to
the perceived quality of the therapeutic relationship, suggesting that
they use therapy relatively independent of the therapeutic relationship.
For those in the middle range of perfectionism, the quality of the
therapeutic relationship contributed substantially to the therapeutic
outcome. Those with high levels of perfectionism were not able to
benefit extensively from the treatment. They noted that the quality of
the therapeutic relationship as reported by clients after the second
treatment hour was independent of the pretreatment level of perfectionism and did not differ for the two psychotherapy modalities, "suggesting that the quality of the therapeutic relationship may be related
in part to personal aspects of the therapist" (Blatt, Zuroff, et al., 1996,
p. 169). These researchers concluded that therapeutic outcome is not

predicted by the type of treatment but by the qualities that client and the therapist bring to the therapeutic process.

There is some research that shows how particular therapist characteristics contribute to the positive therapeutic relationship. In the TDCRP study, the most effective therapists were more psychologically minded, eschewed biological interventions (medication and ECT) in their ordinary clinical practice, and expected outpatient treatment of depression to take longer than did moderately and less effective therapists (Blatt, Sanislow, Zuroff, & Pilkonis, 1996).

Burns and Nolen-Hoeksema (1992) demonstrated that therapeutic empathy had a moderate-to-large causal effect on recovery from depression in CBT treatment. Those participants with the most empathic and warmest therapists showed the most improvement. "This indicates that even in a highly technical form of therapy such as CBT, the quality of the therapeutic relationship has a substantial impact on the degree of clinical recovery" (Burns & Nolen-Hoeksema, 1992, p. 447). It has been argued that the early improvement (by the 3rd week) seen in many CBT studies is attributable to the therapeutic alliance and not to particular CB techniques (Ilardi & Craighead, 1999).

## IS A PARTICULAR TREATMENT BETTER FOR WOMEN?

As stated previously, generally, studies have found no significant differences among particular treatment conditions. Among the empirically supported therapies, there is scant information available to determine if a particular treatment approach is more effective for women. Only recently was the TDCRP data analyzed to investigate the effect of patient gender and therapist gender: Patient gender or therapist-patient gender matching was not related to outcome in that study (Zlotnick, Elkin, & Shea, 1998). This topic is discussed in more detail in chapter 4. One major difficulty in assessing whether any particular treatment approach is more effective for women is that women make up the majority of participants in treatment outcome studies (Thase, Frank, Kornstein, & Yonkers, 2000).

There are some data that suggest that IPT may be more effective than CBT for more severely depressed women due to its less structured methods and emphasis on social roles, role disputes, unresolved grief, or social deficits, and the more structured approach of CBT may require more cognitive clarity than a severely depressed woman can tolerate (Thase et al., 2000). However, there are currently insufficient data to form any far-reaching conclusions. If fact, with the exception of Thase and colleagues' article, the efficacy of treatment modality based on gender has not been addressed in the research literature. There is a small body of literature in which clinicians address the special needs of depressed women in regard to CBT and IPT, which is summarized below.

## COGNITIVE BEHAVIORAL THERAPY

### Overview of Treatment Approach

CBT is a time-limited (usually 20 sessions), active, directive, structured, psychoeducational approach based on Beck's theory of depression (Beck, Rush, Shaw, & Emery, 1980). The major underlying assumption is that a depressed person's affect and behavior are determined by the way in which she views self, the world, and the future. Another important assumption is that cognitions can be self-monitored by the client and communicated. A third major assumption is that modification of these cognitions will lead to changes in behavior and affect. Key elements in the therapy are a weekly activity schedule, graded task assignments, identifying, monitoring, and challenging dysfunctional automatic thoughts, and problem solving. The process of CBT is often viewed as "collaborative empiricism," with the therapist and client working together to disconfirm core depressive beliefs. The therapist behaves in a teacher-like manner by coaching the client to recognize and alter dysfunctional patterns of thinking and behavior.

### CBT and Women

According to the CBT approach, depressed women generally assume excessive responsibility for negative life events, overestimate their responsibility in relationships, and underestimate their ability to affect important outcomes (Beck & Greenberg, 1974; McGrath et al., 1990). Worrell and Remer (1992) developed a modified CBT approach for working with depressed women that includes feminist strategies such as sex-role analysis, power analysis, and assertiveness training. The APA Task Force on Women and Depression (McGrath et al., 1990) generally supported the use of CBT with depressed women and therapies that focus on action, mastery, and distraction from depressed rumination. It described CBT as (a) an approach that can address cultural influences and gender role stereotypes that contribute to distorted cognitions, (b) a means to regain a sense of mastery over depression by learning to control cognitions, and (c) a method to regain a sense of power by learning to minimize unpleasant activities. An update to the APA Task Force Report (Sprock & Yoder, 1997) endorsed cognitive therapies that teach more adaptive methods of coping and problem solving and challenge maladaptive, negative cognitions. Lewis (1994) endorsed CBT as having a number of advantages for women of color:

> CBT can be utilized to facilitate a woman's coping and her ability to take action in discriminatory situations. Crucial to this process is strengthening a woman's ability to encounter internalization of negative messages from the external world. (p. 231)

Stoppard (1989) cautioned that CBT is inadequate in addressing the issues of depressed women when their negative cognitions are interpreted to be the result of distorted negative processes or dysfunctional attitudes rather than exploring the possibility that negative cognitions may reflect a negative reality. The risk of victim-blaming may be reduced by including information about the person's environment and including sex role and power analysis.

## INTERPERSONAL THERAPY

### Overview of Treatment Approach

IPT is a time-limited (usually 12 to 20 sessions), manualized treatment based on the interpersonal theories of Meyer (1957) and Sullivan (1953), which draw from psychodynamic therapy techniques. IPT is based on linking depression with interpersonal functioning. For clinical purposes, the causality of depressive episodes is irrelevant (Klerman, Weissman, Rounsaville, & Chevron, 1984; Markowitz & Weissman, 1995; Weissman & Markowitz, 1994). The IPT therapist takes a directive, active stance, providing encouragement, exploring options, and offering directive suggestions. IPT stays in the here-and-now, rather than exploring the past, and focuses on feelings surrounding interpersonal situations rather than cognitions as in CBT. The goal is to develop more effective ways of interacting. Specific techniques are reassurance, clarification, improving communication, testing perception and performance through interpersonal contact, and decision analysis, which is helping clients explore different possibilities and their consequences. IPT has three phases. The first phase (one to three sessions) consists of diagnosing depression, eliciting an interpersonal inventory, establishing the interpersonal problem area, developing a treatment plan, giving the client the "sick role," and making an interpersonal formulation of the individual's depressive episode. The second phase focuses on one of four interpersonal problem areas: grief, role disputes, role transitions, or interpersonal deficits. In the final phase, treatment gains are summarized, stressing the client's role in achieving such gains, and preventative measures for the future are discussed.

## IPT and Women

According to McGrath et al. (1990), IPT may have particular relevance for women because it teaches the use of a potential repertoire of relational talents that many women already possess. The APA's Web page on women and depression recommends IPT for women of color due to the importance of close relationships in their lives (APA, 2000). Thus far, research with individuals of color and IPT is limited (Rossello & Bernal, 1999). McGrath and colleagues (1990) recommended that therapists treating depressed women become aware of the utility of IPT and how to practice it with the caveat that "an examination of the relation between societal expectations and women's depression may be an important adjunct to IPT" (McGrath et al., 1990, p. 57). An additional strength of IPT is that its effectiveness in increasing time until recurrence of depression (Frank et al., 1990) suggests it may be an appropriate treatment for pregnant women and nursing mothers who do not want to take antidepressants (Weissman & Markowitz, 1998).

## WOMEN'S EXPERIENCES OF RECOVERY

Seldom have researchers asked participants what was most significant or most helpful in their recovery. Two qualitative studies attempted to identify the process of depressed women's recovery by asking them to share their experiences. Schreiber's (1996) study of 21 women who had recovered from depression described a process the author called "(re)defining myself" (p. 469) consisting of six phases: my self before, seeing the abyss, telling my story, seeking understanding, clueing in, and seeing with clarity. The author concluded that the results of the study supported Stiver and Miller's (1997) view that women's depression is the result of unacknowledged and mourned losses women experience throughout their lives and also reinforced Jack's (1991) relational view of women's depression. Clueing in, a process that translates insight into action, was identified by the participants as vital in their recovery. In this phase the women experienced both cognitive and emotional knowing, examining information about themselves and the world, resulting in (re)inventing her self and discarding the "not me," which for many meant giving up the "good girl" role and having needs of their own. During this phase, the women's view of themselves and their worlds shifted. The women who were most recovered spoke about becoming whole by "owning the missing parts of my self" (Schreiber, 1996, p. 485). All the women in the study expressed a belief that they were now better at understanding compassion and could appreciate that people, including themselves, were vulnerable and flawed. The study does not specify how many of the women had any kind of treatment for their depression.

Peden (1991) interviewed seven women who had at some time in the past been hospitalized for depression and considered themselves to be recovering from depression. The women experienced recovery as dynamic, nonlinear, moving back and forth between categories and phases. The first phase was labeled the "turning point" during which the women began the process of recovery and which was for many of the women involved a crisis such as a suicide attempt. Recovery proceeded through the women's crucial decision to work on herself. Occurring simultaneously with the turning point was the availability of professional support, including inpatient and outpatient services. For all the women, there was the identification of a particular mental health professional with whom there was a "fit," a new experience despite previous interactions with mental health professionals. The second phase consisted of four categories that did not have any particular order of occurrence: determination (to get well), work over time, support of friends and family, and successes. Phase three consisted of two categories: Self-esteem, which occurred as a result of gains in the prior phase; and maintaining balance which was related to the struggle to maintain a positive sense of self-esteem and a reduction in negative thoughts. The author described each woman's commitment to recovery as key to the process.

In a research project designed to understand women's experiences of psychotherapy, Lott (1999) surveyed 274 women and interviewed 120. Part of her motivation for the project was that she had found little in the literature describing how actual clients felt about their therapy experiences. In her study, she found a disparity between what actual clients were saying about their therapy experiences, good and bad, and what therapy outcome researchers have been touting as the most effective therapies:

When I look at the slew of outcome studies that have been published over the past few years, studies that, for example, find ten or fifteen sessions on a specific cognitive behavioral regimen effective in the treatment of "clinical depression," I'm not sure how widely these findings apply. The subjects studied, with their single diagnoses, scarcely resemble the complex women of my interviews. Would these women, who may be more representative of those who seek psychotherapy in the real world, fare as well? In the long term, do the patients in those outcome studies consider themselves cured or happy, able to go on, and have more satisfying lives? Or have they simply, perhaps temporarily, learned to define "successful treatment" in their practitioner's terms? Are ten or twelve or even fifteen sessions, conveniently the number of sessions for which providers are willing to pay, enough to change deeply ingrained psychological patterns that are tied to the soul-suffering that the women in my book reported? (Lott, 1999, pp. 285–286)

After combing the available literature about women and depression, I concur with Lott (1999) that the voices of real women clients are largely missing. Until empirically supported therapies integrate the realities of real life clients with real life clinical situations, we can only take their applicability to our women clients with a grain of salt. However, we can look to this body of data as a resource from which to make informed choices about what we as therapists do in therapy.

## SUMMARY

Taken together, the outcome research highlights the importance of the therapeutic alliance and suggests the need for longer-term treatments to prevent recurrences. Table 3.1 summarizes important findings (or lack of findings) of depression treatment outcome studies.

Despite the large body of empirically supported therapies for depression, the particular needs and issues of depressed women have not been a focus for researchers. In 1990, the APA Task Force (McGrath et al., 1990), made a number of recommendations for research to further knowledge about therapies with depressed women that appear not to have been heeded. Ten years later, the Task Force's recommendations regarding treatment interventions remain relevant. I have summarized the most important points from the report in Table 3.2.

In the remaining chapters of the book, I will describe Integrative Relational Therapy (IRT), which incorporates these recommendations. The next chapter discusses special issues with women clients and the therapeutic relationship, one of the important variables in depression treatment outcome.

TABLE 3.1  **Findings of Depression Treatment Outcome Studies**

1. Psychotherapy is more effective than no therapy.
2. CBT and IPT are the most studied psychotherapies.
3. Studies have shown there is little or no difference between CBT and IPT.
4. Studies have shown there is no difference between psychotherapy and pharmacotherapy, although psychotherapy may have more long-term effects.
5. Findings are mixed as to whether combination therapy (antidepressants and psychotherapy) is more effective than monotherapy.
6. There is a lack of research comparing combination therapy utilizing SSRIs and monotherapy.
7. Longer treatment is most effective.
8. Client factors and therapeutic relationship factors have been related to positive outcome.
9. There have been few studies on the efficacy of psychological treatments to prevent recurrences.
10. There is little data available to determine if one treatment approach is more effective than another for women.

TABLE 3.2  **Summarized Recommendations of the APA Task Force on Women and Depression (McGrath et al., 1990)**

All therapists working with depressed women must be knowledgeable about
1. Women's risk factors and treatments of the depressions.
2. The psychology of women and gender differences in the etiology and treatment of depression.
3. The realities of depressed women clients' lives, including those associated with membership in specific cultural, ethnic, racial, social, and other special populations.
4. Women's special needs.
5. Women's different modes of expressing depression.
6. Psychopharmacologic treatments and their side effects.
7. Gender- and culture-aware treatment strategies.
8. Gender role analysis.
9. Action and mastery elements of psychotherapy.
10. The relation between societal expectations and women's depression.
11. Conceptual and practical eclecticism, when necessary, to meet the unique needs of individual clients.

# The Therapeutic Relationship and Special Issues with Women

Several years ago an acquaintance met me for coffee to talk about his interest in becoming a psychotherapist. He was in his early 40s and thinking about a career change. By the time we sat down at our table with our lattes, he had annoyed me so much that I was not inclined to encourage him in this new career direction. What he had said that annoyed me so much was that doing therapy seemed like it would be really easy, because all you do is "just sit there and listen."

Although "just sit there and listen" is *not* all we do, the casualness he implied by his comment indicated to me that he had not the foggiest idea of what it meant to really *sit* there with someone, to really *be* there with someone. Psychotherapy is a craft that requires a high degree of concentration, alertness, and emotional availability, an ability to be fully present with individuals who are often feeling deep and troubling emotions. One of the challenges for therapists is to be able to be truly present with the client without being distracted or influenced by their own reactions and preconceived templates of who a client is and what she is feeling. Many of us have been raised in families in which the expression of emotion was muffled, silenced, or discouraged. Yet our task is to create a healing space in which the client feels safe to express deeply private thoughts and intense feelings. We must not only become comfortable in the presence of people in deep distress, but we must also know how to attend to their distress in such a way as to encourage growth and healing.

Martha Manning, a psychologist who has written eloquently about her own struggle with debilitating depression, described the importance of being present for the client:

> Despite the dead ends and infuriating blind alleys, despite the frustration and embarrassment, despite every awful drug side effect, having a companion on the journey helps. It is so easy for me to forget the importance of the

companionship itself when things aren't going well for my patients. I tend to only look at actual outcomes to judge my goodness as "doctor." But my memories of my own doctors remind me that the process of just walking down the road with someone is so important. The communication of hope, the administration of gentleness, and the sharing of some part of the self can make a long lonely journey, in all its circuitousness, almost bearable. (Manning, 1994, p. 150)

In this chapter I will discuss particular aspects of the therapeutic relationship that allow the therapist to be "a companion on the journey." At the heart of an integrationist approach is a relational and interpersonal framework that has three key premises:

1. The self develops in an interpersonal context.
2. Relational images and templates are influenced by sex role socialization, family of origin, and culture.
3. The client-therapist relationship presents a vehicle for understanding current relational styles and learning new relational styles.

This chapter will focus on the third concept and describe ways that the therapist can contribute to the development of a positive therapeutic relationship, creating an environment in which change may occur. "The therapy relationship itself can represent a therapeutic intervention. The experience of a trusting and safe environment facilitated by the therapist's availability, responsiveness, and constancy, in which clients can explore past and present feelings and interactions may initiate change" (Bachelor & Horvath, 1999, p. 162). Integrative Relational Therapy (IRT) goes further in its emphasis on the therapeutic relationship. Many symptoms can be understood as adaptive efforts to maintain connection with others, efforts that result in disconnection from one's own experience, which then constrains the quality of connection with others. A key goal of therapy is to learn new models of connection that promote a fuller sense of connection with self and others. The therapeutic relationship provides the vehicle for learning new relational images and templates. It is the critical variable in working with women (Comas-Diaz, 1994).

So "just sitting and listening" becomes an awesome task, one which requires the therapist to be emotionally available, responsive, and consistent. The therapist must have the capacity to be emotionally moved by the client while not becoming overwhelmed with affect. The therapist must have access to emotions in order to be responsive to the client, but must not respond based on personal associations and memories. Simultaneously, the therapist cannot be distant or removed.

Table 4.1 lists the specific therapy skills that will be discussed in this chapter: mutual empathy, mutual empowerment, seeing, listening, empathic attunement, authenticity, collaboration, and recognition of transference and countertransference. Although these skills are relevant with ANY client, therapy with women clients demands an acute awareness of women's unique issues and their implications for creating a truly healing and facilitative therapeutic relationship.

## A MUTUALLY EMPATHIC RELATIONSHIP

Miller and Stiver (1997) described a healing therapeutic relationship as one arising out of mutual empathy and mutual empowerment. What is mutual is that two people are participating in an equally emotionally

**TABLE 4.1   The Therapeutic Relationship: Specific Skills**

Mutual empathy
    Client's experience as focus
    Therapist is moved by the client
Mutual empowerment
Listening
    Awareness of historical and sociocultural silencing of women and minorities
    Translation of client's problem into nonpathologizing language
    Contextualization of client's complaints
Seeing
    Awareness of women's hypervisibility and invisibility
    Attention to nonverbal behaviors
Empathic Attunement
    Affective element
        Visceral reactions
        Associational empathy
    Cognitive element
        Mental inquiry
        Identifying patterns, issues, and schemas
        Theoretical and case conceptualization
        Choosing interventions
Authenticity
Collaboration
Recognition of Transference and Countertransference
    Familially based relational images
    Sociocultural experiences: hierarchy, sexism, racism, etc.
    Actual circumstances in therapeutic situation

present manner. Mutuality in therapy places the client's experience at front and center, with the therapist only sharing to the extent that the client is helped. This is not a dependent relationship, but a connection that results in two kinds of movement: the client's movement into action and the therapist's feeling of being moved by the client. The therapist's movement—being moved by the client—arises out of feeling empathy. As I discuss in more detail below, empathy is an essential element in change processes in therapy. When the therapist feels a sense of empathy toward the client, the client experiences a different kind of relationship than those she may typically have had. In our culture, women are often seen as "too emotional." Women face enormous pressure to fulfill gender role stereotypes of being a "good woman," a "good girl," a "good daughter," or a "good wife." These templates of goodness demean and ridicule expressions of negative emotion. To be complaining or unhappy, then, often seems selfish or "bad." The therapist offers the client an opportunity to express her conflicts or dissatisfaction with demands and expectations without the criticism that the client either anticipates from others or heaps upon herself. By empathizing with the client's unhappinesses, dissatisfactions, and conflicts, the therapist provides a new context for the client, one in which she no longer has to disown parts of herself that she has seen as selfish or bad.

The therapist needs to be acutely aware of women's familial and cultural contexts of being discounted, unheard, or criticized. For many women, feeling heard and understood by a therapist will provide a pivotal experience that will be a catalyst for change processes to begin. Lott (1999), who interviewed 120 women about their therapy experiences, concluded:

> The women in my book agreed about the one experience in therapy that was the most profound, that held the greatest prospect for change. That was the experience of being "gotten"—of being understood, truly seen and heard in one's humanity, all one's complexity, all one's conflict—by another human being. (p. 292)

The experience of being "gotten" facilitates mutual empowerment in the therapy relationship. The client feels that I, as the therapist, "get" her. Feeling an increased sense of connection with me and with herself, she is then empowered to be ALL that she can be as a person. As a therapist, I feel that the client "gets" me, thus empowering me to bring all of myself to the therapy relationship and to be the very best therapist that I can be.

The therapeutic relationship provides the vehicle by which the client can resolve the "central relational paradox" (Miller & Stiver, 1997,

p. 81): On one hand, the woman longs for and seeks connection; on the other hand, her relational history causes her to protect herself by keeping important parts of herself and her experience out of connection. When the therapist creates a context in which a woman client can express her negative emotions and her conflicts with being "good," the therapeutic relationship facilitates changes in her sense of self through several processes:

1. She experiences a sense of acceptance, particularly in regard to cut-off or disowned parts of herself and negative emotions.
2. She is exposed to new templates of the self in connection that encourage her to more fully be herself in relationships and promote a more authentic sense of self.
3. The expression of negative emotions has the potential to move the depressed woman from immobility to activity.
4. The experience of "being gotten" and feeling the therapist's empathy moves the client into action.

## SEEING AND BEING SEEN

To be "truly seen" evokes our society's overemphasis on female beauty and attractiveness. Women live in a culture that overvalues their physical appearance and undervalues the person who lies behind the appearance. Women's hypervisibility results, paradoxically, in a heightened sense of invisibility (Kaschak, 1992). The experience of being truly *seen* by a therapist has the potential to create a profoundly different kind of relationship, one that promotes growth and healing.

Having been silenced for so long, many women will enter therapy without the language or the safety that will allow them to voice their thoughts and feelings. The therapist can support and nurture the woman client's ability to put forth her authentic self by carefully observing her nonverbal body language. A sigh, a flush of color, a tear, a postural shift—these nonverbal behaviors reflect affective experiences. By making comments such as, "You look stunned. Can you tell me what is happening for your right now?", the therapist lets the woman know that her thoughts and feelings are important, facilitating translation of the nonverbal to the verbal, from the invisible to the visible.

Another result of the overemphasis on women's physical appearance, attractiveness, and desirability, is the feeling of being constantly under the male gaze. Many women see themselves "from the outside in" (Kaschak, 1992, p. 103), internalizing a constantly vigilant and judgmental perspective that is preoccupied with how men view them. This has implications for the therapy relationship. A client comes into the session with a new haircut, a new dress, or new glasses. To comment reinforces an overemphasis on appearance and attractiveness. To not comment reinforces her invisibility. The therapist needs to be aware of the complexities involved in these kinds of exchanges and to be highly attuned to the client's issues and conflicts concerning her physical self.

## LISTENING

To be "truly heard" evokes women's personal and political history of being silenced. Because so many women will enter therapy with a history of feeling unheard, it is incumbent upon the therapist to know how to truly listen to clients. The basic counseling skills of reflection, summarization, and clarification become incredibly powerful means to convey to the client that she has been heard and understood. It is the combination of the therapist's empathy, of truly being present with the client as she articulates her thoughts and feelings, combined with the therapist's counseling skills of reflection, summarization, and clarification that will convey to the client that she is heard. Although these are skills that therapists may take for granted, they form the cornerstone in building an effective therapeutic relationship and are particularly meaningful when working with people who have experienced disconnection, isolation, oppression, or any degree of marginalization.

Nineteen-year-old Jennie, a survivor of sexual abuse and assault who was depressed, told me: "When I hear you say back to me what I've said about myself, my feelings seem more real and my words have more weight and I realize how I have been seeing things." Because depressed women can feel so negative and tentative about themselves, honoring and valuing their words is a vital part of the therapy process. Most of us have been trained as therapists to be good listeners. Working with depressed women, however, requires that we listen in a particularly attuned and alert manner:

> We must become bilingual to understand women's speech about their lives. We need to be aware of how women employ negatively valued words— dependent, passive, insecure, immature—as they attempt to represent aspects of a subjective reality that, as yet, have no other names. So to become bilingual means to listen to patterns and meanings behind the negatively valued words, and then to translate those meanings into less negative terms that more accurately reflect the experiences the women are trying to convey. (Jack, 1991, p. 27)

Listening, then, is not a receptive, passive experience for the therapist, but, rather, is an active process that involves several crucial steps.
First, as the therapist listens to the client, she or he wants to convey
that the client is heard and understood. This can be accomplished
nonverbally with facial expressions and body postures that express attention and concern and verbally by reflecting, summarizing, or clarifying
what the client is saying. However, it is in the verbal reflection that
the therapist goes beyond merely reflecting back the client's words,
"translating" the client's comments by placing them in the context of
a larger social reality and using destigmatizing language. To accomplish
this, the therapist must not only be well versed in the conditions of the
client's life, but also in the larger social, cultural, and familial contexts
that are relevant for the client, including risk factors for depression. For
example, Laura, whom I discussed in chapter 2, a 29-year-old Caucasian
woman, married with three children all under the age of 5 and who
provided childcare in her home for six children, became depressed
after the birth of her third child. She described her sense of inadequacy
and despair in the first session:

> "I don't know what's wrong with me. I feel that I am a horrible mother. How
> could I be so unable to cope? I have always coped. Actually, I have more
> than coped. I have always succeeded in whatever I have done. But now, I am
> such a failure that I can't even bare to face another day."

I translated Laura's experience, explaining,

> It's completely understandable that you are having a hard time managing
> things at home, feeling so overwhelmed by how much there is to do, and
> feeling terrible about yourself because you feel you cannot cope. In the past,
> you've been a perfectionist and always had very high standards for yourself.
> And because you had such a bad childhood, you have planned to be a great
> mother—different than your own mother. Yet financially you have to work
> and your childcare business leaves you exhausted and desperate for some
> time to yourself. In the meantime, your husband is often traveling for his
> job so you are often left with more responsibilities than any human being
> could handle alone. Many women find having three young children over-
> whelming and suffer from depression as a result, but to have three children
> and a childcare business, most women would find it very hard to keep their
> heads above water. So you have these expectations to be a great mother and
> yet, given your situation, that is humanly impossible and you blame yourself
> and feel inadequate and hopeless.

In order to contextualize Laura's experience and translate for her,
I needed to know about her history, her expectations for herself, her

current life situation, and about risk factors for depression. While Laura located her problem within herself ("I'm a failure"), I translated her problem to be located outside herself (too much to do, too little resources) and within herself (expectations to be a great mother). If Laura had been lesbian or from a minority racial or ethnic group, I would have included in my contextualization the additional stress of being a member of an oppressed group.

## EMPATHIC ATTUNEMENT

The exchange with Laura also illustrates another crucial aspect of the therapist's stance, which is to convey a sense of empathic attunement. The client often presents herself in a self-critical and denigrating way. The therapist empathizes with the client's experience and by doing so presents the client with a different view of herself, one that locates difficulties at an intersection between external and internal factors. I felt for Laura an incredible sense of empathy, envisioning how stressful her days must be and how shocked she was that she could not live up to her vision of who she was supposed to be as a mother. I conveyed my empathy nonverbally and verbally as I looked directly at her with a concerned expression on my face, leaning forward in my chair, speaking in a softer tone of voice.

Empathy consists of two simultaneous elements: the affective and the cognitive (Kaplan, 1991a). The affective encompasses physiological feelings of the therapist such as postural shifts, muscle tension, and tearing of the eyes, in which the client's emotional state is transmitted to the therapist as a visceral experience. The therapist may also experience associational empathy, which occurs when the therapist takes on the client's emotional state and transfers it to something in her own experience. As I listened to Laura, I suddenly found myself remembering my mother as angry and depressed during my childhood. My mother had four children and, similarly, my father was often away on business. After the momentary memory "flash" of my angry and depressed mother, I recalled the sadness and helplessness I felt as a child, the firstborn child and eldest daughter who was supposed to be competent and in charge, feeling unable to ease my mother's distress. This recall lasted for a matter of seconds and demonstrated the sense of identification I had with Laura. This type of brief, momentary "flashback" by the therapist to a personal experience demonstrates the degree of identification the therapist feels with the client. It is a moment of very much being with the client and being moved by the client. The therapist then integrates this affective experience with cognitive processes. This usually takes the form of internal questions the therapist asks to determine the next intervention and may include identifying issues, patterns, or schemas; developing a case formulation; and attending to theoretical concepts. For example, with Laura I asked myself whether I should self-disclose that my mother felt similarly overwhelmed. I asked myself whether anger, which seemed to be one of my mother's responses to her life situation but was not yet apparent in Laura, was an emotion I should explore with Laura. Finding that none of these directions fit with where Laura was at this moment, I refocused on what Laura had just disclosed, deciding to translate or reframe her problem.

My choice at that moment was dependent on a number of variables including how much time was left in the session, the phase of therapy, the strength of the therapeutic relationship, our treatment goals, and my knowledge about Laura's ego strength and ability to tolerate affect. I needed to be certain that if I made an intervention that would contain and curtail further expression of affect, it was based on the client's needs and not on my own. When we become affectively involved with associational memories and feelings that our clients elicit, we face the danger of acting on our own needs. In the session with Laura, I could have stayed with my childhood feelings of helplessness, becoming paralyzed as a therapist. With training, supervision, and experience, the therapist becomes more facile at quickly having internal conversations like the one I described above, integrating affective with cognitive processes. A relationally oriented therapy demands that the therapist attend to internal processes while simultaneously being fully present with the client. Such a dual presence is demanding and can be exhausting.

There is no single recipe or way of being that will result in the creation of the "right" kind of therapeutic intervention. In fact, it will be the therapist's ability to adjust to each individual client's need at each particular moment in the therapy process that will most likely lead to the optimal kind of therapeutic relationship.

The specific therapist responses that best foster a strong therapeutic relationship vary from client to client. Attitudes such as warmth, empathy, and so on and interventions and strategies such as support, directiveness, or deeper exploration appear to be differentially productive. Sensitivity to clients' differential responsivity seems important. Verifying with the client his or her expectations and perceptions and the perceived helpfulness of particular responses could aid in adjusting these to the client's individual needs. Factors such as phase of therapy, the client's readiness for change, and interpersonal dynamics also need to be considered. (Bachelor & Horvath, 1999, p. 162)

As a psychologist who often sees clients who have previously seen a graduate student therapist and found that therapy unsatisfactory, a not uncommon complaint that I hear is that the previous therapist was too reassuring. For example, Alexandra complained of her previous therapist: "She was always trying to tell me how great I was and I couldn't stand to hear that. I felt that she really did not understand how I felt about myself. After a while, I realized that I wasn't telling her a lot of stuff about myself." So reassuring Laura that she was actually a good or adequate mother to her children would have probably been an ineffective intervention, causing Laura to feel that I did not truly understand how bad she was feeling about herself. Empathic attunement involves being able to be present with the client and attuned to her affective state. Empathy does not need to be conveyed in words, but by "going with" the client into her immediate experience (Miller & Stiver, 1997). When the therapist begins an intervention from a place that is quite affectively different from where the client is, there is a lack of attunement resulting in disconnection.

The way that I conveyed my empathy for Laura at this point in our therapy reflected the newness of our relationship as well as Laura's own self-described discomfort with telling another person that she was having a hard time. I was quite careful not to express too much emotion or to be too self-disclosing with her. I struggled for a way to be authentic without overwhelming Laura with more intimacy than she could handle.

## AUTHENTICITY

As the client experiences a different, accepting, healing kind of relationship with the therapist, she feels an increasing freedom to be authentic in the relationship. As I will discuss further in chapter 9, strengthening the client's connection with her authentic self is a powerful and important task in the therapy. While the concept of authenticity as applied to the client seems well understood, the concept as applied to the therapist warrants further discussion. For in order to nurture and support the client's authenticity, the therapist also needs to be authentic in the therapy. "When we are fully present with another human being and in our own self, we are able to create an environment that is encouraging and affirming of the other's emerging selfhood" (Hertzberg, 1990, p. 204).

Not to be confused with transparency and self-disclosure, authenticity on the part of the therapist allows the therapist to be truly moved by the client, to be emotionally present and available to be with the client, and to go with the client into her pain and her struggles. My empathy for Laura was authentic and real. I was experiencing a depth of emotion with her and for her. By deciding to keep my own associations to her pain to myself, I was not being inauthentic, but rather, I was being attuned to Laura and the relational context we had created up to this point.

> Authenticity, then, means that the therapist tries to be with the thoughts and feelings occurring in the relationship. It also means that the therapist tries to be with the movement toward connection, the fear of that movement, and the strategies of disconnection. She should be "in" this moment-to-moment interplay. She should try to convey that she has felt with the patient and raise questions when she hasn't, questions that will help them move both toward (mutuality). This moment-to-moment responsiveness is the most important part of authenticity. (Miller et al., 1999, p. 2)

Authenticity, then, is a different attitude than the traditional model of the therapist as "blank screen." The therapist is actively present and involved with the client. When therapist and client experience being authentic together, there is an alive sense of connection, a connection that feels like an increase of vitality, aliveness, and energy, a greater sense of "zest" (Miller & Stiver, 1997, p. 30).

The emphasis on authenticity, then, challenges the therapist who experiences a sense of disconnection from the client. For example, when Ellen, a 28-year-old nurse and single parent, told me she had gotten back together with her emotionally abusive boyfriend for the third time, I found myself spacing out and emotionally distancing myself from her in the session. I lost the moment-by-moment connectedness between us. As I attended to my loss of connection, I identified feelings of frustration and disapproval, acknowledging that my defensive strategy had been to become emotionally disconnected from Ellen rather than to truly feel these feelings. Sharing these feelings would have done nothing to help Ellen leave a bad relationship and might have caused her to drop out of therapy. Recognizing that my frustration and disapproval came from a power-over stance of believing that I, as the therapist, knew what was best for Ellen, I refocused on Ellen's experience of telling me news that she probably knew would disappoint me and what that must be like for her. This internal dialogue beginning with the recognition that I had lost connection (spacing out), leading to feelings of even greater disconnection (frustration and disapproval), led me to a solution that brought me back in connection with Ellen (empathizing with her anticipation of my disconnection). This moment-to-moment involvement with the client's and the therapist's own experience is hard work, but work that has the potential to be a powerful resource for the client's growth.

## SELF-DISCLOSURE

As we consider a therapeutic relationship that is mutually empathic, mutually empowering, and authentic, what does this mean about self-disclosure on the part of the therapist? First and foremost, self-disclosure is only helpful to the extent that it promotes and supports the client's growth. Authenticity is not synonymous with self-disclosure and an authentically present therapist may self-disclose very little. In fact, self-disclosure may feel burdensome or intrusive to the client.

> Sometimes in the service of "being a good role model" for the patient, a therapist might tell a patient how he or she managed a particular event in the past, conveying to the patient that the patient should do the same. We see this instance of disclosure as particularly harmful since it intensifies the power inequities in the relationship, suggesting that the "therapist knows best," and it does not respect or encourage the patient's growing capacity to cope with that particular event in her own unique way. (Miller & Stiver, 1997, p. 145)

So before making a self-disclosure, the therapist must answer these questions:

- How might this be helpful to the client?
- How might this be unhelpful to the client?
- If I self-disclose, am I demonstrating my superiority or supporting a power-over type of relationship with the client?
- Will my self-disclosure nurture the client's growth and invite her to solve a problem in her own unique way or will it limit how she sees or solves the problem?

Simultaneously, it is important to keep in mind that at times *not* making a self-disclosure may be detrimental. When the therapist is preoccupied by serious life events, the ability to be present with the client will be altered, and the client will most likely feel or sense this. Leaving the client to wonder why it feels different to be with her therapist may result in the client blaming this change in connectedness on herself, as many women are likely to take responsibility for relational disconnections upon themselves. This self-doubting on the part of the client leads to a kind of double disconnection—first, when the therapist is more distant due to emotional exhaustion or preoccupations and, second, when the client withdraws due to her own sense of self-blame, confusion, or isolation. The decision to self-disclose or not, therefore, is one that should not be taken lightly.

On the other hand, the therapist has to be able to be spontaneous with clients and not turn every question into a profound interaction. Out of mutuality comes an excitement to connect and a striving to be genuine. Each therapist needs to come to a conclusion as to what information is shared and which is private, with an awareness of the potential impact of this kind of information with each particular client at each particular point in the therapy. As with any element of the therapy process that has "grey" areas and raises ethical issues, as therapists we must continue to be open to challenging our decision making and consulting with colleagues.

## COLLABORATION

The client-therapist relationship is one holding an asymmetry of roles and inequality of power. The client, feeling inadequate, helpless, or downtrodden in some way, seeks out an "expert" to help with her problems. The most familiar models we have of healing relationships in our culture come from the medical model of treatment, which places the patient in the hands of a healing professional, "the expert," who prescribes a treatment or does something to make the person well. Sheila, who was profoundly depressed over her inability to get out of an emotionally abusive relationship, told me in her second session that she wanted me to "fix" her. I responded by telling her, "*Together* we will figure out how you can make the changes you want to make." Sheila was feeling powerless in her life, as many women feel when they are depressed. By seeing the client as an expert about her own problem and enlisting her in a collaborative approach to the therapeutic work, the therapist can minimize a power-over type of relationship. When the therapist takes an inclusive stance, continually drawing the client into the process of directing and delineating the therapy, the depressed woman becomes more empowered not only in the therapy but also in her life. Because words such as "should" and "need to" mirror women's culturally devalued position, the therapist is cautioned to employ language that is inclusive, collaborative, and nonauthoritarian.

A recent reevaluation of factors that influence therapy outcome concluded that "the client's capacity for self-healing is the most potent factor in psychotherapy. It is the 'engine' that makes therapy work"

(Tallman & Bohart, 1999, p. 91). This has important implications for therapists:

> We believe therapists should be much more willing to listen to clients, respect their frame of reference, and genuinely collaborate with them. Collaboration means more than client participation and compliance. It means that therapy must be thought of as the meeting of two minds, each possessing its own expertise and competence, with goals and solutions co-created through mutual dialogue, instead of being chosen and applied to the client by the therapist. (Tallman & Bohart, 1999, p. 117)

Collaboration is not foremost among most women's relational associations and experiences. Women are often in the background or excluded from decision making at home, at work, at school, in the community, in the nation, and in the world. The therapist, then, is faced with a challenge by trying to create what may be a new kind of relationship for many clients.

## DIFFERENCE AND POWER

Collaboration may be even more of a challenge when the differences between client and therapist mirror differences that represent inequalities of the dominant Anglicized, heterosexual culture. Differences in gender, age, able-bodied status, sexual orientation, race, ethnicity, class, and economic status in the therapeutic dyad represent a microcosm of power-over relationships that exist in our culture. Templates that both client and therapist bring to the therapy room include not only familial relational images, but also culturally determined, stereotypical images.

Connie, a graduate student of color, repeatedly expressed her anger at society, often beginning her comments in therapy with the words, "You guys," thus implicating me, a Caucasian professional, as a member of the oppressive power structure. Although few clients will go so far as to verbalize this view, it is important for the therapist to recognize that these types of power-over relational images are part of many clients' experiences, whether they are conscious of them or not.

When differences in a therapeutic relationship mirror power-under roles—for example, a Chicana woman therapist and a White male client—the therapist is challenged to empathize with the client's potential discomfort with this role reversal and set aside her own feelings and experiences concerning social power inequities.

The realities of many therapeutic situations are that clients and therapists have a limited range of possibilities in choosing each other. We all will inevitably work with clients who are quite different from us, often in ways that replicate power-over relationships. It is the therapist's responsibility to be aware of such differences and be attuned to their potential impact on the therapeutic encounter.

When I have worked with college students who are sometimes decades younger than myself, who come from different geographic and social environments as myself, I consider our relationship to be cross-cultural. Cross-cultural encounters can be conceptualized as client-therapist dyads representing such different identities as gender, race, ethnicity, generation, sexual orientation, religion, and social or economic class. We are challenged as therapists when working with individuals whose world views differ markedly from our own.

> Within the cross-cultural encounter, clinicians may be able to empathize at a cognitive level, but not necessarily at an affective level. In cognitive empathy therapists can study the client's culture and confer with colleagues who share the client's cultural background. Kleinman (1989) has termed his concept *empathic listening*, where the therapist recognizes his or her ethnocultural ignorance of the client's reality and reaffirms, through empathic witnessing, the client's experience and reality. The emergence of empathy for the emotional experience of the culturally different client may be difficult, and recognizing this difficulty is a useful element of managing the therapeutic relationship within the integrative framework. (Comas-Diaz, 1994, p. 295)

## THERAPIST GENDER

Do women clients do better with women therapists? Although many women may prefer a female therapist, it is difficult to come to any clear conclusion from the research owing to the lack of uniformity of types of therapy and presenting problems that are studied. One finding has been that experience was unrelated to outcome for female therapists but that less experienced male therapists had more negative outcomes (Kirschner, Genack, & Hauser, 1978; Orlinsky & Howard, 1980). Overall, the research suggests that the impact of gender in psychotherapy is related to a complex interaction of factors, with client factors also being an important variable.

> All of counseling is an ongoing, mutually influencing interaction. A female client once told a male counselor that she was feeling inferior to him. When quizzed as to why, she thought for a minute and blurted out, "You're a man!" That was a very powerful realization for both of them and helped bring into the counselor's awareness, and into the counseling, ways he and the client were "doing gender." (Gilbert & Scher, 1999, p. 150)

"Doing gender" may, thus, be a two-way street, with client and therapist mutually influencing subtle cues and behaviors that support stereotyped gender roles. A female client may fall into her automatic stance of deferring to a male, and the male therapist may fall victim to his own privilege, accepting the role of expert and authority. It may be difficult to identify with whom such dynamics actually begin. Both client and therapist come into therapy with their own storehouse of relational experiences, biases, and expectations. As therapists we are challenged to be attuned to our own contribution to relational dynamics and to respond consciously, authentically, and helpfully to our clients. We may be equally challenged when working with a client from a similar group as ourselves by overempathizing or overidentifying with her, failing to truly listen and see who she is. The bottom line is that we must be awake to our own biases and stereotyping, noticing overconnections and disconnections, being open to explore our own issues through supervision, consultation, and our own psychotherapy.

## TRANSFERENCE AND COUNTERTRANSFERENCE

Transference and countertransference are useful conceptualizations for understanding the dynamics of the therapeutic relationship, including the issues of difference and gender discussed above. Historically, the terms have had a range of definitions (Chin, 1994; Pearlman & Saakvitne, 1995). In IRT, the definitions of transference and countertransference are adapted from Pearlman and Saakvitne.

Transference is defined as

1. The client's affective, ideational, and physical responses to the therapist and the therapist's countertransference.
2. The client's conscious and unconscious ways of coping with the affects, conflicts, and associations related to the therapist.

The woman client discussed previously who, with her therapist, was "doing gender," had an affective response to the therapist; we do not have enough information to determine the full range of her affective responses, but the brief excerpt reveals that she was feeling submissive and we can surmise that she may have also felt fear, intimidation, or anxiety. She was having an ideational response: "You're a man!". She may have had a variety of associations and relational experiences related to and aroused by this cognition, including being raised in a family in which women were subservient to men, having a history of abusive relationships with men, or working in a job in which women held lower status positions. Having no information about her physical sensations, we can only speculate that she may have felt some degree of bodily tension during therapy sessions. Her conscious and unconscious ways of coping with these responses may have included behaviors such as following behind her therapist as they walked from the waiting room to the office, avoiding eye contact, choosing a particular chair in the therapist's office, waiting for the therapist to initiate topics, agreeing with the therapist even when she did not agree, holding back information, and being passive.

Transference is not restricted to negative responses, but also includes positive responses. For example, the therapist may have reminded the client of her favorite uncle or a friend may have seen the same therapist and told her he was wonderful, creating positive expectations. She may have wanted to see the most qualified therapist and, based on her own biases and internalized misogyny, may have believed that an older, experienced male therapist was the best choice.

Transference may be based on three sources. The first two are related to prior experiences that predispose the client to have particular conscious and unconscious assumptions about relationships:

1. From the client's early familial relationships, including parental and sibling relationships. For women clients this includes, father-daughter, mother-daughter, and sibling-sibling relational images and may occur regardless of the gender of the therapist.
2. From the client's sociocultural contexts, which include experiences of sexism, racism, discrimination, hierarchy, and misogyny including interpersonal violence.
3. From actual experiences happening in the therapeutic context, including the therapist's behaviors and environmental circumstances.

In IRT, the focus is on understanding how transference responses influence the way the client experiences connection and keeps herself out of connection. Familially based transference reactions can be aroused by feeling vulnerable in the therapeutic encounter, eliciting a childlike feeling state in relation to the therapist, which then triggers early relational templates. This has the potential to impact the therapeutic encounter and, for women clients in particular, may include feelings of helplessness, passivity, dependency, defensiveness, or resistance to help. While a traditional view of transference is concerned with identifying specific types of early transference reactions (i.e., oedipal, etc.), in IRT a more general understanding of familially based transference responses is sufficient.

It should now become apparent that the client's transference reactions can be elicited and influenced by the therapist's countertransference and vice versa, resulting in an interactive, reflexive, mutually influencing relational encounter. The definition of countertransference is a mirror of transference: (a) the therapist's affective, ideational, and physical responses to the client, and (b) the therapist's conscious and unconscious ways of coping with the affects, conflicts, and associations related to the client.

As with transference, countertransference has three sources: familial relational images, sociocultural contexts, and actual experiences that occur in the therapeutic situation. An awareness of countertransference reactions not only can assist the therapist in identifying conscious and unconscious biases, stereotypes, and assumptions, but also can provide useful information to the therapist in identifying the client's transference reactions. For example, in the case illustration first noted, if the therapist had noticed the client's submissive behaviors, he may have been able to initiate a discussion of gender differences as well as minimize his dominant behaviors.

In this chapter I have given two examples of my own countertransference reactions that illustrate other ways that this information can enrich or facilitate therapeutic work. In the first example, I had an associational memory of feeling helpless and sad as a child in response to Laura's experience of being left at home with three children. While I chose not to use this information at that point in the therapy, recognition of my feelings prevented me from becoming immobilized by them, allowing me to shift into a cognitive frame. I mentally filed the memory for possible use in the future when we would work on differentiating specific feelings from a general sense of depression. In the second example, I recognized that I was feeling disconnected from Ellen when she told me about her third reconciliation with her boyfriend. Noticing my disconnection led to finding a way to restore connection. Identification of countertransference reactions has the potential to provide solutions to therapeutic impasses.

## SUMMARY

To truly facilitate healing, to be "a companion on the journey," we must be willing to go with our clients into their pain, to be authentically and collaboratively present with them, to deeply listen and see, to be aware of the many contexts and pressures of our clients' lives, and to be willing to examine our own issues, biases, and responses. "This is not a profession for the faint of heart" (Gilbert & Scher, 1999, p. 150).

IRT emphasizes the therapeutic relationship as a key element in psychotherapy. This chapter has identified and discussed specific skills that are crucial in the development of a healing, facilitative psychotherapeutic relationship with women clients. These essential building blocks are summarized in Table 4.1. The collaborative, mutually empathic, and mutually empowering therapeutic relationship described in this chapter will form the foundation for all of the therapeutic tasks related to the five elements of therapy discussed in the remaining chapters.

# CHAPTER FIVE

# Assessment: Philosophy and Standards of Care

A ssessment is one of the most powerful tools we have as therapists, second only to the client-therapist relationship. Through assessment we give the client's problem a name, form hypotheses about why the client has such problems, develop a plan for addressing problems, and often must share this knowledge with third parties such as insurance companies and the legal system. Our assessment influences the way the client and many others see herself and her problems.

IRT incorporates traditional, relational, and feminist methods for assessment to create a professionally responsible and culturally sensitive approach that is user friendly for client and therapist. In IRT, assessment is not only a tool for the therapist, but it also will become a self-assessment tool for the client to use independently between therapy sessions and once therapy has ended.

Table 5.1 lists the elements of IRT assessment, which include: philosophy, "standards of care," case conceptualization, and treatment planning. IRT provides four conceptual maps that give client and therapist a framework from which to understand how the client came to be depressed and how to build of vision of who the client can be, enhancing strengths and minimizing vulnerabilities to future depressive episodes. The four conceptual maps are: (a) biopsychosocial risk factors, (b) a relational view of symptoms, (c) aspects of the self, and (d) elements of therapy.

The four conceptual maps are IRT's unique contribution to therapy with depressed women. These maps will facilitate case conceptualization and treatment planning, providing a simple yet sophisticated guide for therapist and client. This chapter describes the philosophy of assessment in IRT and standards of care, including assessment of imminent danger and the role of antidepressant medication. The next chapter describes the four conceptual maps. Chapters 5 and 6 comprise the fundamentals of assessment according to IRT.

**TABLE 5.1   IRT Approach to Assessment**

Philosophy of assessment
    Collaboration and education
    Empowerment through self-assessment
    Nonpathologizing perspective
    Strengths and competencies
    Cultural literacy and cultural competency
    Informed consent
"Standards of care"
    Assessment of imminent danger
    Symptoms including seasonal timing and comorbidity
    Previous depressive episodes and treatment history (request records)
    Family history of depression or other psychiatric problems
    Evaluate for medication referral
Case conceptualization
    Biopsychosocial risk factors
    Relational view of symptoms
    Aspects of the self
Treatment planning
    Five elements of therapy
    Prioritization of treatment tasks: stabilization, transformation, future orientation
    Financial or institutional resources available
    Relapse prevention plan

# THE IRT PHILOSOPHY OF ASSESSMENT

In addition to providing several distinct conceptual maps, IRT brings
a particular philosophy to the assessment process. Assessment is a collaborative endeavor in which case conceptualization and treatment planning are coauthored and co-created by client and therapist. The process
of assessment is guided by a relational approach to therapy that emphasizes mutual empowerment and cultural sensitivity. The therapist is
responsible for engendering a climate of respect, support, and empathy.
Although the therapist has the tools to give the assessment process
structure and direction, the therapist works in concert with the client
in determining areas for exploration and ways of articulating the client's
strengths and vulnerabilities. In addition, the client is empowered to
become adept at self-assessment to gain a multidimensional perspective
on herself and her problems so that she will be able to handle more
effectively her day-to-day life, to make meaningful contributions to her
therapy, and, ultimately, to take steps that will contribute to relapse
prevention.

As will be apparent as each element of therapy is discussed, one element will be the primary focus at any particular point in the therapy, but several elements will usually be addressed simultaneously. During the assessment process, each element is included in the following way. Assessment is only accurate and effective to the extent that the client feels a sense of safety with the therapist. The client is empowered to become actively involved in the assessment process and to be a coauthor of the case conceptualization and treatment planning. Furthermore, she is activated to become adept at assessing herself and her problems in a more empowering way. Through the positive connection between client and therapist, the client shares intimate knowledge about herself, which is essential in the assessment process. The meaning of the client's symptoms are contextualized and depathologized into a story of hope and transformation.

Assessment is an ongoing endeavor. Client and therapist are continually refining and reevaluating the case conceptualization and treatment plan as a result of changes that occur as the therapy unfolds. The client may feel freer to share more intimate information as her feelings of safety and connection with the therapist increase. As she becomes activated through her connection with the therapist, she may initiate activities outside of the therapy that will result in positive changes in her life circumstances as well as in her sense of self. And finally, the meaning that she makes of her depressive symptoms and her distress may change as she gains a more multidimensional perspective.

## COLLABORATION AND EDUCATION

Because therapists possess a professionized lens through which to view the client, they must be sensitive to the power imbalance inherent in the assessment process. By using a collaborative and educative approach, the therapist can empower the client and minimize the power differential. Each brings an expertise that together form the basis of a valid assessment: The client is an expert on herself, her life, and her world while the therapist is an expert on women's issues, depression, and psychotherapy.

Typically, I explain to clients why I am asking questions and include the client in developing hypotheses and conceptualizations. Collaboratively, we piece together the client's life history and life story to formulate an explanation that makes sense to the client. The therapist brings a sense of vision to this endeavor that engenders "a way of telling the story of who this person was at the beginning of this journey through life and how this person came to today's place of distress, in a manner that leads to a liberating, empowering, and healing vision of who she or he can be" (Brown, 1994, p. 154).

Throughout the therapy, the therapist engages the client in an ongoing process of co-creating a narrative about the client's problems that is not self-blaming and that considers the role of multiple factors in the client's depression. The client is encouraged to develop the tools to more objectively evaluate herself and her problems, leading to an autonomous ability to assess herself once therapy has ended in order to prevent relapse and solicit professional help if appropriate.

## A NONPATHOLOGIZING PERSPECTIVE

IRT emphasizes a nonpathologizing perspective on the client and her problems and a respectful approach to assessment. The therapist can facilitate this perspective by avoiding professional jargon and explaining the reasoning behind asking questions. For example, before I ask the client a series of questions about symptoms based on the diagnostic criteria for major depression, I always explain that there are certain symptoms associated with depression. Because depression has taken on meaning in the popular vernacular that may be stigmatizing or minimizing, I discuss how the mental health field actually defines depression, describing symptoms in a nonblaming way, and emphasizing the reality of depression as a frequent occurrence in women.

In IRT, symptoms are seen as adaptive efforts to cope with conflicts or difficulties. The client's responses and symptoms are viewed with compassion and understanding and as the best efforts that the individual could make given her personal resources, personality, or life circumstances. Symptoms are also seen as having meaning in the context of the individual's life, often as signs of resistance or rebellion from untenable circumstances. Symptoms may offer useful information potentially providing solutions to life problems.

In IRT, the therapist addresses the whole person rather than symptoms or diagnoses. This does not mean that the therapist avoids making diagnoses, but, rather, recognizes the danger of misusing and overrelying on diagnoses as a way to understand the client. There have been numerous critiques of the Diagnostic and Statistical Manual (DSM) as biased against women and as overly pathologizing of women's problems (Brown, 1994; Caplan, McCurdy-Meyers, & Gans, 1992; Figert, 1996; Hamilton & Gallant, 1990; Parlee, 1992; Worrell & Remer, 1992). Subsequently, diagnostic labels are to be used conscientiously with the understanding that they represent only one dimension of the client's problem.

## STRENGTHS AND COMPETENCIES

The therapist actively seeks out the client's strengths and competencies during the assessment process. By exploring who the client is underneath the depression and prior to the depressive episode, a fuller picture of the client's strengths and competencies emerges. The therapist asks not only about the past but also about what the client has been doing to cope with her recent distress. Frequently when I ask, "Is there anything that helps you feel better, even for a few minutes?" I gather important information that we will incorporate into the treatment plan. By bringing forth coping strategies that are working for the client, no matter how insignificant, the therapist is reinforcing the client's sense of instrumentality.

It is not unusual for the client to have limited awareness of her strengths and competencies during a depressive episode. It is possible, however, for the therapist to extrapolate from the client's stories about herself and her life specific examples of resilience and capabilities. When pointing out strengths and competencies, the therapist must not minimize the client's pain and distress. In this manner, the therapist models ways that the client may partake of a balanced self-assessment, identifying strengths as well as vulnerabilities.

## MULTICULTURAL LITERACY AND COMPETENCY

IRT recognizes the role of multiple identities in clients' lives including race, gender, sexual orientation, ability and disability, religion, and class. The therapist is responsible for acquiring familiarity with the clients' cultural and ethnic heritage (Greene, 1996), which may require doing additional reading and consulting with colleagues. In describing her own therapy with a White therapist in the book, *Willow Weep for Me: A Black Woman's Journey Through Depression,* Meri Nana-Ama Danquah (1998) wrote,

> I am black; I am female; I am an immigrant. Every one of these labels plays an equally significant part in my perception of myself and the world around me. If I am expected to investigate the events of my life with a therapist, then

I expect him/her to have a working, if not fundamental knowledge of how what I have lived factors into who I am and the ways I cope. A knowledge, preferably, *that I do not have to give him/her* (emphasis added). (p. 225)

While seeking out resources and becoming knowledgeable about culturally diverse identities, the therapist also recognizes that there are within-group differences. The therapist is careful not to stereotype and seeks to understand the client in all her complexities and uniquenesses. Cultural literacy does not require that the therapist be the same culture as the client, but, rather, "it refers to an attitude of respect toward and a willingness to know a client's life context as fully as possible" (Greene, 1996). Appendix A lists some references for psychotherapy with specific multicultural populations.

Cultural competency refers to the technical skills required to apply the concepts of cultural literacy in the therapy (Greene, 1996). The therapist must be willing to explore not only the client's ethnic and cultural context and oppressions related to such contexts, but also must be willing to investigate the client's personal strengths, vulnerabilities, resources, and barriers. Client and therapist work together to find a balanced conceptualization that incorporates external and internal factors, coauthoring a multidimensional narrative that pieces together the many facets of the client's realities and experiences. The therapist respects the culture of the client while simultaneously challenging dysfunctional responses that are culturally sanctioned (Comas-Diaz, 1994). The therapist will be more effective in challenging such dysfunctional responses when there is a strong therapeutic alliance or only after client and therapist have some shared positive therapeutic experiences.

Cultural competency also means using gender neutral language that is sensitive to all sexual orientations. For instance, when inquiring about information related to relationship status, the therapist is advised to ask "Are you involved with anyone romantically?" rather than "Are you married, single, or divorced?" A culturally competent therapist does not make assumptions about a client's sexual orientation and conveys openness and acceptance not only through verbal language, but also nonverbally.

A culturally competent therapist introduces the topic of differences (or similarities) in the therapeutic dyad, providing the client with an opportunity to acknowledge her concerns, questions, doubts, or thoughts on the matter. Early in therapy the client may feel uncomfortable sharing any concerns, but as the connection between client and therapist deepens, leading to an increasing sense of safety and trust, to share on this topic. Similarly, as the therapy develops an increased understanding of the tal, and institutional factors, she may develop ɔ articulate what earlier in the therapy went e therapist provides the opportunity for the ; and similarities throughout the therapy.

informed consent is a basic ethical norm for all psychological practitioners" (Brabeck & Brown, 1997, p. 20). Typically, an informed consent form is a document that describes the therapist's credentials, training, and treatment approach or orientation and types of interventions that will be utilized. It can also include exceptions to confidentiality and explanation of fees. Rather than seeing informed consent as necessary but unimportant, the therapist can incorporate informed consent into a collaborative and ongoing process with the client. Informed consent can facilitate the client's empowerment and autonomy (Brabeck & Brown, 1997).

In the state of Washington where I practice, state law requires that psychologists provide a written informed consent form at the outset of therapy. In the first session with a client named Kelly, the process of discussing exceptions to confidentiality described on the form helped us clarify and agree on a plan of action if she were to become actively suicidal. When I asked Kelly, as I typically do at the start of the first session, if she had any questions about the informed consent form or if there was anything she wanted to discuss, she initiated a discussion about her fear that I would call the police if she were suicidal, an event that had occurred with a previous therapist. She asked me, "What happens if you feel I am more than you can handle?" We were able to come to an agreement as to how we would approach decisions about her safety, beginning with my asking her if she would be able to be honest with me if she became more than *she* could handle. Together we were able to arrive at a plan that protected her integrity, included her in the decision-making process, and clarified the specific circumstances in which I would consider involuntary commitment. The therapist makes every effort to preserve the client's autonomy and to reinforce the collaborative nature of the therapeutic alliance, discussing exactly how decisions will be made and why.

## "STANDARDS OF CARE" IN THE ASSESSMENT
## OF DEPRESSED INDIVIDUALS

The standards of the mental health field require that the therapist gather certain specific types of information when completing an intake interview or assessing a depressed individual. The ethics of professional practice support incorporating the so-called "standards of care" into our clinical practice. At this point, psychologists, counselors, and social workers have not established any formal "standards of care" in the treatment of depression. I use the term "standards of care" to represent a consensus in the literature and in the mental health field.

IRT supports following "standards of care" while integrating the philosophical approach just described. Following such standards contributes to the sense of *safety* in the therapy relationship in that the therapist is protecting both the client and the therapist: The client is assured of receiving ethical, professional treatment and the therapist is assured that the steps taken are those that any competent and ethical therapist would take in assessing a depressed individual. Following "standards of care" is a form of quality assurance. Such "standards of care" are listed in Table 5.1 and include: assessment of depression and other diagnoses, assessment of imminent danger, inquiring about previous depressions and previous mental health treatment, requesting records of previous mental health treatment, inquiring about family history of depression and other psychiatric problems, and evaluation for a medication referral.

The best way to assess the client's depression is through a clinical interview (AHCPR, 1993a). The therapist can easily ask about the symptoms of major depressive and dysthymic disorders by conversationally asking about each of the symptoms listed in the diagnostic criteria in the *DSM–IV* (APA, 1994). It is always essential to ask about manic or hypomanic symptoms as well to determine which kind of affective disorder the client may have. As was mentioned in chapter 1, individuals with bipolar disorder may be destabilized if prescribed medication for unipolar depression and a thorough evaluation of symptom history is essential. Similarly, the therapist wants to evaluate whether the client has other comorbid diagnoses. As mentioned in chapter 1, IRT is appropriate for clients with anxiety symptoms and for those with so-called personality traits (which in IRT are referred to as vulnerabilities in self capacities as defined in chapter 6).

The most important of the treatment tasks related to standards of care is assessment of imminent danger and should be included in the first session.

## ASSESSMENT OF IMMINENT DANGER

Therapists have the challenging task in the first session of balancing several different agendas. They must (a) gather certain kinds of critical information including level of depression and imminent danger, (b) allow the client the opportunity to speak freely about herself and her reasons for coming to therapy, (c) begin to form a mutually empathic, mutually empowering, and collaborative therapeutic relationship, and (d) give the client reason to want to return for another session. Although it may not be possible to complete a thorough assessment of the vicissitudes of the client's depression in the first session, it is essential to determine the risk of imminent danger, and the presence of symptoms and risk factors related to the risk of imminent danger.

Certain risk factors have been associated with suicide and suicidal behavior. Although the research shows that men have more completed suicides and women have more suicidal behaviors, the clinician cannot rely on this gender dichotomy to assess risk. Table 5.2 is a checklist for

**TABLE 5.2 Checklist for Assessment of Imminent Danger**

_____ Previous suicide attempts
_____ Familial history of suicide or suicide attempts
_____ Drug or alcohol abuse or excess
_____ Alone, or isolated
_____ Serious health problems
_____ Recent significant personal loss
_____ Panic attacks
_____ General psychic anxiety
_____ Anhedonia (lack of interest or pleasure in usually pleasurable activities)
_____ Diminished concentration
_____ Global insomnia (difficulty falling asleep, intermittent awakening, and early morning awakening)
_____ Significant hopelessness
_____ Attraction to death
_____ Suicidal thoughts
_____ Suicidal plan
_____ Homicidal thoughts
_____ Homicidal plan
_____ Lethal or highly lethal plan
_____ Means to carry out plan are available
_____ Low self-control
_____ History of impulsive behavior
_____ Moderate to high intent to kill self
_____ Moderate to high intent to harm others

assessment of imminent danger adapted from several sources (Peruzzi & Bongar, 1999; Pope & Vasquez, 1998; Sommers-Flanagan & Sommers-Flanagan, 1995, 1999). The checklist incorporates items that have been associated with a high risk for suicide including: previous suicide attempts, drug or alcohol overuse or abuse, severe psychic anxiety, hopelessness, panic attacks, being alone or socially isolated, poor physical health, recent loss, decreased ability to concentrate, and global insomnia. "An absence of these factors in an individual client is no guarantee that he or she is safe from suicidal impulses" (Sommers-Flanagan & Sommers-Flanagan, 1999, p. 248). Probably the most important indicators of serious risk are the presence of both hopelessness and impulsivity. Alcohol use when added to these two indicators increases the risk of suicide. A review of suicide assessment instruments (Range & Knott, 1997) recommended three: Beck's Scale for Suicide Ideation, Linehan's Reasons for Living Inventory, and Cole's self-administered adaptation of Linehan's structured interview called the Suicidal Behaviors Questionnaire.

With an attitude of respect and concern, the therapist asks about suicidal thoughts, facilitating a collaborative working relationship with the client. It is important for the therapist to ask about lethality in a calm and matter-of-fact manner, neither over-reacting to clients' suicidal statements nor minimizing the importance of safety. By normalizing the frequency with which people tend to think about suicide, the therapist facilitates a discussion of the topic.

Asking about suicidal thoughts can be included in a discussion of symptoms. Depending on the circumstances of the first session, the therapist can use the checklist in a more formal and structured way or as an informal guide. When Laura and I began to evaluate whether she had symptoms of depression, I assessed for imminent danger in a conversational way:

SLS:     You said earlier that you have been feeling really down. Have you been thinking about suicide?
Laura:   Yes.
SLS:     Today?
Laura:   Yes.
SLS:     What were you thinking?
Laura:   I was thinking it would be better for my children if I were dead.
SLS:     Did you think about how you would kill yourself?
Laura:   No, I just thought it might be better to be dead than to be alive and be like this.

SLS:        Have you been thinking about being dead often?

Laura:      Lately, only about once or twice a day, but right after my son was born, I thought about it all the time.

SLS:        Do you think about actually doing something to make yourself dead or do you just wish you were dead?

Laura:      I never think about doing something, it is more like a wish that I not be here.

SLS:        Do you ever think about killing the children or your husband or anyone else?

Laura:      No! I would never think that!

It is important to ask about homicidal ideation as well as suicidal ideation. A seriously depressed person may not be thinking clearly and could potentially construct a plan to resolve her problems that includes others' deaths. In the case of a recent relationship breakup there may be homicidal ideation or wishes to harm the ex-partner or ex-partner's possessions. Although serious homicidal intentions may be an infrequent turn of events, it is one for which the therapist should evaluate and be prepared.

In Laura's case, I concluded that she was at low risk because she denied having a specific plan or an active intention to kill herself or to harm her family, and by the end of the first session she expressed a sense of hope about the prospect of recovery. By the end of the interview, I had covered all of the items of the list, determining that Laura had never made a suicide attempt in the past, nor had anyone in her family as far as she knew. She described symptoms of panic as well as difficulty concentrating, sleep difficulties, and anhedonia. I requested that she call me in the event that her suicidal thoughts increased before our next appointment. Although no treatment has been shown to be more successful than any other in preventing suicidal behaviors, "prolonged and repeated contact in any form, by telephone or interview may be of benefit" (Hirsch, Walsh, & Draper, 1983, p. 310). Throughout the therapy, Laura agreed to continue to keep me informed should suicidal ideation return or intensify. Therapist and client want to maintain communication in an ongoing manner about suicidal thoughts and impulses. "What is crucial is that the therapist must not neglect an adequate assessment of the client's suicidal potential at adequate intervals" (Pope & Vasquez, 1998, p. 251).

When an assessment indicates that the client is at high risk, the therapist wants to work collaboratively with the client to develop a safety plan. The therapist starts with the least restrictive option as a means to protect the client from self-harm, maintaining the client's integrity and autonomy to the greatest extent possible. The least restrictive plan of action is to develop a verbal or written contract that the client will not harm herself and that she will call in the event that she has any doubt about her ability to keep herself safe. The effectiveness of such a contract is dependent on a positive therapeutic relationship: The more connected the client feels to the therapist, the more likely she will be to follow such a contract and maintain communication with the therapist. In addition, the therapist must work with the client to remove access to instruments the client could use to commit suicide. Another strategy is to help the client make plans to spend time with close friends or relatives, increasing her social support as well as providing her with distracting activities. Safety plans for the high risk client are discussed again in chapter 7.

Increasing contact through phone calls or additional therapy sessions is also advised. This is a time to let the client know that you care about her. We all have our own unique ways of communicating caring to clients based on our personalities, theoretical orientations, and values. "One of the most fundamental aspects of this communication of caring is the therapist's willingness to listen, to take seriously what the client has to say" (Pope & Vasquez, 1998, p. 254). Working with a suicidal client can be quite stressful for therapists, and we must be willing to spend extra time, now and again making extraordinary efforts to maintain contact, express concern, and work with the client to find a safe and supportive environment. Consulting with colleagues is recommended when working with high-risk clients.

When the client is unable to agree to a safety contract with certainty, a discussion of involuntary hospitalization may be appropriate. Carefully evaluate with the client the pros and cons of hospitalization. If the client is a serious suicidal risk, cannot agree to a safety plan, and is refusing hospitalization, the therapist is placed in the difficult position of deciding whether to initiate involuntary hospitalization.

Another standard of care concerns evaluating the client in order to determine if a referral for antidepressant medication is an appropriate option.

## CONSIDERING A MEDICATION REFERRAL

IRT supports psychotherapy as the first line of treatment and strives to balance the often competing pulls of (a) the therapist's ethical responsibility to follow standards of care, (b) the personal views of the client about taking medication, (c) the perspective that women's depression is a complex, multidimensional problem, and (d) the available financial resources of the client. On the one hand, the therapist wants to offer the client whatever treatments may reduce her suffering. On the other hand, an over-reliance on medication has the potential to minimize the client's own healing capacities. Women are particularly vulnerable to having their depression dismissed as a "chemical imbalance," ignoring the interpersonal as well as the larger social and cultural factors involved. Historically, women's problems have been overpathologized and overmedicalized. Medication has the potential to disempower the woman client's sense of self-efficacy as an agent in her own recovery. Therefore, when a decision is made to make a medication referral, the therapist is in need of locating a sensitive, competent practitioner who values psychotherapy, sees medication as only one element of an overall treatment plan, and is willing to work collaboratively with the client and therapist. The therapeutic triad of client, therapist, and pharmacotherapist has the potential to magnify dynamics of power and control, particularly for women of color (Comas-Diaz & Jacobsen, 1995) and socially or economically disadvantaged women. Splitting is also a danger. Ideally, the members of the therapeutic triad work as a collaborative team with an awareness of these potential pitfalls. Often this is a challenge and therapists may find themselves in the position of dealing with patronizing or unenlightened practitioners either due to the limitations of insurance coverage or due to clients' preference of practitioner. While the preferred practitioner is one trained in psychopharmacology, such as a psychiatrist, this is often not viable for a variety of reasons.

Drug companies have spent buckets of money advertising antidepressants in magazines and on TV. The result is that many people not only have an overblown expectation of the efficacy of medication, but are also ill prepared for their own active participation required in psychotherapy. One wonders what the impact would be if psychotherapy were advertised in a manner similar to antidepressants!

As was discussed in chapter 3, the research is unclear as to the benefits of combination therapy, and recommendations in the literature are contradictory. Although research with people who experience chronic depression is beginning to suggest that combination therapy may be the most effective treatment for this subtype (Keller et al., 2000), the decision to refer should be made on a case-by-case basis. The reality is that there are no studies on the long-term effects of SSRIs and each individual client will have to make a decision as to whether medication is right for her, given her unique symptoms, severity and chronicity of depression, reaction to medication, beliefs, and financial resources.

## *For Whom Is Medication Appropriate?*

A discussion of medication seems appropriate in the first session with individuals who have psychotic symptoms with a depression. For other clients, if there is no improvement by the third to sixth session, particularly in the case of serious suicidal ideation, it is appropriate to raise the topic (AHCPR, 1993b; Duncan et al., 2000a). For those who have had recurrent depressions and found benefit from medication in the past, it is important to determine if they are taking medication or why they might have decided not to at this point. Guidelines for considering a medication referral are listed in Table 5.3.

An important factor to consider is whether the client has the financial resources to pay for antidepressants. Some prescribing practitioners will give out free samples and some drug companies have programs for those in need, but it may be difficult for clients to rely on these sources over the long term. The therapist should become familiar with any resources in the community that can assist those with limited financial means and be prepared to develop realistic treatment plans.

## *Discussing Medication*

As mentioned above, the client's beliefs about medication are paramount in determining whether to make a medication referral. In my practice over the years I have seen a large number of women clients who have been absolutely opposed to taking medication and they have truly taught me about the power of psychotherapy as a healing modality.

**TABLE 5.3   Some Guidelines for Considering a Medication Referral**

In the first session:
  Psychotic symptoms
  Poor candidate for psychotherapy
  Client request
In the third to sixth session:
  Little to no improvement
  Serious suicidal ideation
  Client request
Beyond the sixth session:
  Limited improvement
  Client request

Alternatively, I have seen individuals who are convinced that medication is essential for their recovery and I believe it is important to support the client's ideas about what will help. As discussed in chapter 3, client expectations have been identified as one of the major contributors to improvement (Lambert, 1992). I respect the client's views about medication while simultaneously exploring underlying assumptions, particularly when they are on one extreme of the continuum— medication is an evil or a panacea. It is not unusual for people to loath the idea of taking antidepressants because to do so would feel overly stigmatizing. As one of my client's exclaimed, "Taking Prozac would mean I am really off my rocker, really nutso, and then I would feel even worse about myself." It is of the utmost importance to provide information and psychoeducation to the client in order to support her empowered participation in the decision to take medication. These issues are particularly salient for women of color who have historically been overmedicated (Comas-Diaz & Jacobsen, 1995).

The therapist explains that medication, if chosen, is an adjunct to psychotherapy. Antidepressants have the potential to reduce distressing symptoms, allowing the client to be more effective in doing the transformative work of psychotherapy. Once client and therapist have agreed upon a case conceptualization that delineates the combination of factors implicated in the depressive episode, the roles of medication and psychotherapy will become clear. In other words, the case conceptualization will highlight areas for change, thereby clarifying that psychotherapy is the primary modality.

As part of a discussion about a referral for medication, the therapist may need to educate the client about the neurophysiological action of antidepressants, explaining what is known about how they work. The therapist discusses potential side effects and, if the client chooses to take medication, the therapist and client maintain communication about any side effects that the client experiences. Due to the inconsistency and lack of predictability concerning the amount of information the prescribing practitioner shares with the client, I always mention the potential for sexual side effects of relevant SSRIs.

An issue that clients often discuss with therapists is discontinuing medication either because they do not like the side effects, because it is not helping, or because they feel sufficiently recovered. Antidepressants often can take up to 6 or 8 weeks to be fully effective and individuals have idiosyncratic reactions to specific types of medication so that if one medication is ineffective or has troubling side effects, another may be more effective. When SSRIs are suddenly stopped rather than slowly being tapered to a lower dosage, the result can be SSRI discontinuation syndrome, which includes a number of distressing reactions such as the return of depressive symptoms and flu-like symptoms (which does not occur with Prozac due to its long half-life). Clients should be urged to discuss discontinuing medication with the prescribing practitioner (Rivas-Vazques, Johnson, Blais, & Rey, 1999).

The role of medication in relapse prevention should be determined on a case-by-case basis. Studies show that continuing on an antidepressant after recovery for at least 6 months decreases the risk of relapse by 70% (Mulrow et al., 1999). While maintenance medication appears to increase the length of time between recurrences, psychotherapy is also effective (Blackburn & Moore, 1997; Frank, Kupfer, Perel, et al., 1990; Frank, Kupfer, Wagner, McEachran, & Cornes, 1991; Reynolds et al., 1999). As stated above, the effects of taking medication over a period of years is not known and many people cannot tolerate side effects indefinitely, particularly sexual problems.

## Special Medication Issues for Women

There are special issues for women regarding medications about which the therapist should be aware, and, when appropriate, discuss with the client. As mentioned in chapter 2, reproductive hormones appear to interact with medications (Ackerman, 1999; Raskin, 1997; Stewart, 1998). Women have a 15% greater blood flow to their brains, which means that antidepressants and antianxiety agents will affect women's brains faster (Sichel & Driscoll, 1999).

Race may also influence the way that medications are metabolized (Lin, Poland, & Nakasaki, 1993). For example, African Americans may need lower dosages and slower increases (Ackerman, 1999; Smith & Lin, 1996). According to some of my colleagues, psychiatrists and medical practitioners do not routinely receive training in the differential response to medication based on gender or race. "A gender-based blind spot persists in much of the literature available to clinicians and researchers (Jensvold, Halbreich, & Hamilton, 1996, p. 5). In fact, historically, NIMH made policy decisions not to support research into women's differential responses to medications and it was not until 1990 that these issues were seriously considered by developing an Office on Research on Women's Health (Comas-Diaz & Jacobsen, 1995). There is little research on the differential effects of medication based on race, culture, and ethnicity. Thus, the therapist may need to be an advocate in helping the client receive appropriate treatment. Special medication issues are summarized in Table 5.4.

For the menstruating woman, one possible scenario is that there may be a decrease in medication levels premenstrually resulting in an increase in depressive symptoms at that time and an increase in medication levels postmenstrually with a resulting increase in side effects (Ackerman, 1999; Jensvold, 1996; Raskin, 1997). When this problem appears to produce distressing symptoms, a change of dosage or type of antidepressant should be discussed with the prescribing practitioner.

An alarming development is the recent marketing of fluoxetine as Sarafem in "a pretty pink and lavender capsule, available in a light blue box" (Kramer, 2000, p. 17). The Eli Lilly company is spending a great deal of money to market this "new" drug for PMS and progressive practitioners are expressing concern that women will be overprescribed and that their distressing symptoms will be dismissed. Resources for addressing PMS with diet and exercise are listed in Appendix A.

Certain medications interact with birth control pills. For example, estrogen-containing birth control pills cause the heterocyclic and tricyclic antidepressants to remain in the system longer (Janowsky, Halbreich, & Rausch, 1996; Raskin, 1997). The therapist should make sure that the client discusses these issues with the prescribing practitioner and should not assume to have expertise in this area. As discussed in chapter 2, the effect of oral contraceptives (OCs) on mood is unclear. However, it is prudent to evaluate whether a depressed woman is taking OCs and whether the onset of depressive symptoms coincided with the introduction of OCs.

Despite the popular belief that postpartum depression is best treated with antidepressants, a comprehensive review of drug efficacy studies concluded that data are insufficient to determine the efficacy of SSRIs

**TABLE 5.4 Special Medication Issues for Women**

Sexual side effects.
Gender and ethnicity can influence dosage.
Menstrual cycle-related changes are possible.
OCs can interact with SSRIs and TCAs.
OCs may cause mood worsening.
The long-term effects of SSRIs are not known, particularly during pregnancy and breast-feeding.
Hormone replacement therapy does not alleviate major depression.
Progestins may cause mood worsening.

for postpartum women (Mulrow et al., 1999). The therapist may have to work against assumptions about an over-reliance on medication in postpartum women and their medical practitioners, educating them about the role of psychosocial factors in their depression (Swendsen & Mazure, 2000) and the potential benefits of psychotherapy.

For pregnant and nursing women, the decision to take medication for depression or anxiety should be made with care. Although the research currently shows that there are no short-term effects of antidepressants passed to children in utero or through breast milk, the long-term effects are not known (Llewellyn et al., 1997; Raskin, 1997; Wisner, Perel, & Findling, 1996). For women with disabling panic or anxiety symptoms or a history of severe recurrent depression particularly with a history of suicide attempts, the benefits of taking medication may outweigh the risks. The therapist may need to assist the client in obtaining sufficient information to make an informed decision that is most suited to her as an individual.

Menopausal women do not show increased rates of depression. In fact, the risk of major depression decreases after age 44 (Weissman et al., 1988). However, there appears to be a slight increase in mood symptoms in the immediate premenopausal period and in women who undergo surgical menopause (Yonkers & Bradshaw, 1999), particularly as a result of hot flashes and night sweats, which disrupt sleep. Given the preliminary findings of the Women's Health Initiative study (NIH, 2000) that hormone replacement therapy (HRT) may increase risk of stroke, blood clots, and heart disease after two years, the current wisdom is to prescribe HRT for a limited time for disruptive symptoms of perimenopause or menopause. Thus far, the data is inconclusive as to whether HRT reduces the risk of heart disease over the long term, increases the risk of breast cancer, or reduces the risk of osteoporosis. More definitive knowledge about HRT and cancer will not be known for several years.

There is now a small body of research concerning the effects of HRT on mood in perimenopausal and menopausal women. One review of the few studies of estrogen treatment of depression found that estrogen improves mood only for those women who do not have major depression (Burt et al., 1998). Another review concluded that estrogen alleviates milder mood disturbances in peri- and postmenopausal women and that it may be more effective in perimenopause than in postmenopause (Yonkers & Bradshaw, 1999). Women who undergo surgical menopause have the most consistent benefits from estrogen (Yonkers & Bradshaw).

Many women are prescribed combined hormone therapy of estrogen and progesterone due to the tempering effects of progesterone on the negative effects of estrogen. Findings are contradictory as to whether progestins precipitate mood disorders. A review published by the American Psychiatric Association Press concluded that "there is little support for the view that progestins cause mood worsening" (Yonkers & Bradshaw, 1999, p. 128), while a report by the National Women's Health Network (NWHN, 2000) asserted that progestins may cause depression or mood changes. Findings are unclear as to whether HRT facilitates antidepressant activity (Amsterdam et al., 1999; DeBattista, Smith, & Schatzberg, 1999). In addition, "little is known about possible effects of menopause per se on pharmokinetics" (Hamilton & Yonkers, 1996, p. 37).

In conclusion, the therapist needs to be knowledgeable about psychopharmacologic treatments of depression, their indications, contraindications, and side effects. In addition, women's neuroendocrinology suggests the need to be familiar with reproductive-related issues and events and their impact on mood. The therapist may need to educate prescribing practitioners about the potential impact of reproductive-related events, OCs, and HRT. As will be discussed in chapter 6, the therapist should gather information about such issues from women clients as part of the assessment process.

In my own practice, I have been surprised by the frequency with which medical practitioners ask my opinion about which antidepressants to prescribe and, although I place the responsibility back on the prescribing practitioner, I engage in a discussion of the pros and cons of particular choices, appreciating their collaborative efforts. It is particularly important to communicate about the presence of anxiety or agitation because fluoxetine (Prozac), the most activating of the SSRIs, is usually contraindicated. Additionally, with clients who are actively suicidal, tricyclic antidepressants are contraindicated owing to their potential lethality, emphasizing the importance of maintaining ongoing communication with prescribing practitioners. Table 5.5 lists the numerous areas that the therapist should address with the client in discussing medications.

I get many of my referrals from medical practitioners in the community who have already prescribed medication by the time I see the client, in which case I seek to find a way to be collaborative with the medical practitioner while continuing to honor my own values and those of the client. The bottom line is that it is vitally important that we as therapists be extremely knowledgeable about medications.

## PHOTOTHERAPY

Although the prevalence of winter depression or seasonal affective disorder is not well researched at this point, studies have found that women

**TABLE 5.5   Discussing Medication**

A comprehensive discussion about medication with clients should include
1. The client's beliefs and underlying assumptions about antidepressants.
2. Past experience with medication including type, dosage, length of treatment, responses, and side effects.
3. The neurophysiological action of antidepressants.
4. Potential side effects.
5. The role of medication as an adjunct to psychotherapy.
6. The role of medication in relapse prevention.
7. Special issues for nursing and pregnant women.
8. Financial resources available for medications.
9. Ongoing monitoring of side effects.
10. Discontinuation syndrome.
11. Querying the client about the use of herbal remedies.

have higher rates than men (APA, 1994; Leibenluft et al., 1995; Sato, 1997). The effectiveness of phototherapy has been demonstrated in several studies and may be helpful for individuals living in regions at higher latitudes that typically have shorter days in winter, such as Alaska, the northern part of the United States, and Canada. The problem may be especially acute for persons who have recently moved from a more southern latitude. It may be appropriate for a psychotherapist to recommend phototherapy when a depression is clearly seasonally related, although it may be difficult to accurately diagnose SAD, particularly for someone having a first depressive episode (Sato, 1997). Those who are initially identified as having winter depressions may not necessarily continue to have purely seasonally related depressions (Schwartz, Brown, Wehr, & Rosenthal, 1996).

To meet the DSM–IV (APA, 1994) criteria for winter depression, the individual must have had two major depressive episodes beginning in fall or winter and remitting in spring during the last two years without nonseasonally related episodes in that interim, and seasonal depressive episodes must substantially outnumber the nonseasonal episodes during the individual's lifetime. It should be noted that there is little research comparing phototherapy with other treatments including medication and psychotherapy. IRT espouses phototherapy as an adjunct to psychotherapy for winter depression for clients who have access to lights and are motivated to use them regularly. Psychotherapy encourages the client to mobilize herself in order to utilize the most optimal coping strategies, including light therapy.

Lights with sufficient intensity are expensive and results are not assured, so this is not a treatment for those without sufficient financial resources. At this point, there are no standardized treatment protocols for light therapy. While typical treatment protocols involve suddenly exposing individuals to unnaturally high levels of light, there is some evidence that dawn simulation is effective due to the gradual exposure to light intensity. More research is needed in this area.

After reviewing treatment outcome studies, Sato (1997) made several recommendations which I summarize in Table 5.6.

## HERBAL THERAPIES

Not only have herbal therapies gained in popularity in recent years, particularly among middle-class Anglo Americans, but the use of alternative therapies and home remedies have a long history among many ethnic minority groups. It is important to ask about the use of such remedies and to understand the client's beliefs about any such remedies (Comas-Diaz & Jacobsen, 1995). There is increasing popularity in the use of St. John's wort (hypericum) and other herbal remedies. It is not unusual for people to believe that herbal preparations are superior to antidepressant medications because they are so-called "natural" substances. There is no scientific basis for this conclusion and there is actually very little knowledge about the long-term effects of herbs and their interactions with other herbs and drugs.

Mulrow and associates (1999) reviewed 14 studies of hypericum (St. John's wort), most of which were conducted in Germany. The researchers concluded

### TABLE 5.6  Light Therapy Recommendations (Sato, 1997)

1. Sufficient light intensity is 2,500 lux.
2. Studies show effectiveness with full spectrum lights and ordinary fluorescent lights.
3. Sufficient exposure time is 30 minutes to 2 hours on a daily basis during the winter.
4. Morning treatments appear to be most effective.
5. At the first signs of depression, one week of treatment may be sufficient to prevent emerging winter depression from developing into full-blown depression.

> Hypericum appears more effective than placebo for the short-term treatment of mild to moderately severe depressive disorders, but data are limited and subject to positive publication bias. Whether hypericum is as effective as standard antidepressant agents given in adequate doses is not established. (p. 59)
>
> Evidence regarding the efficacy of hypericum is lacking in many areas. Neither the most appropriate preparation nor the most effective dose is known. . . . There are no long-term maintenance or prevention of relapse data. (p. 60)

Recently, NIMH issued a public alert on St. John's wort because of its adverse interactions with indinavir, a protease inhibitor used to treat HIV, and cyclosporine, a drug used to reduce the risk of organ transplant rejection (NIMH, 2000). St. John's wort may also reduce the efficacy of oral contraceptives (State of the art, 2000). In regard to other herbal remedies such as kava kava or valeriana, there are no trial data assessing their efficacy at this time (Mulrow et al., 1999).

While it is inappropriate for a psychotherapist without specialized training to recommend herbal remedies, it is not unusual for clients to ask for the therapist's opinion about such remedies, whether the client is a current user or is contemplating use. In such situations, I inquire about usage, explore with the client her beliefs about symptoms and recovery, educate the client that knowledge is very limited about herbal remedies, and caution against combining herbal remedies and prescribed medications, recommending consultation with the pharmacist. I also recommend the client use the lowest possible dosage and increase only after giving a low dosage sufficient time to work. In other words, I provide education and support the client in being a critical consumer.

## TRADITIONAL CHINESE MEDICINE

Traditional Chinese Medicine (TCM), which consists of acupuncture and medicinal herbs, is becoming increasingly popular and slowly becoming a complement to Western medical practice. In fact, even in the rural backwater where I live, the local hospital has received a mandate from its corporate office to develop an integrative medicine program including massage therapy and acupuncture.

Therapists may find that their clients have been utilizing TCM or that clients are interested in trying this modality. Western-style research is just beginning. TCM may be especially helpful for clients with fibromyalgia, chronic fatigue, migraine headaches, and reproductive-related problems. Chinese medicinal herbs are based on complex formulas, and clients should be cautioned about diagnosing and treating themselves.

## SUMMARY

This chapter has provided the fundamentals of assessment, presenting a philosophical framework and guidelines for following standards of care in treating depressed individuals. IRT incorporates traditional, relational, and feminist methods for assessment to create a professionally responsible and culturally sensitive approach that is user friendly for client and therapist. In IRT, assessment is not only a tool for the therapist, but it will become a self-assessment tool for the client. The major elements of the IRT philosophy of assessment are: collaboration and education, empowerment through self-assessment, a nonpathologizing perspective, focus on strengths and competencies, cultural literacy and cultural competency, and informed consent. Standards of care include assessment of imminent danger, symptoms including seasonal timing and comorbidity, previous depressive episodes and treatment history, and family history of depression or other psychiatric problems. Psychotherapy is viewed as the primary treatment modality with pharmacotherapy as an ancillary treatment option offered to clients based on a range of factors, including motivation for psychotherapy, symptom severity, and beliefs about treatment. In regard to medication, there are special issues for women that require specialized knowledge on the part of the clinician.

The next chapter will describe four conceptual maps that are unique to IRT and that, when combined with philosophy and standards of care, form the essentials of assessment in IRT.

# CHAPTER SIX

# Assessment: Case Conceptualization

"There's something wrong with me. I feel like a failure." These were Laura's words to me in our first session. Her view of herself placed the source of her problem squarely on her shoulders: she was to blame for her depression. She was the problem. As you may recall, I contextualized Laura's problem, describing the complex interrelationship of factors that contributed to her depression. By utilizing several conceptual maps, I was able to collaborate with Laura to develop a case conceptualization that was no longer self-blaming and that led us to the development of a treatment plan.

One of the most important questions the therapist should ask the depressed woman at the outset of therapy is, "What in your life is making you unhappy?" (APA, 2000). While some women enter therapy with a clear picture of the reasons for their depression, others will be so debilitated or self-blaming that they fail to see beyond their own perceived inadequacies. Asking about the source of unhappiness frames the problem of a woman's depression as encompassing external as well as internal factors and paves the way for discovering potential solutions. To aid in developing such a multidimensional case conceptualization, IRT provides four unique conceptual maps from which to understand the client's problems. These maps bring relational, feminist, and multicultural perspectives to the assessment of depression and address affective, cognitive, behavioral, somatic, and systemic aspects of depression.

The four conceptual maps are: (a) biopsychosocial risk factors, (b) a relational view of depressive symptoms, (c) aspects of the self, and (d) elements of therapy. The first three items comprise the framework for case conceptualization. The treatment plan will flow from the case conceptualization and will be based on the elements of therapy, which will be prioritized according to the phase of therapy: stabilization, transformation, or future orientation.

108

# PSYCHOSOCIAL RISK FACTORS

As discussed in chapter 2, a complex interrelationship among a number of psychosocial risk factors contributes to women's high rates of depression. Identification of each client's specific risk factors is an essential part of IRT. Because biopsychosocial risk factors represent factors over which larger forces have come to bear, identification of such risk factors may immediately reduce the client's depression by providing her with an explanation for her problems that is not self-blaming. However, with clients who have numerous, serious risk factors there is the danger of both therapist and client becoming overwhelmed, discouraged, hopeless, and helpless about the client's life situation. In these cases, it is important for the therapist to be able to convey a sense of hope and support, remembering that a caring, empathic, positive therapeutic relationship may be of enormous help to the client even in the face of immutable, overwhelming life events.

Table 6.1 provides a checklist for biopsychosocial risk factors that may be used as an informal guide to help therapist and client gather and integrate a large amount of information. Because so many women take their lives for granted or minimize problems, it is often helpful to ask about specific types of events and situations. Ultimately, identification of risk factors leads to the beginning of a new narrative about the client's depression that is not self-blaming. Through identification of risk factors, client and therapist can develop a treatment plan aimed at reducing or buffering against risk factors. Following, I discuss the most salient issues in assessing psychosocial risk factors.

## BIOLOGICAL FACTORS

As discussed in chapter 2, biological factors of interest are: endocrine, genetic, chronic pain or illness, substance abuse, and a history of prior depressive episodes. The implications of these factors should be discussed in terms of treatment planning. A family history or client history of depression indicates the client's heightened vulnerability to the depression-inducing aspects of stressful events and suggests the need for a relapse prevention plan.

A health history including a reproductive history should be a part of assessment. A reproductive history may include asking about events that may implicate hormones as well as life stressors. For example, reproductive events such as pregnancy, recent birth, miscarriage, abortion, and infertility may be related to stress rather than hormonal factors.

**TABLE 6.1   Psychosocial Risk Factors Checklist**

*Biological Factors*

Reproductive-related
_____ Substantial affective lability related to premenstrual phase
_____ Hormone replacement therapy (ask about type)
_____ Birth control pills
_____ Hysterectomy
_____ Perimenopausal or menopausal
_____ Illness or chronic pain
_____ Substance overuse or abuse
_____ Prior depressive episode
_____ First degree relative history of depression

*Life stressors*
_____ Relationship conflict
_____ Employment stress or discrimination
_____ Interpersonal violence
_____ Sexual assault
_____ Harassment
_____ Pregnancy
_____ Miscarriage
_____ Childbirth
_____ Infertility
_____ Childcare
_____ Eldercare
_____ Homemaker role
_____ Role strain
_____ Single parent
_____ Single-again status
_____ Isolation
_____ Recent loss
_____ Poverty or serious financial hardship

*Societal factors*
_____ Lower status job
_____ Inequality in workplace
_____ Inequality in family responsibilities
_____ Inequality in financial responsibilities
_____ Inequality in access to financial resources
_____ Career change to lower status or decreased income
_____ Member of racial, ethnic, religious, sexual, or age minority group
_____ Disabled

*Developmental factors*
_____ Childhood loss of parent
_____ Childhood trauma or neglect
_____ Developmental transition

The therapist asks about reproductive events and develops an individualized treatment plan based on the complex factors involved in each client's situation, the client's goals for therapy, and the client's appropriateness for a medical evaluation or medication referral. As discussed in chapters 2 and 5, the research on pharmacological and psychosocial treatments of reproductive-related depressions is limited and therapist, client, and, when appropriate, medical practitioner, will be faced with devising an individualized treatment plan based on the unique needs of each woman. As the baby boomers come into menopause, there is a growing body of integrative health knowledge. Appendix A lists so-called alternative resources for reproductive-related events.

For clients with chronic pain or chronic illness, there may be a need for a more aggressive pain management program or a support group for clients with similar problems. The long-term nature of this risk factor also suggests a focus on hope-inducing and meaning-making types of activities. Psychosocial treatments for these particular problems may be more appropriate than IRT or may be integrated into the IRT model.

The initial sessions should include a thorough assessment of substance use or abuse. Serious substance abuse warrants an evaluation for referral to inpatient, residential, or intensive outpatient programs. It is not unusual for a client to feel unsafe about reporting substance-related behaviors and for this kind of information to be disclosed later in the therapy. When a client is not improving, a re-evaluation of substance use may lead to recognition that this had been a hidden problem.

## LIFE STRESS FACTORS

The therapist gathers a picture of the client's life stressors by asking about the client's current situation and her life history. Because many women take their lives for granted and minimize the stressfulness of their lives, the therapist may need to ask about specific types of events. Simply because a client minimizes the impact of a situation like caring for an aging parent, does not mean it is not stressful. The therapist may have to help the client develop a more realistic view of the demands on her life and the impact such demands may have on her. Identification of stressful life events begins the process of helping the client manage and reduce stress in more effective ways, which is discussed in chapter 8.

## SOCIETAL FACTORS

Recognition of the potential role of societal factors to increase stress and distress is important in developing a comprehensive and accurate case conceptualization. Here I briefly discuss the potential impact of minority group membership and roles of unequal status.

## Identification of Minority Status

Being a member of a less privileged or minority group is a risk factor due to the impact of racism, homophobia, ageism, and discrimination against the disabled. For example, for a Hispanic graduate student, being from a different race and socioeconomic background than her professors and peers often caused her to feel alienated, angry, and misunderstood. For a lesbian client, being closeted in her job created daily stress and strain, contributing to feelings of self-doubt, anxiety, and depression. Naming these issues is vital in developing an accurate, culturally literate case conceptualization.

## Unequal Status

Having unequal status at home or at work can have an insidious, negative impact on the client, eroding self esteem, increasing stress, and promoting hopelessness. As part of assessment, it is important to identify significant life situations of inequity. Because so many women take their status for granted and may not even be aware of the fact that they are in oppressive or in unequal situations, it is important to purposefully and systematically explore this issue. Power analysis involves exploring the client's power status within important interpersonal environments in the client's life, including family, work, and community groups.

Consider Donna, a 40-year-old Caucasian administrative assistant with a master's degree in business administration who came to therapy baffled by her first depressive episode:

> My life is great so I don't understand why this is happening to me. I get along really well with my two girls (a high school senior and a college sophomore), I am about to get married to a great guy, I had a good childhood, and I love my job.

Donna was in excellent health, was an amateur athlete who trained and competed regularly, had several good friends, and was financially on solid ground. She was puzzled by her symptoms of being irritable and tearful at work, feeling exhausted by the end of the work day, and experiencing dread at getting out of bed each weekday, yet she stated repeatedly that she loved her job. In fact, she claimed it was the best job she had ever had. It was only through examining Donna's role at work and identifying her subservient place in a workplace hierarchy that the eroding influence of powerlessness on her mood became apparent.

Donna supervised several clerical workers and had a large number of responsibilities that required that she meet deadlines. She worked in a large medical facility in which the doctors were constantly running to her and demanding that she immediately complete certain tasks that were not among her job responsibilities. She felt powerless to refuse and when she did get up the courage to do so, she was met with arrogance and hostility from the doctors. It was only through identifying the stressful elements of her position while joining with her reverence for her current position, "the best one I ever had," that I was able to help Donna acknowledge and address this problem.

For survivors of sexual abuse or other forms of interpersonal violence and victimization, being in positions of lower status or less power may recapitulate the dynamics of their previous victimization, eliciting trauma-related affects of depression, helplessness, and hopelessness. Particularly for individuals who have already had a successful round of therapy focusing on trauma resolution, the return of these symptoms can be confusing, puzzling, and demoralizing. It can be extremely helpful to be able to identify and name the source of the client's distress.

While the therapist initially takes the lead in identifying risk factors related to minority group membership and unequal status, as discussed in chapter 8, an eventual goal of therapy will be for the client to develop critical consciousness so that she will independently identify the role of social factors in distressing interpersonal situations.

## A RELATIONAL VIEW OF SYMPTOMS

In IRT, the therapist is interested in going beyond the diagnostically derived symptoms of depression to develop a comprehensive picture of the interpersonal and uniquely individual manifestations of the client's affective, cognitive, physical, behavioral, and systemic experience. In addition, there is attention to strengths as well as problems. These pieces will be directly addressed in the specific treatment tasks related to the elements of therapy and will be important in developing a relapse prevention plan. A relational view of symptoms acknowledges the key role that relationships play in women's lives and in their depressions. As stated in chapter 1, many women lose connection with themselves in order to maintain connection with others. The loss of connection with self leads to depression, and depression serves to further this loss of connection with self and others. Many symptoms may be viewed as adaptational because they represent the woman's efforts to manage her emotions to maintain relationships. Helping a woman reframe her symptoms as her best efforts at adaptation reduces blame and paves the way for her to learn new ways of coping.

It will probably take therapist and client several sessions to get a comprehensive picture of the numerous manifestations of her depression. This section will briefly describe a relational perspective on symptoms and the subsequent chapters on treatment interventions will give more specific details and case examples of how this approach will contribute to the therapeutic process. Table 6.2 shows a list of topics that may be used as an informal guide in exploring depressive symptoms from a relational perspective. Chapter 10, which discusses connection with self and others, will illustrate how this material is integrated into the therapy.

### AFFECTIVE EXPERIENCE

There is a wide range of affective experiences that depressed individuals report. Among the predominant emotions that depressed clients de-

**TABLE 6.2   Relational Perspective on Depressive Symptoms**

Affective experience
  Prevailing affect
  Underlying emotions
Cognitive experience
  Internal conversations:
    Statements of negative voice
    Statements of self-nurturing voice
  Personal meaning of depression
  Metaphoric meaning of depression
Physical experience
  Visceral experience of depression
  Metaphoric language
Behavioral manifestations
  Authentic connections
  Disconnections
Systemic experience
  Narratives of parents and grandparents
  Cultural history and heritage
  Stories from the client's childhood
  Description of the client's day-to-day life

scribe are feelings of numbness, excruciating pain, overwhelming sadness, anger, constant irritation, fear, anxiety, and shame. Initially, some clients may report a general, undifferentiated sense of depression. As client and therapist engage in deeper exploration, however, more complex emotions may emerge or appear to be present. The therapist can assist the client in describing her affective experience by asking the client to talk about what she feels, reflecting back the client's own descriptions, incorporating the client's own words, asking for clarification, and gently offering her own observations.

The identification of underlying emotions will be particularly relevant for the middle phase of therapy once the client has stabilized and she begins to focus on specific issues that may be related to her depression. Many women are unable to express sadness and anger at life circumstances or at the important people in their lives. The therapist must appreciate that there are cultural differences in the way that emotions are expressed, developing a framework that is sensitive to the client's multiple identities. A relational conceptualization of depression includes an understanding of the familial, social, and cultural influences that foreclose women from being able to directly express and name their negative emotions, limiting their ability to take actions that will restore lost connections and promote recovery.

## COGNITIVE EXPERIENCE

### Internal Conversations

In addition to the cognitive symptoms of depression that affect memory, concentration, and decision-making abilities, IRT is particularly concerned with the client's internal conversations. Consistent with IRT's focus on strengths and competencies, the therapist and client are interested not only in listening to distorted or negative cognitions, but also in hearing inner voices of strength, nurturance, and resilience. The focus on inner voices of strength differentiates IRT from traditional cognitive therapy, which strives to identify and correct negative cognitions through rational, step-by-step cognition-based reasoning. By carefully listening to both sides of internalized conversations, by hearing the voices that talk back or resist the self-denigrating voices of depression, and by increasing awareness of cognitive manifestations of the authentic self, IRT leads to restoration of the self and recovery from depression. Listening to internal conversations is described in more detail in chapter 9 in which therapy tasks related to connection with self and others are discussed.

## Meaning of Depression

Another element of the client's cognitive experience is the meaning the client has made of her depression or depressive symptoms. Often clients suffer what I call "the double whammy of depression." Not only is the individual depressed, but she is depressed about being depressed. Her sense of hopelessness is intensified by the meaning she has made of being depressed: "I'm a failure. I'm inadequate. I shouldn't be feeling this way. This proves I cannot cope. I'm no good."

Part of recovery will involve a transformation of meaning about the depressive episode, as the client and therapist seek to untangle the larger meaning of her depression in the context of sociocultural, interpersonal, and intrapersonal factors. Thus, the personal meaning the client has made of her depression (i.e., "I am a failure") is translated into a contextual and multidimensional meaning based on a combination of internal and external factors (i.e., "My life is too stressful and I was unprepared to cope with such stress"). Meaning is the fifth element of therapy and treatment tasks related to transformation of meaning are described in chapter 11.

### PHYSICAL EXPERIENCE

Depression is a mind-body phenomenon that can be physically as well as emotionally encompassing. Depressed individuals can have physical symptoms ranging from agitation to immobility. Some people can describe extremely vivid, visceral experiences such as

I feel a heavy, black cloud in my chest.

My veins are filled with molasses.

I am in a deep, dark cave with no way out.

I am mired in quicksand.

All my joints ache. It hurts to move at all and the biggest pain of all is in my heart.

Helping the client articulate the physical experience of depression and describe any metaphors or images can be helpful in a number of ways. First, determining whether the client is physically agitated or immobilized will facilitate determining particular treatment tasks that may bring some relief from these symptoms. Second, metaphors often can be used to explore solutions to problems. Third, the client may be able to identify when the depression is lifting by recognizing the absence of these symptoms. Finally, as part of relapse prevention, noticing the return of these symptoms may be an early warning sign that will signal initiation of prevention activities.

In addition to physical symptoms, the client's attitude about her body may be an important area to explore. Many women experience intensified body image dissatisfaction with depression (Joiner et al., 1995). Furthermore, efforts to cope with life stresses may create body alienation from weight gain, inactivity, and the use of unhealthy coping mechanisms such as smoking, overeating, or substance abuse. Healthy sexuality may become suppressed or buried. Recovery from depression entails restoring a healthy connection with both body and mind. Treatment tasks related to connection with the physical self are described in chapter 8, entitled "Activation."

## BEHAVIORAL EXPERIENCE: CONNECTIONS AND DISCONNECTIONS

Many women silence themselves or keep important parts of themselves hidden to maintain significant relationships (Jack, 1991, 1999). In IRT recovery from depression involves reinforcing relationships that support the client's authentic sense of self, restoring significant relationships that have become inauthentic, and resolving relationships that ultimately will never be healthy for the client. Relational changes and positive changes in the client's sense of self occur in a mutually reinforcing way: As the client engages in increasingly authentic interactions, her authentic sense of self is strengthened; likewise, as the client's sense of authentic self is strengthened, she is motivated to interact more authentically.

As part of the assessment process, client and therapist examine connections and disconnections with important people in the client's life, identifying relationships that support authenticity and those that do not. While the initial phase of therapy, particularly for the seriously depressed client, will usually focus on identifying supportive others and ways that the client can utilize supportive relationships in her recovery, the middle to late stages of therapy will more likely address relational disconnections and conflicts. Specific interventions will be discussed in chapter 10.

## SYSTEMIC EXPERIENCE

There are a number of ways that depression is influenced by systemic factors and ways that systemic factors may support recovery. In other words, the client is part of a number of larger systems that may influence, even indirectly, her mental health. These systems include her immediate family of residence, her extended family including past generations, coworkers or significant individuals at the workplace or school, and community groups and organizations. Through telling stories, the client develops a narrative of systemic experience that encompasses her daily life and the historical influences on her sense of self and sense of possibilities.

Connie, a 25-year-old Hispanic graduate student and the oldest daughter in a family of six children constantly felt guilty about not being available to her family because she was away at school. (Although some Hispanic individuals may prefer a more specific ethnic identifier, for purposes of confidentiality, I will use the more general term, Hispanic.) She told countless stories of her mother's self-sacrifice for the family and of her mother's frequent phone conversations to tell her the latest family crisis, eliciting enormous guilt in Connie. When I asked Connie to tell me about her grandmothers, she described two women who defied convention to pursue their own goals: One grandmother had been an artist of some note and the other had left her husband to seek a better life in United States. Bringing her grandmothers into the picture expanded her role models and, ultimately, helped her begin to construct her own vision of who she wanted to be, with the recognition that her mother's path was not her only choice. She could begin to construct a vision of a self who pursued her own goals while remaining close to her family.

Mothers and grandmothers provide important models that may help the client understand the conflicts she faces, the choices she has made, and the patterns she may be repeating. Naming these influences has the potential to activate the client into making new choices, forming new meanings of her experiences, and developing a more affirmative and integrated identity as will be discussed in chapter 11.

## THE ASPECTS OF THE SELF MODEL

Recovery from depression entails reclaiming the self and often transforming aspects of the self (Jack, 1991, 1999; Lerner, 1988). The aspects of the self model (Pearlman & Saakvitne, 1995) provides a nonpathologizing template with which to organize information about the client's strengths, vulnerabilities, and diverse aspects of identity. As discussed in chapter 3, psychotherapy outcome research has shown that the client's positive sense of self is one of the best predictors of outcome in short-term treatment for depression (Ablon & Jones, 1999; Asay & Lambert, 1999). Having a concrete conceptual map from which to delineate the client's sense of self facilitates the development of a realistic treatment plan. Does the client possess a generally positive sense of self, suggesting that therapy will be short term? Or do aspects of the self suggest the need for longer term work in order to fortify strengths and decrease vulnerabilities?

The aspects of the self model is adapted from Constructivist Self Development Theory (McCann & Pearlman, 1990; Pearlman & Saakvitne, 1995), which was developed for therapy with trauma survivors. An integrative model that incorporates self psychology (Kohut, 1977), constructivism (Mahoney & Lyddon, 1988), and relational theory (Jordon, 1991), the aspects of the self model can be used as an assessment tool for any client regardless of diagnosis. Its integrative, relational, and nonpathologizing orientation combined with its attention to diverse identities and cognitive schemas are consistent with IRT. I have adapted Pearlman and Saakvitne's (1995) model to focus on those aspects of the self most salient for depressed women.

There are three major aspects of the self that are particularly relevant for depressed women: frame of reference, self capacities, and core cognitive schemas. Table 6.3 lists these aspects of the self and their subcategories. The aspects of the self will be discussed throughout the book and numerous case examples will assist the reader in learning this model, which is an extremely valuable tool in case conceptualization and treatment planning. By the third or fourth session, the therapist should be able to have a clear picture of the client's strengths and vulnerabilities related to aspects of the self that will aid in development of a meaningful treatment plan. Recovery and relapse prevention involve utilizing and reinforcing strengths while minimizing vulnerabilities related to aspects of the self as well as reducing biopsychosocial risk factors.

## FRAME OF REFERENCE

Frame of reference is the lens through which the individual sees herself and her world. Seeing the world as the client does allows the therapist to access the client's language and viewpoint, which is essential for the

**TABLE 6.3    Aspects of the Self**

*Frame of reference*

Framework of beliefs through which the individual interprets experience:

    World view: self-efficacy and optimism

    Identities & roles

    Larger sense of meaning

*Self capacities*

Intrapersonal abilities that enable the individual to maintain a sense of self and manage emotions

    Ability to tolerate strong affect

    Ability to be alone

    Ability to self-soothe

    Ability to use an activating coping style

    Ability to maintain a positive sense of self

*Core cognitive schemas*

Beliefs, assumptions, and expectations related to self and the world.

Schemas related to self-esteem and control will be particularly salient

*Note:* Adapted from Pearlman & Saakvitne, 1995.

creation of a healing alliance and meaningful psychotherapy. "Frame of reference incorporates the manner in which an individual relates to and interprets [her] own experience. It is fundamental to an individual's perception and interpretation of life experiences" (Pearlman & Saakvitne, 1995, p. 61). There are three aspects of frame of reference: world view, identity, and a larger sense of meaning. Each of these aspects inform who the client is and how she views her world. The therapist will be able to recognize frame of reference through the client's stories of the past, present, and future. Therapy issues related to the three aspects of frame of reference are discussed in chapters 8 and 12.

## World View: Self-efficacy and Optimism

World view embodies the client's overall beliefs about the world including life philosophy, moral principles, causality, and locus of control. World view encompasses the client's attitude about interpersonal and nonpersonal events. For the purposes of working with depressed individuals, there are two specific aspects of world view that therapist and client want to identify and understand: self-efficacy and optimism. Self-efficacy is particularly salient for women who, through sex role socialization, are often trained to have an external locus of control, relying on others to dictate what they will do or not do and how they should feel or not feel. Specific theories and research regarding vulnerability to depression through a lack of self-efficacy were discussed in chapter 2 (Bromberger & Matthews, 1996a; Helgeson & Fritz, 1998; Lewis, 1994; Ritter, 1993). Self-efficacy is synonymous with empowerment, a long-standing concept in feminist therapy.

Laura, the client with three small children and a day care center in her home had a sense of self-efficacy; she was someone who tended to "take the bull by the horns" in life, seeing herself as able to solve any problem through hard work and diligence. Although this kind of self-activating approach will ultimately favor a faster recovery because the individual already possesses a self-empowered world view, it can contribute to the epigenesis or maintenance of a depression. The self-activating person is often disoriented, confused, or stymied by not being able to use her normally gung-ho approach to solving life's problems. Women who espouse a superwoman world view have difficulty accepting help, recognizing their vulnerabilities, or acknowledging obstacles. However, through the support of a positive therapeutic connection and through education about depression, the self-efficacious person is usually able to reconnect with the empowered self. As Laura stated at the beginning of the second session, "I left here feeling I had a treatment plan and I did not have to be alone with this." She described a new sense of hope and activation as a result.

On the other hand, the individual who lacks self-efficacy and is buffeted about by life's events allowing things to happen to her and to control her, has a longer road to recovery. Sex role socialization influences women to be passive and dependent on others. Ultimately, the woman client who lacks self-efficacy will have to develop a new world view that will not only facilitate her full recovery from depression, but minimize her vulnerability for recurrence. In recovery from depression, the client strengthens and mobilizes self-efficacy through self-care, activating coping strategies, and problem solving, which are discussed in chapter 8. Rigid and limiting core cognitive schemas contribute to a lack of self-efficacy, and therapeutic interventions related to these issues are discussed in chapter 11.

The second aspect of world view that has particular relevance for depressed women is whether she views the world through an optimistic or pessimistic lens. The client's underlying world view of optimism versus pessimism may not be apparent until after the client has stabilized or her depression has lifted. A pessimistic attributional style has been linked with depression (Seligman, 1991), and learning an optimistic cognitive style has been shown to decrease risk for depression (Seligman,

Schulman, DeRubeis, & Hollon, 1999). Thus, if the client sees the world as malevolent and unjust, her feelings of hope about the future are eroded and her interest in taking action on her own behalf is jeopardized. Alternatively, the client who has an optimistic world view has the capacity for hope and the willingness to work toward change. A pessimistic world view suggests a much longer course of recovery, and therapeutic work will usually involve significant changes related to all elements of therapy.

## Identities and Roles

Identity includes but is not limited to racial, maturational, gender, cultural, and vocational identities, as well as roles, idealizations, and projections of roles. The influence of gender and culture on role prescriptions is salient in IRT, as women strive to understand the forces that have come to bear on their sense of self and their life choices. Attitudes toward particular identities and roles that are ambivalent, negative, or rigid may have important implications for the client's vulnerability to depression. Likewise, conflicts between particular identities or roles may be pivotal in the underlying causes of depression. Affirmative identity is an important goal in IRT. Toward this end, the identification of internalized oppressions is an important part of the healing process. Internalized oppression is defined as negative beliefs about facets of identity that are considered to be nondominant identities within our Anglo, male-dominated, heterosexual, Christian culture. Internalized misogyny, internalized racism, internalized homophobia, internalized ageism, and internalized antisemitism are all examples of internalized oppressions that impact the individual's sense of self and confer a vulnerability to depression. Identity issues may be particularly complex and important for adopted women and women from multicultural backgrounds. The therapist is advised to become acquainted with models of identity development relevant for a given client (e.g., see McCarn & Fassinger, 1996; Sue & Sue, 1990), and these issues are discussed further in chapter 11.

## Larger Sense of Meaning

A larger sense of meaning describes a sense of connection with something beyond oneself, which acts as a buffer against depression by presenting beliefs that engender hope and optimism, by offering the means to access positive emotions, and by offering skills that enhance coping (Frederickson, 2000). Aspects of a larger sense of meaning include the ability to experience "spiritual moments"; a relationship with nature; belief in a higher power; belonging to a church, religious, or spiritual community; participating in altruistic or political activities; and engaging in creative endeavors. The therapist evaluates with the client to what extent she embraces an expansive sense of meaning and supports the client in strengthening or building meaning-making activities and skills that are consistent with her values, culture, and sense of self. Specific interventions and case examples are described in chapter 11.

## SELF CAPACITIES

Self capacities, listed in Table 6.3, involve those activities that regulate and manage one's inner state and one's emotions (Pearlman & Saakvitne, 1995); they are intrapsychic abilities. Through self capacities, the individual is able to maintain a consistent sense of self across time and across experiences. Self capacities include the ability to engage in activities, both mental and actual, that facilitate positive affect states and include: the ability to tolerate strong affect, the ability to be alone, the ability to self-soothe, the ability to have an activating coping style, and the ability to maintain a positive sense of self. Self capacities will have significant impact on case conceptualization and treatment planning.

Laura possessed well-developed self capacities in that when she was not having a depressive episode she typically recovered quickly from hurts and disappointments. Laura's strong self capacities indicated that therapy would probably be short term. On the other hand, Renata, a 50-year-old attorney, tended to ruminate over hurts and had difficulty refocusing herself on external endeavors as she would feel overwhelmed by her negative internal experience. For Renata, therapy would include strengthening self capacities.

The category of self capacities provides a nonpathologizing way to describe intrapsychic strengths and deficits needed to manage emotions. Individuals who have severe deficits in self capacities may resort to self-destructive behaviors in order to manage their emotions and would be considered in the language of the *DSM–IV* (APA, 1994) to have a personality disorder. IRT for depression is most appropriate for individuals with mild to moderate deficits in self capacities.

The individual who has strong self capacities is able to become mobilized to manage her emotional state through self-care, activating coping strategies, problem solving, and productive internal conversations. The work of therapy will include teaching and reinforcing skills that strengthen self capacities. For the client who has deficits in this area, therapy will have a longer course. While all elements of therapy address self capacities, those most relevant for strengthening and mobilizing self capacities are related to activation as described in chapter 8 and connection as described in chapter 9.

## CORE COGNITIVE SCHEMAS

Core cognitive schemas (CCSs) are basic assumptions and beliefs around which the client organizes information about herself and the world. They are fundamental templates that consciously and unconsciously guide the individual, influencing her sense of self, her life choices, her relationships, and her day-to-day decisions. As experiences arise, they are filtered through existing schemas and such experiences will either be fitted into or will reshape existing schemas (Hollon & Beck, 1979; Pearlman & Saakvitne, 1995; Piaget, 1971). Schemas will be apparent in the client's descriptions of daily life, in her inner dialogues, and in her narratives about her life. The therapist listens carefully, noticing and naming underlying schemas, looking to the client to confirm or disconfirm whether the named schemas fit for her. Statements of the client's negative or critical inner voice will usually lead directly to identification of dysfunctional negative self-schemas.

Depressed women typically assume excessive responsibility for negative life events, overestimating their responsibility in relationships while simultaneously underestimating their ability to affect important outcomes (Beck & Greenberg, 1974). Cultural factors, gender role stereotypes, and family experiences influence the development of resulting schemas. Standards for the ideal self form the basis for schemas that are used to judge the actual self (Jack, 1999). Schemas related to being "good" and "lovable" will be salient for many depressed women. Identification of dysfunctional CCSs will include assumptions the client has about gender roles, which usually involve beliefs about being a "good girl," "good woman," "good wife," "good daughter," and so forth. Dysfunctional CCSs are usually absolute, dichotomous, inflexible, or moralistic in tone. Perfectionistic schemas (Blatt, 1995; Blatt, Quinlan, Pilkonis, & Shea, 1995) and tenacious, rigid schemas usually indicate a longer course of recovery.

Particularly salient for depressed women are schemas related to esteem (being good, perfect, or lovable) and control (responsibility, instrumentality, or passivity). Table 6.4 lists examples of dysfunctional schemas related to esteem and control.

As you may recall from the discussion of Laura, she had the beliefs that she should be able to handle anything and that she should be a perfect mother. Identifying such schemas is an important part of the therapeutic work. While such schemas may seem obvious to the clinician, the client is often surprised when such schemas are identified and named as they conflict with important values that the client holds. Recognizing, naming, and challenging schemas can be a powerful part of the transformational work of therapy, which is discussed in chapter 11.

## SUMMARY OF ASSESSMENT

As described in chapters 5 and 6, assessment in IRT comprises a number of pieces that form a cohesive whole leading to case conceptualization and treatment planning. The foundation of assessment is a philosophy based on a collaborative, nonpathologizing, and culturally sensitive approach. The client is empowered to use self-assessment to contribute to the ongoing therapy process, to maintain perspective on her life after therapy, and to monitor potential signs of relapse. The therapist follows standards of care in assessing the client's symptoms, personal history, treatment history, family history, and risk of imminent danger

**TABLE 6.4 Dysfunctional Core Cognitive Schemas of Depressed Women**

*Examples of dysfunctional schemas related to esteem*
 I must be loved and approved by every person in my life.
 Other people's needs count more than mine.
 I am unlovable. No one will ever love me.
 I am undeserving.
 It is selfish to have any needs or wants.
 I must be a "good" wife, mother, daughter, and so forth.

*Examples of dysfunctional schemas related to control*
 I should be able to handle anything.
 It's my fault that I am depressed.
 I should do everything perfectly.
 I should not need any help.
 It is easier to avoid life's problems.
 If I get emotional, I will lose control.
 No matter what I do, it does not make any difference.

to self or others. Psychotherapy is viewed as the primary treatment, and referral for a medication consultation is based on a number of factors including clinical appropriateness and the client's beliefs and wishes.

The case conceptualization is coauthored by client and therapist and comprises (a) biopsychosocial risk factors, (b) a relational view of symptoms, and (c) strengths and vulnerabilities of the aspects of the self. Depression is considered to be based on external factors and their interface with vulnerabilities in the client's sense of self. Through identifying, celebrating, and reinforcing strengths and uniquenesses, as well as naming vulnerabilities, therapist and client create a treatment plan that is realistic and empowering. Case conceptualization and treatment planning are ongoing, interactive, and dynamic processes. The case conceptualization generates the treatment plan, which consists of (a) the elements of therapy, (b) prioritization of treatment tasks based on phase of therapy (stabilization, transformation, or future orientation), (c) the financial or institutional resources that dictate the number of sessions available, and (d) a relapse prevention plan. Chapters 7 through 11 address treatment tasks based on the remaining elements of therapy: safety, activation, connection, and meaning. Chapter 12 discusses relapse prevention.

# CHAPTER SEVEN

# Safety

Connie, a 23-year-old Hispanic graduate student came to see me upon the recommendation of her academic advisor. She felt embarrassed and overwhelmed by the referral and followed through because she felt it was what a "good graduate student" should do. She had never been to a therapist or counselor before. She told me that she believed she should be able to handle her own problems, but after trying to do so for several months, she still felt miserable, was unable to concentrate on her academic work, and was in danger of being asked to exit her doctoral program with a terminal masters degree. During the first session she rarely made eye contact with me and spoke in a barely audible voice. My task with Connie from the moment she sat down in my office was to facilitate a sense of safety and give her reasons to try to trust me.

Safety is the second element of therapy. It is the premier task of the therapist. The therapist must create a safe environment in which the client can feel free to share her most intimate thoughts and feelings. Without safety, therapy will be ineffective and assessment will be inaccurate. In this chapter I will discuss the treatment goals related to safety (see Table 7.1).

As will be the case for each of the five elements of therapy, therapist and client assess which of the treatment goals fit for a particular client based on her unique needs. The first two safety tasks, creating a safe and facilitative therapeutic environment and developing a safety plan for the high-risk client, have long been recognized as essentials in working with clients. The last tasks, planning a zone of safety for the seriously depressed client and developing safe and secure life circumstances, have particular relevance for women clients and are consistent with the philosophy of IRT. Clients are at risk for longer-lasting depressions or recurrences if they are unable to reduce exhausting or overwhelming demands of daily life, which is especially an issue for women with multiple roles. A zone of safety creates a temporary respite

**TABLE 7.1   Safety: Treatment Goals**

1. A safe and facilitative therapeutic environment
2. A safety plan for the high-risk client
3. A zone of safety for the seriously depressed or low-functioning client
4. Safe and secure life circumstances
5. Grounding skills

from the burdens of life during the most acute stage of depression. The fourth element of safety, developing safe and secure life circumstances, addresses risk factors related to sex role socialization and social inequities: Many women may be in physically or emotionally dangerous relationships or in economically insecure circumstances. Furthermore, women often find themselves in inferior, low paying jobs, increasing their stresses and eroding their spirits. Only when a woman feels safe and secure in her daily life is she truly able to reduce her vulnerability to depression and decrease her risk of recurrence. Although this safety task usually involves long-term goals and may not be addressed until the final stage of therapy, the other safety tasks are relevant early in the therapy.

The interrelationship of the therapy elements is apparent in the way that safety tasks lead to or suggest activities related to assessment, activation, connection, and meaning. For example, a safe therapeutic environment not only allows for more accurate and meaningful assessment but also for a greater sense of connection between client and therapist. Connection and safety catalyze the client into activation. Experiences of safety with the therapist have the potential to transform the client's meaning structures and such changes increase the client's willingness to become further activated, resulting in a cascade of interrelated changes.

## A SAFE AND FACILITATIVE THERAPEUTIC ENVIRONMENT

As Connie sat down in my office for the first time, I noticed that her hands were shaking and her eyes were brimming with tears. "I'm scared," she whispered. Never having been to a therapist before and coming from a family in which one kept one's problems to oneself, she found the experience of being in my office intimidating and disorienting. Connie and I had several obstacles to overcome in forging a trusting therapeutic relationship. In addition to her discomfort and unfamiliarity with psychotherapy, we were from different age, ethnic, and class backgrounds.

The essential strategies involved in creating a safe and facilitative therapeutic environment have been discussed in previous chapters and will be summarized here. Specific skills that the therapist uses toward this end, which were discussed in chapter 4 and chapter 5, include mutual empathy, mutual empowerment, listening, seeing, empathic attunement, authenticity, recognition of transference and countertransference issues, education, collaboration, a nonpathologizing perspective, recognition of strengths and competencies, cultural literacy, cultural competence, and informed consent. Specific interventions that the therapist can undertake that manifest these skills are listed in Table 7.2.

The development of a safe, trusting, and facilitative therapeutic relationship is one of the cornerstones of IRT and will be one of the primary tasks throughout the therapy. Through empathic attunement, the therapist is able to discern which of the previously listed skills will be emphasized. Empathic attunement is the paramount skill that will allow the therapist to know how to nurture a safe, healing, and accepting atmosphere in the therapy. By attending to each client in a present, moment-by-moment way, the therapist becomes attuned to each individual's unique verbal and nonverbal communications and to each interaction's multiple layers of meaning. By being truly present with the client, the

---

**TABLE 7.2   Interventions: Safety in the Therapeutic Encounter**

The therapist can facilitate the client's sense of safety in the therapeutic encounter by

1. Being empathically attuned to the client and fully present in the moment-by-moment interaction.
2. Conveying accurate empathy through reflecting and summarizing the client's thoughts, feelings, and concerns.
3. Educating the client about the process of psychotherapy.
4. Explaining confidentiality.
5. Seeking informed consent through written documents and verbal discussion.
6. Collaborating with the client to identify treatment goals and choose treatment interventions.
7. Providing a succinct, understandable, and nonpathologizing case conceptualization that includes strengths as well as problem areas.
8. Seeking the client's feedback about the process of therapy.
9. Initiating a dialogue about multicultural differences between therapist and client.

---

therapist offers the client what for many women will be a new experience of being accepted, respected, and understood. Such experiences lead to the development of a safe, facilitative therapeutic relationship.

In the first session with Connie, I acknowledged the courage it must have taken her to come to my office (mutual empathy, recognition of strengths, listening, and seeing) and asked her if she would like me to explain therapy to her, making a point of explaining confidentiality (education, collaboration, and informed consent). I then asked Connie what she would like to work on in therapy, emphasizing that therapy would be aimed at exploring her goals, not the goals of her advisor who had made the referral (collaboration and education). I also asked her what it was like for her to see a White therapist (cultural competence, recognition of transference issues).

Thus, in our first session, I established a framework that encompassed acceptance, understanding, collaboration, and caring while simultaneously introducing difficult issues. The therapist contributes to a facilitative therapeutic environment by directly addressing the client's problems and issues, thus creating an expectation that therapy sessions are a place for work. Although it may feel uncomfortable for the therapist to raise potential problems and conflicts, to do so sends the message that therapy is a place where difficult issues can be discussed. The therapist must strike a balance between easing the client's anxiety and involving her in the challenging work of psychotherapy.

In addition to the previously listed skills, the therapist can also facilitate safety through maintaining professional boundaries and being consistent. Knowing what to expect from the therapist may reduce some of the client's anxiety, thus paving the way for increased feelings of safety and trust. Caring may be communicated within the framework of a professional relationship. Establishing appropriate professional boundaries not only protects the client from having unrealistic expectations of the therapist, but provides a context in which the client feels freer to unburden herself. So often women feel constrained against disclosing pain for fear of burdening or overwhelming the listener. Establishing boundaries and a frame for a professional, yet caring relationship can offer the client a safe environment for talking about her troubles, which she may ordinarily be unwilling to do.

The sense of safety in the therapy relationship is one that unfolds over time. For example, in our initial sessions, Connie felt too anxious to voice many of her true thoughts and feelings. As she became more comfortable with me and with the process of therapy, however, she was able to voice her concerns that therapy was a middle-class endeavor that would force her to deny her roots and distance herself from her family. We were able to have open, challenging discussions about the purpose of therapy and about her fears. These discussions led to a deeper sense of mutual understanding and trust.

Trust, therefore, is an important issue in establishing a safe and facilitative therapeutic environment. The therapist needs to be alert to issues of trust that the client may bring into the therapy, which may come from being a member of a nondominant group, through victimization experiences, or through prior negative encounters with mental health professionals. It can be important for the therapist to identify trust as an issue and bring forth this issue into a therapeutic dialogue. When a client comes to know that the therapist can handle her feelings of distrust, the stage can be set for powerful change processes that strengthen the client's trust in herself and her own feelings as well as her trust in the therapist.

The client's sense of safety is strengthened when the therapist is attuned to the client and is able to accurately reflect the client's feelings and thoughts as well as make effective interventions. The therapist's accurate empathy facilitates instillation of hope in the client, which is of vital importance for successful recovery. When the therapist demonstrates understanding, knows about depression, and is aware of strategies that will lead to recovery, a sense of hope is instilled in the client. Most clients will feel safer with a therapist who is active. An inactive therapist can elicit feelings of anxiety that are not helpful for the depressed client.

A safe and facilitative therapeutic environment and relationship will increase the likelihood that client and therapist can successfully navigate the rough waters of crises, particularly those that involve suicidal episodes.

## A SAFETY PLAN FOR THE HIGH-RISK CLIENT

One of the first priorities in working with a depressed client is establishing whether she is a danger to herself or others. While assessing safety is always part of the initial session as discussed in chapter 5, assessment of safety and suicidal risk is an ongoing part of the therapy. Safety may require making verbal or written contracts as well as referring the client to a more containing environment such as an inpatient unit.

Creating a sense of safety within the context of the therapeutic relationship will maximize the likelihood that the client will be forthcoming about suicidiality and that a plan for the client's safety will be successful. It is essential that the client be an active and collaborative participant in developing her own safety plan and that the therapist resist becoming paternalistic or overly controlling so as to support the client's sense of being an agent in her own recovery. However, there will be some suicidal clients who are so depleted or confused that the therapist may be called upon to take charge or direct the client in order to maintain safety. These situations call for extreme sensitivity and caution in protecting the integrity of the client and the therapeutic alliance. The therapist starts with the least restrictive alternative and proceeds in a stepwise fashion in order to develop an effective and respectful safety plan. The essential ingredients of developing a safety plan for the high risk client in IRT are summarized in Table 7.3.

For example, Marcia, a client I had seen for three sessions, called me at 10:00 p.m. on a Friday night to tell me that she was planning to kill herself by taking an overdose of sleeping pills and drinking a fifth of vodka. On the phone she was crying, sounding confused, slurring her words, and admitting to having had several shots of vodka. I tried to engage Marcia in a discussion to come up with a safety plan that involved having her spend the night with friends or family. However, she was too upset to problem solve with me and refused to involve anyone else. When I determined that Marcia was not willing to go to the hospital voluntarily and she continued to assert that she was going to kill herself, I explained to her that I felt I had no choice but to protect her life by sending the police to her house to begin the process of involuntary hospitalization. (According to the relevant state law, this was the process by which involuntary hospitalization is to be initiated.) I asked Marcia to stay on the phone with me while waiting for the police but she hung up. By the time the police arrived, Marcia had flushed her pills down the toilet. The police decided she was not an imminent

---

**TABLE 7.3   Interventions: Safety Plan for the High-Risk Client**

The therapist can maximize the success of a safety plan with a high risk-client by
1. Maintaining an attitude of respect and collaboration toward the client.
2. Involving the client in decision making.
3. Starting with the least restrictive alternative.
4. Working with the client to remove any potential means of lethality.
5. Encouraging the client to enlist the support and presence of friends or family members.
6. Making frequent contact and follow-up.
7. Communicating with other members of the treatment team and, when appropriate, involving them in the decision-making process.
8. Consulting with colleagues.
9. Documenting.

risk, confiscated the bottle of vodka, and called to tell me that they were not going to transport her to the hospital. By that point, Marcia had calmed down enough to problem solve with me, explaining "seeing the police at my door kind of brought me back and I realized that I didn't really want to kill myself." We were then able to make a plan for Marcia to spend the night at a friend's house. With Marcia's permission, I spoke to the friend on the phone, enlisting her to become involved with our safety plan. I then arranged to speak to Marcia on the phone in the morning, at which point we would decide how to proceed.

Even though it was the weekend, I ended up seeing Marcia in my office on Saturday afternoon. With a suicidal client the therapist must be prepared to go to great lengths to have ongoing contact with the client and to convey caring. As was discussed in chapter 5, repeated contact is the best approach for the at-risk client (Canetto & Lester, 1995). With a suicidal client the therapist's immediate and simultaneous goals are the protection of the client's safety and the protection of the client's integrity. A discussion of the existential nature of life and death is not appropriate for the at-risk person and is only to be pursued if the client initiates such a discussion and is stabilized.

The clinician is more likely to encounter situations that have a higher degree of ambiguity than the one I described with Marcia. For example, what might I have done if during our first phone contact Marcia had tentatively agreed to not kill herself but refused to participate in any other safety plans while continuing to sound distressed and confused? In other words, what would I have done if I doubted Marcia's ability to follow through on her agreement, particularly if she were a client that I did not know very well? Or what if Marcia lived nearby, raising the option of my going to her home myself or accompanying the police? Each crisis presents options and nuances that can only be assessed in the moment based on the unique parameters of the client, the therapist, the therapeutic relationship, and the circumstances of that particular encounter. Calling a colleague for a consultation is always a good strategy in dealing with ambiguous situations. Often there are no simple or definitive answers in responding to suicidal clients and such work can be draining and scary for therapists. Therapist self care, which is particularly important when working with suicidal clients, is discussed in chapter 14.

## A ZONE OF SAFETY FOR THE SERIOUSLY DEPRESSED OR LOW-FUNCTIONING CLIENT

In IRT there are two types of safety plans. The first, described previously, is a plan for the safety of the suicidal or high-risk client, which is

designed to protect the life of the client. This type of safety plan is well
known to most mental health professionals. The second type of safety
plan is also for the seriously depressed, low-functioning client and is
aimed at creating a safety zone within which healing and recovery can
occur. Such a plan may involve taking time off from work or otherwise
reducing responsibilities. Although many mental health professionals
may encourage the client to develop such a plan, IRT makes suggestion
of such a plan an explicit part of the recovery process.

Because women are typically so compelled to overfunction and such
overfunctioning may be a contributing factor in their depressions, suggesting a break can be a crucial step toward recovery. By developing a
zone of safety, the client is given permission to be depressed, to listen
to her symptoms, attend to herself, and preserve her energies for the
most crucial tasks and responsibilities. For the seriously depressed or
low-functioning client, the therapist suggests that she take a brief break
from work, school, or major responsibilities. This is meant to be a short-
term plan to allow the client to focus on recuperation and recovery.
The therapist is attuned to the client and collaborates with her in
developing a plan that is realistic, feasible, and, above all, is based on
the client's desire to follow such a plan. Suggesting that the client
arrange a break is particularly important when a client is not functioning
well and is barely able to fulfill work, school, or family responsibilities.
Such a break may include taking sick leave, dropping out for the semester (most universities grant medical leaves), bringing in friends or family
members to help with child care, or temporarily withdrawing from
social or civic activities. Although such a reduction in responsibilities
during the acute phase of a depression may appear to be an obvious
strategy, many clients may be too self-critical to allow such a change
or too cognitively compromised to appropriately organize all but the
simplest arrangements. The therapist can offer a richer, more complex
variety of suggestions and solutions.

Establishing a zone of safety is meant to be a brief respite. While
some clients will do better having the structure of their daily responsibilities, others will become further depleted with each task and may jeopar-
dize their work, career, or academic success if they continue to function
in their depressed state. This will be particularly true for clients who
are experiencing cognitive symptoms such as memory loss, poor concentration, or indecisiveness. Some clients will be greatly relieved by the
therapist's suggestion that they temporarily withdraw from certain responsibilities. However, other clients who obviously could benefit from
a break may resist the notion of any kind of respite. When the client
expresses disinterest in a plan to take a break, the therapist respects

the client's choice to continue in her life as usual. Creating a zone of safety is an intervention for the low-functioning client and is to be differentiated from the lifestyle changes that accompany the middle phase work of transformation. For some clients, reducing responsibilities will be a middle-phase task of the therapy that will be accomplished only through the deconstruction of core cognitive schemas related to control, esteem, or perfectionism. Because of the strong relationship between stress and depression, an investigation of the clients' attitudes about roles and responsibilities will be a crucial part of most therapies but may only be successfully addressed in the middle phase of therapy.

## SAFE AND SECURE LIFE CIRCUMSTANCES

Safety is also addressed in regard to the client's relationships with others and with her environment. As the client gets down to the work of therapy, she evaluates her life circumstances: significant relationships, economic conditions, work, home, and school environments. She explores the degree of physical as well as emotional safety she feels in those aspects of her life and begins to identify areas that will require her to take action toward attaining the goal of safe relationships and secure life circumstances. While identifying an unsafe environment may be an early phase task, effectuating change is frequently a middle-to-late-phase task. Table 7.4 lists ways the therapist can help the client attain safe and secure life circumstances.

**TABLE 7.4   Interventions: Safe and Secure Life Circumstances**

The therapist can help the client develop safe and secure life circumstances by
1. Asking the client to identify relationships that may endanger herself or her children.
2. Asking the client to identify relationships that are supportive and empowering.
3. Working with the client to evaluate the safety of home and work environments.
4. Working with the client to evaluate her economic security and autonomy.
5. Collaborating with the client to make short-term plans for immediate safety from others or from dangerous environments.
6. Collaborating with the client to make long-term plans for safety from others or from dangerous environments.
7. Collaborating with the client to identify long-term goals for greater economic security and greater autonomy.
8. Identifying resources (social service agencies, books, etc.) that will support the client in meeting long-term goals for safe and secure life circumstances.

Safety may be a long-term goal for women in abusive relationships, as well as for women living in unsafe neighborhoods, working in hazardous jobs, or enduring workplace harassment.

Safety also includes developing a long-term life plan that leads to increased economic security. When women feel financially dependent on others (partners, parents, a terrible job, the welfare system), they can feel trapped, scared, and disempowered, which can inhibit recovery from depression or precipitate relapse. The therapist works with the client to develop a realistic plan for increased financial independence. This work may include helping the client have a sense of hope and motivation over the length of time it may take to effectuate change in these areas and reduce risk factors. Helping the client develop financial autonomy may also involve challenging her premises about money and deconstructing and reconstructing such premises (Katz, 1994). Establishing financial security may involve a continuum of therapy activities ranging from identifying new career goals, supporting the client as she pursues life changes, making a referral to a financial consultant, or simply naming the need to address these issues in the future. As with numerous other therapy goals, developing safe and secure life circumstances frequently involves an interrelationship of therapy activities related to all five elements of therapy.

Laura, the client who was having a postpartum-related depression, felt financially insecure not only due to her limited income but also due to her husband's irresponsible spending. Moreover, she dreamed of eventually starting her own consulting business and leaving the childcare business behind once her youngest child entered first grade. While our therapy was short term, as part of our relapse prevention plan we discussed the importance of her continuing to sustain her vision of a future career change as well as finding ways to enlist her husband in a more collaborative approach to managing their money. By emphasizing the importance of these goals, I was able to make explicit their important role in Laura's long-term well being.

The work of transforming life circumstances may take years and the client may do this work in a variety of ways ranging from continuous, ongoing therapy to brief intermittent contacts with a therapist. For some women, the simple act of recognizing and acknowledging that unsafe or insecure situations contribute to depression may be a goal. Often the therapist will refer the client to other agencies, groups, or community resources either as an adjunct to psychotherapy or, when appropriate, as the sole source of support for the client after therapy has terminated. The therapist works with each client to co-create a plan for safe and secure life circumstances that makes sense for each individual client. Because of the influence that women's lower social and economic status has on risk of depression, relapse prevention, which is discussed in chapter 12, must address these aspects of clients' lives.

## GROUNDING SKILLS

Depression is viewed as a normative developmental event that follows stressful events and precedes re-integration, typically leading to a woman's recognition that situations in her life are causing unhappiness. Until she gains the equilibrium and insight to begin to make changes, this may be a destabilizing and confusing experience, eliciting feelings of fear, anxiety, anger, or immobility. The client will benefit from learning how to ground herself, which will assist her in maintaining a holding environment (Winnicott, 1965) within herself outside of the therapy office. An effective tool toward this goal is grounded breathing which the client may be encouraged to practice regularly and use during stressful times. The therapist may also benefit from using grounding skills in doing the work of psychotherapy and in coping with stress.

## GROUNDING THROUGH BREATHING

The advantage of grounding through breathing is that it can be used at any time or place. Its subtlety allows it to be used in public places.

1. Teach the client to breath diaphragmatically, so that the diaphragm expands on the inhalation. The diaphragm can be located by placing the hand on the abdominal area and feeling the stomach expand outward on the inhalation.

Therapist: "Breathe evenly and calmly, feeling the diaphragm expand with oxygen on the inhalation and feeling it deflate on the exhalation. All of your attention is focused on expanding and contracting the diaphragm with each breath."

2. Therapist: "Each exhalation is accompanied by saying a number to yourself. Count 10 exhales. If you still need help calming yourself after 10 breaths, continue to count in groups of 10 until you feel ready to stop."

3. After the client tries counting, she can try saying a calming statement to herself on the inhalation. She should choose a calming statement that feels right to her. This intervention may be effective in times of mild stress without counting the breaths. I first ask the

client to try the following statement which I adapted from a meditative verse by Thich Nhat Hanh (1990). The smile has been found to elicit positive emotions in depressed individuals (Schwartz, Fair, Mandel, & Klerman, 1976). I practice this along with the client.

On the inhalation: "Breathing in, I calm my body."

On the exhalation: "Breathing out, I smile."

4.  If the client does not resonate with this statement, I offer a number of suggestions and brainstorm with her to find one she likes. Another variation is: "I am inhaling calm air; I am exhaling anxiety." Clients who experience anxiety as a result of heightened awareness in the throat, chest, or abdominal area during deep breathing may find relief by focusing on the sensation of the breath against the nostrils, a classic meditation technique.

## SUMMARY

This chapter has discussed safety, the second element of therapy. Safety is an essential feature in an effective client-therapist relationship, allowing the client to truly share herself and the reality of her life with the therapist. For the suicidal client, a safety plan that respects the client's integrity is developed collaboratively, starting with the least restrictive alternatives. For the severely depressed or low-functioning client, a zone of safety provides a temporary respite from the demands of daily life, allowing the client to preserve her energies for recovery. To create a life that supports recovery and relapse prevention, the client is encouraged to embrace the goal of safe and secure life circumstances. Such a goal may be long term and often involves resources beyond the therapist. The next chapter discusses activation, which will further mobilize the client to pursue her goals.

# CHAPTER EIGHT

# Activation

Connie, the graduate student mentioned in the last chapter, came into her fourth therapy session with a look of excitement in her eyes. "I was able to have a good weekend. I took care of myself and it worked." In previous sessions, we had identified a number of factors that had collectively contributed to feelings of misery as a graduate student, recognizing that living alone for the first time in her life was a major source of distress. Not only was living alone a new and foreign experience for her, but also, as the oldest daughter in a large family, her life had been dominated by taking care of her extended family including siblings, cousins, aunts, uncles, and grandparents. Now, several hundred miles from home, she was alone and without the usual demands of taking care of others. It was a surprise to Connie that living alone was difficult because she had longed to be on her own since high school. In reality, Connie did not have the foggiest idea how to go about spending time alone. Over the weekend, Connie discovered that by actively undertaking self-care activities, she could reduce her feelings of misery.

Activation, the third element of therapy in IRT, is synonymous with empowerment for the depressed woman. Movement into action is a vital ingredient of recovery from depression. As with all elements of therapy, activation is interconnected to safety, connection, and meaning, and ways to refine and understand activation activities are continually revised through assessment. When the depressed client feels connected and safe with her therapist, no longer feeling alone and hopeless, she is catalyzed into action (Miller & Stiver, 1997). Activation tasks involve body, mind, and spirit, comprise short- and long-term goals, and encompass early-, middle-, and late-phase tasks. Activation addresses not only the client's day-to-day well-being, but also her long-term life circumstances and life direction. Activation refers to an attitude that encompasses the areas listed in Table 8.1.

The length of time that it takes clients to become activated will vary and will take many forms depending on the phase of therapy, the

TABLE 8.1   Activation: Treatment Goals

1. An empowered state of mind
2. A proactive approach to daily life
3. A mobilized and healthy body

client's level of depression, the client's self capacities, and the client's life circumstances. Some clients will be activated into restoring their predepressive empowered selves while others will learn how to become empowered for the first time. Activation tasks involve being both active and proactive.

Activation is one of the priorities of therapy with depressed individuals. Clients with acute symptoms can be greatly helped by introducing early in the therapy activities that reduce distressing symptoms and promote more positive affects.

## AN EMPOWERED STATE OF MIND

Women face a double challenge in recovering from depression: not only do they have to struggle against the immobilizing impact of depressive symptoms, but also they often have to overcome culturally and socially sanctioned roles of passivity and accommodation. Depression can offer a way to covertly rebel and unconsciously resist life's difficulties that is more congruous with traditional female roles than with active confrontation (Gilligan, 1982; Jack, 1991). However, recovery from depression demands that the client take a stance of active resistance and the transition from passivity to activity may be quite a challenge for some women, particularly those who lack self-efficacy. IRT encourages the client to make a commitment to ongoing growth and to embrace an attitude of empowerment in all aspects of her life. She is urged to cultivate an alert and awake mental attitude, to develop critical thinking skills, and to take action to remedy disempowering situations.

### CRITICAL CONSCIOUSNESS

Because so many women respond to interpersonal distress with self blame, an essential skill in becoming empowered in one's approach to life is the ability to critically evaluate interpersonal situations that elicit negative affect, to engage cognitive processes to identify multiple factors that contribute to distress, and to problem solve effective ways to respond to distressing interpersonal situations. Toward this end, IRT adapts the concept of critical consciousness (Comas-Diaz, 1994) as a necessary condition for all women in order to achieve recovery and to increase resilience against relapse. The concept of critical consciousness was articulated by Lillian Comas-Diaz (1994) for psychotherapy with women of color and involves an awakening of consciousness leading to the capacity to analyze critically one's place in the world and to take logical action aimed at transformation. Although critical consciousness is akin to feminist consciousness, an integral part of feminist therapy (Brabeck & Brown, 1997), critical consciousness is more specific in its attention to the multiple oppressions of race, culture, gender, economics, sexual orientation, age, ability, and linguistic status.

The critically conscious individual views herself and the world with awakened eyes and is committed to taking action when inequities or problems are clarified through the use of this politicized lens. Critical consciousness represents an awakened capacity to critically analyze interpersonal situations, to recognize the influence of societal and systemic contexts of oppression on the individual's sense of self, to cope with emotional reactions in an empowered manner, to take constructive action to remedy oppressive situations, and, for some clients, to attend to others' oppressions. Table 8.2 defines the skills involved in the development of critical consciousness.

**TABLE 8.2   Interventions: Cultivating Critical Consciousness**

The therapist assists the client in cultivating critical consciousness by
1. Helping the client to recognize when sociocultural factors (gender, race, culture, sexual orientation, religion, age, economics, ability, or linguistic ability) play a role in the dynamics of distressing situations.
2. Teaching the client to engage in power analysis to recognize the potential role of power inequities in distressing situations.
3. Collaborating with the client to identify self care and affect management skills that increase self-mastery in disempowering situations.
4. Collaborating with the client to problem solve ways to improve disempowering situations in her own life.
5. Educating the client about the value of a commitment to ongoing personal growth and empowerment.
6. Exploring with the client whether working to improve others' oppressions through altruistic or political activities is of interest. (Usually a late-phase or post-termination task.)

The therapist collaborates with the client to assist her in developing the awareness and action orientation of critical consciousness. Initially, the therapist guides the client in engaging in the skills involved in critical consciousness and encourages the client to independently use such skills outside of therapy. The client learns to analyze situations so that she no longer sees problems as entirely due to her own shortcomings and develops the perceptual capacities to identify the multiple factors contributing to her mental state. The critically conscious client no longer responds to difficulties by concluding, "there must be something wrong with me" or by being overwhelmed with negative affect. She is able not only to name her part in problems but also to recognize contributing external, contextual factors. She engages in power analysis to understand the possible impact of power dynamics in disempowering and distressing interpersonal interactions. She experiences self-mastery by taking action to improve oppressive situations and by utilizing affect management skills and self-care to manage her distressing emotions. She does not allow herself to be overwhelmed or immobilized by emotion, but knows how to manage her emotions to effectively access problem-solving skills. Some clients will be moved to participate in altruistic or political activities to fight other people's oppressions. In short, through critical consciousness, the client is committed to her well-being and the well-being of others.

Connie, who came into therapy feeling immobilized and depressed, presents an example of the benefits of teaching the client to develop critical consciousness. Connie described constant feelings of guilt and inadequacy, and concluded "I'm not smart enough to succeed in grad school." As Connie and I deconstructed her situation, it became apparent that she was being pulled by conflicting cultural values and roles. As the oldest daughter in a close-knit, extended family, she had grown up with the expectation that she should be a "good daughter" by helping and taking care of the family. As the first in her family to attend graduate school, however, she felt pressured to be the "perfect student." In her first semester away from home, she confronted countless situations in which she was unable to be simultaneously a "good daughter" and a "perfect student." Inevitably, phone conversations with family members left her feeling emotionally paralyzed, as she experienced guilt for not being home to help her family. On numerous weekends, she made the long drive home to help her family, which often prevented her from completing school assignments on time.

As we began to identify the cultural and identity conflicts Connie was experiencing, she became armed with a way to understand her distress. Eventually, Connie began to speak to other Hispanic women students about these conflicts and discovered that she was not alone in her struggle. The capacity to critically analyze her distress and name the sociocultural factors that contributed to her bad feelings catalyzed a series of change events that moved Connie toward recovery. Rather than being immobilized by guilt and inadequacy, Connie had an intellectual framework from which to understand her problems, which spurred her to problem solve. Eventually, Connie was able to address her beliefs about being "good" and "perfect." While there were no easy solutions for the conflicting cultural values Connie was navigating, having an intellectual perspective from which to understand her problems allowed her to become more action oriented and less depressed. While the therapist may initially lead the way in naming sociocultural dynamics involved in a client's distress, through critical consciousness, the client develops the ongoing capacity to utilize cognitive processes to name disempowering dynamics on her own as they continue to arise. Identity conflicts such as those experienced by Connie are discussed in more detail in chapter 11.

The client can learn to use her critical consciousness in-the-moment or retrospectively when interactions seem tense, uncomfortable, or negative at home, at work, at school, and in the community. By using analytic processes to move beyond the negative feeling states that interpersonal interactions may evoke, the client can feel intellectually engaged and empowered rather than undermined and depressed. The development of critical consciousness catalyzes a series of interrelated changes that impact the client on multiple levels, encompassing all of the elements of therapy. By recognizing how her thinking has been subverted by various forms of oppression, the client comes to challenge her meaning structures related to self image and to reconstruct beliefs about herself and others. The client develops a more integrated and positive identity, stimulating change events discussed in the next four chapters. Moreover, the critically conscious client is activated to transform oppressive conditions in her own life, thus reducing risk factors. Through critical consciousness, the client no longer tolerates unsafe life circumstances or oppressive relationships. She becomes empowered to work on her own behalf to develop positive life goals. She recognizes her own emotional agitation and is empowered to use effective coping skills to calm and soothe herself while simultaneously engaging in problem solving. Through critical consciousness, some clients may be moved to work on improving the conditions of other oppressed peoples through activist endeavors, developing an expansive sense of meaning that is further discussed in chapter 11. Although critical consciousness is presented as a form of activation, it will be interwoven into all of the therapy elements, impacting the client in the realms of self-assessment, safety, connection, and meaning.

## THE "POOP DETECTOR"

As a way to facilitate the use of critical consciousness in significant relationships, I have adapted Gottman's (1999) concept of the "poop detector." While critical consciousness refers to an overall world view, the "poop detector" refers to a specific evaluative ability in intimate relationships. In research designed to identify the differences between successful and unsuccessful marriages, Gottman discovered several dimensions of perception through the use of mathematical modeling of marital interactions. In the happy, stable marriages that were studied, women had a lower threshold for their husbands' negativity, which Gottman dubbed the "marital poop detector." When these wives perceived negative behavior from their spouses, they noticed it, brought it up, and engaged their spouses in problem solving. In other words, they did not let problems go unnoticed and made sure they got resolved. In unhappy marriages, the women raised their threshold for negativity, attempting to ignore problems and made statements to themselves such as, "I shouldn't let this bother me unless it gets much worse." In other words, they kept resetting their "poop detectors."

This research challenges feminine injunctions of goodness that it is best to "just go along with things" or "not rock the boat" in relationships. Often women disregard negative behavior from a partner or spouse because they doubt their perceptions or minimize their own needs in the service of maintaining harmony in a relationship. Although Gottman's research was with married, heterosexual couples, as a concept, the "poop detector" can be applied to partnered couples of all sexual orientations as well as to romantic and nonromantic close relationships. Not only do clients find the term, "poop detector" memorable and humorous, but they also resonate with its sentiments. The "poop detector" is yet another tool that discourages a self-blaming or passive stance and supports self-efficacy.

Some clients judge themselves as "bitchy" or "intolerant" when they first notice their "poop detectors." A woman who has been socialized to be passive and accommodating may become extremely uneasy when she stops resetting her "poop detector" to a higher negativity threshold. For such a woman, the work of therapy may be longer as she struggles to trust her own perceptions and becomes more empowered to take action when interpersonal problems arise.

# A PROACTIVE APPROACH TO LIFE

Recovery from depression entails active and proactive behavioral activities that improve the moment-to-moment quality of life. The client is encouraged to embrace an empowered stance in approaching her day-to-day life by engaging in self-care activities, actively participating in daily activities, and problem solving ways to reduce daily stress. The therapist is attuned to the needs and abilities of the client, neither pushing her beyond her readiness nor supporting complacency. The therapeutic relationship provides a safe environment in which the client can begin to experience empowerment and autonomy.

## AN ACTIVE STANCE IN THERAPY AND IN LIFE

The therapist facilitates the client's empowerment by teaching and reinforcing collaboration, continually engaging the client in co-creating a treatment plan and in actively participating in her therapy. Often, the client's language will reveal to what degree she sees herself as an active or passive agent in her recovery. For example, in chapter 4, I mentioned Sheila's statement that she wanted me to "fix her." By listening carefully to the client, the therapist may hear the language of passivity or empowerment. The therapist may sensitively bring the client's language to her attention, engaging the client in an exploration of its possible meanings, and bringing issues of activation into the forefront of therapeutic work. When the client seems passive or the therapist feels she or he is working harder than the client, the therapist may find that naming the relational dynamics that are occurring between client and therapist in the here-and-now facilitates the client's taking more responsibility for herself, or, at the minimum, brings issues of self-responsibility and self-efficacy into the open.

When a woman struggles with taking an active role in her recovery, we examine the familial, social, and cultural influences that may have led to her diminished self-efficacy. Clients with victimization histories may feel afraid of becoming active, mistaking activation for aggression. Some women have been so disempowered by their victimization experiences that they feel that they are not entitled to feel better. On the other hand, some women who harbor longstanding feelings of anger and resentment over a lack of caretaking they experienced as children or over constant demands by others in their adult lives, initially may rebel at the idea of becoming actively responsible for their own well-being. Together client and therapist name and examine these issues.

When antidepressant medication is an appropriate intervention, it can expedite activation, facilitating progress inside and outside of therapy. In fact, it is important for the therapist to explain the role of medication as an adjunct and a support for psychotherapy, which is considered to be the primary means of decreasing vulnerability to depression. An overreliance on medication as the principal agent of change has the potential to reinforce passivity on the part of the client and minimize the importance of self-efficacy, activation, and empowerment.

IRT encourages women to live life with passion, commitment, and direction. The client is urged to develop life goals and to actively pursue them as part of the future orientation phase of therapy. Depending on the resources available to extend the client's therapy beyond the stabilization and transformation stages, therapeutic work may involve merely outlining the need to develop such goals, identifying specific goals, or supporting the client as she pursues such goals. The therapist conveys the importance of sustaining an ongoing commitment to personal growth and empowerment.

## SELF-CARE

An empowered approach to daily life requires a woman to acknowledge that self-care is essential for recovery from depression. Because sex role socialization teaches women that to have needs and attend to them is selfish, self-care is sometimes a challenge. Self-care is important to manage emotions, restore energy, decrease stress, and elicit feelings of contentment and well-being.

In brainstorming with Connie ways to structure her time over the weekend, I was teaching her self-care. The client can undertake cognitive and behavioral self care activities that improve her mood or, at the least, prevent her from becoming more deeply depressed. There are a variety of reasons why a client may be unfamiliar with self-care activities. For 23-year-old Connie, the knowledge gap was developmental: such skills of autonomy and self-nurturance are part of the tasks learned in young adulthood. For a 51-year-old client, Sylvia, a deficit in self-care skills became apparent due to a life transition: As a single mother who had raised four children, she seldom had time to think about herself or spend time alone until her youngest child left home and Sylvia relocated to take a new job. Both Sylvia and Connie were able to actualize self-care skills once their benefit became clear as a result of our discussions. However, for 50-year-old Renata, an attorney who was a workaholic, the concept of self-care was foreign due to her negative sense of self and the belief that she was "undeserving." Activation may be a significant task for women who have diminished self capacities, particularly those who use unhealthy affect regulation activities for self-soothing such as drinking, cutting, or binge eating, are likely to have comorbid diagnoses, and present a more complex diagnostic picture than major depression. For clients such as Connie and Sylvia who have relatively healthy self capacities, engaging in self-care often requires only education and encouragement from the therapist. However, for individuals such as Renata with deficits in self capacities, engaging in healthy self-care activities may involve addressing negative self schemas and transforming negative relational templates, more complex and longer-term therapy tasks, which are discussed further in chapters 9 and 11. Over time, the client comes to strengthen self capacities through internalizing the nurturing and empathic attitude of the therapist.

Self-care in the form of activating coping strategies is particularly important for depressed women. According to response styles theory (Nolen-Hoeksema, 1987, 1990), activating coping strategies have the potential to decrease the length and severity of depressive episodes. Women tend to use ruminative rather than activating coping strategies (Nolen-Hoeksema, 1987, 1990; Nolen-Hoeksema et al., 1999). Strengthening the use of activating and distracting coping strategies is, thus, an important therapy goal. Asking, "What helps you feel better, even for just a few minutes?" may reveal a number of activating coping strategies that the client is already employing without her being fully aware of her own internal resources. Identifying such strategies assists the client in building a repertoire of activating coping strategies that she may more consciously choose to undertake. Such activities not only distract the client from her negative affective state, but often elicit feelings of pleasure, joy, or contentment. Table 8.3 summarizes interventions that strengthen the ability to engage in proactive self-care strategies.

Collaboratively, client and therapist can brainstorm a list of activities that resonate with the client. When clients are too depressed to think creatively, the therapist may sensitively make a number of suggestions that may appeal to the client. The therapist should be aware of a wide range of distracting activities that will be appropriate for clients based on their interests and financial resources. Some examples of distracting behavioral activities include playing video games, gardening, sorting photographs (unless they evoke distressing feelings), drawing, exercising, crafting, reading, baking, and working on jigsaw puzzles. The therapist needs to be careful not to reinforce sex-role stereotypes by suggesting an overabundance of "feminine" activities such as shopping,

**TABLE 8.3   Interventions: Self-Care**

The therapist can strengthen the client's self-care skills by
1. Pointing out coping strategies that the client already uses and encouraging their continued use.
2. Collaborating with the client to identify new self-care and activating coping strategies that the client can try out before the next session.
3. Following up in the next session to celebrate the success of using new strategies.
4. Helping the client to refine her list of coping strategies and encouraging the ongoing use of such strategies.
5. Developing a realistic and specific exercise plan.
6. Teaching relaxation or meditation skills.
7. Gently addressing food and nutrition issues.
8. Teaching sleep hygiene strategies.
9. Teaching informal mindfulness practice in daily life, particularly for clients with ruminating cognitive styles.
10. Coauthoring and monitoring a daily activity schedule for the severely depressed client.

giving oneself a facial, or cleaning—although I have been surprised by the number of clients who rate housecleaning as one of their favorite distracting activities. Clients with strong pre-existing self capacities will most likely be able to identify activities that they enjoyed prior to the current depressive episode. However, clients with undeveloped self capacities or those who are more severely depressed may need more help from the therapist in finding distracting activities, and trying new activities may present more of a challenge for these individuals.

Journal writing is not necessarily a distracting activity if the client becomes focused on topics that elicit negative affect. While journalling may be a more beneficial activity for the client in the middle- to late-phase of therapy who is working on strengthening her connection with herself, it may do more harm than good for the client in the early phase of therapy who is struggling to become mobilized and less depressed. When a client with acute symptoms is an impassioned journaller, I suggest that she monitor her mood when writing and if she finds herself feeling worse, to try something more potentially distracting.

Connie, who had never lived alone, was unaware that actively planning and undertaking simple self-care activities for herself could make a difference in her mood. This illustrates how the therapist cannot necessarily take for granted that the client has basic self-care skills and should ask the client to specifically describe what she does on the weekend and in the evenings after work. While the immobility of depression may be the reason behind some clients' inactivity, lack of skills may be a contributing factor. I helped Connie plan her weekend with simple, distracting, and self-soothing activities, which included shopping on Friday for her favorite comfort food, borrowing several videos from the library, studying for a few hours on Saturday morning, calling a friend to go to the movies on Saturday night, doing her laundry and putting clean sheets on her bed, and taking a long hike with another friend on Sunday. After we planned this schedule, Connie recalled that she had an abandoned cross-stitch project in her closet that she decided to try to restart over the weekend. Her grandmother with whom she felt particularly close had taught her to cross-stitch and the idea of working on the project evoked feelings of comfort.

Connie was only moderately depressed and was able to come up with most of these activities once I described the general idea. As mentioned above, however, more severely depressed clients may need more assistance from the therapist. When the client seems unable to take much initiative or is unable to name activities that have engaged, distracted, or soothed her in the past, the therapist can make suggestions with the intention of involving the client in a collaborative effort. The therapist does not want to do all the work for the client or tell her what to do. By being highly attuned to the client's nonverbal as well as verbal reactions to each suggestion, the therapist may succeed in soliciting the client's participation in this task, ensuring that the client is not just acquiescing to the therapist's ideas. Increasing the client's repertoire of distracting and activating activities is a task that may be repeated as the client progresses in her therapy, particularly when negative self schemas have been displaced or self capacities have been strengthened.

## A PLAN OF ACTION FOR COPING WITH DARK MOMENTS

Together, client and therapist explore the vicissitudes of the client's affective state, gathering detailed information about her day-to-day experience. Some individuals may find that certain events precipitate distress or trigger an even further downward spiral in mood. Having a specific plan of action may provide some relief from particularly distressing moments.

For example, the weekends were particularly difficult for Connie, Sylvia, and Renata. All three responded favorably to my suggestion to make a list of self-care and distracting activities that they could undertake during the weekend. Renata, who at times had difficulty becoming mobilized to undertake activities on her list, revealed that she was often overwhelmed by self-denigrating internal conversations that told her she was not entitled to feel better. When the client is in a seriously depressed state and describes intense, negative internal voices, she may need a more directive cognitive intervention to disempower self-critical inner voices. Although the long-term goal is for the client to engage in a process of challenging negative inner voices and nurturing healthier voices as discussed in the next chapter, the seriously depressed client is often in need of a simple, immediate strategy that interrupts a downward spiral into a deeper depressive state.

Working collaboratively, therapist and client can brainstorm soothing, reassuring, or distracting statements that the client can make to herself when she finds herself in a downward spiral. I usually suggest that the client write down these statements and keep them in an accessible place. For such statements to be effective, they must resonate with the client. For some clients who have histories of recurrent episodes, reminding themselves that "this too shall pass," can break through the belief that the episode will never end, providing a ray of hope. For clients who tend to catastrophize, it may be helpful to remind themselves that "just because I am thinking this way, does not mean it is true." While at this stage of recovery negative self-talk may seem "the truth" to the client, sometimes any challenge to the veracity of such inner conversations gives the client some distance from such negative thoughts. Particularly in the early phase of therapy, elaborate cognitive interventions may require more cognitive clarity than a severely depressed woman can tolerate (Thase et al., 2000). Another intervention that may reduce the power of negative self-talk is to ask the client to imagine the self-critical conversation being stated in the voice of someone she finds to be funny or humorous, such as a cartoon character or a famous person (Yapko, 2000). This intervention usually elicits a laugh when the client first tries it in session and may provide some fleeting relief from persistent negative internal conversations.

Yet another strategy is for the client to add to her list the names of friends or relatives whom she can call if these strategies fail to provide any relief. Together, client and therapist attempt to construct a plan of action with a list of activities and statements that the client can attempt to undertake in dark moments. While these interventions may provide some temporary relief, further work as discussed in the remaining chapters of the book on strengthening a sense of self and transforming negative self-schemas is usually indicated.

## A DAILY SCHEDULE OF ACTIVITIES

It has long been recognized that involvement in daily activities is an important treatment strategy for depressed individuals, particularly those who are more severely depressed (Lewinsohn & Gotlib, 1995; Sacco & Beck, 1995). Being actively engaged in tasks and activities not only distracts the individual from depressive symptoms, but potentially increases positive experiences and counters negative expectations typical of depressive thinking. Because some women are overfunctioning and engaged in too many tasks and activities, client and therapist need to identify ways that daily life can be less stressful, seeking enjoyable or soothing activities that the client can undertake during her week. For women who have been overfunctioning, we attempt to create balance between self needs and the demands of others. For women who have been underfunctioning, we endeavor to increase activities that support connection and aliveness and counter isolation and stagnation.

It is not unusual for depressed individuals to dread activities, particularly social contacts, anticipating that the outcome will be negative. The cognitive mind-set of the depressed individual creates negative expectations that often do not represent reality. When the client actually engages in activities she had dreaded, the result is often much more positive than the client had anticipated. Once a client has the experience of trying a dreaded activity and discovering it was not as bad as imagined, was even mildly pleasurable, or moderately distracting from her miserable internal state, she will be more willing to try again.

Some depressed clients may need to enlist the support of friends or family members to remind them about important tasks or activities or to provide various degrees of assistance in completing such activities. In extreme cases, the therapist may have to act as a "coach" by telephoning the client to remind her about important events or to provide words of encouragement in order to mobilize her. For example, at one point Connie's depression returned and she was having a hard time getting out of bed in the mornings. I called her at home to remind her that she had an important appointment about a summer job, giving her words of support and rehearsing the interview with her.

When the client is immobilized and functioning poorly, it may be helpful to collaboratively identify essential tasks and enjoyable activities and to make a written schedule delineating such activities. This can be particularly helpful for the individual who has depressive symptoms that include memory impairment or reduced concentration.

## PROBLEM SOLVING TO REDUCE DAY-TO-DAY STRESS

The constant demands of a busy life may deplete the client of energy and rob her of opportunities to pursue life-affirming and enjoyable activities. The client's day-to-day life presents numerous opportunities for problem solving ways to reduce stress. Women who hold schemas of control and esteem that result in a superwoman persona will not only overburden themselves with draining tasks but also will resist making changes to decrease their stress levels. I have seen countless women who could afford to hire a housecleaner or buy prepared dinners, whose tenacious beliefs about being a "good mother" or a "good wife" prevented them from being wise about modulating their energies. While the therapist may feel frustrated by some clients' resistance to endorse what appear to be obvious solutions, it is vital that the therapist be attuned to the client and work collaboratively with her in problem solving. Even when the client appears ready to engage in a discussion about reducing her stressors, it may be up to the therapist to suggest solutions. Women who hold relatively traditional gender roles may find such solutions novel, even when they seem obvious, or may feel uncomfortable letting go of doing everything. By making suggestions, the therapist not only offers new solutions but also gives the client permission to be different.

In the early stage of therapy, the therapist helps the client identify events and obligations that are potentially draining, distressing, or stressful, and engages the client in brainstorming to come up with creative and realistic solutions to reduce or eliminate these activities. However, it is important that the therapist not move too quickly into problem solving. When the therapist prematurely initiates problem solving, she not only supports the client's view of herself as passive but also encourages the idea that someone else (the therapist) will take care of her or tell her what to do. In addition, if the client is not ready to take action, she will be unsuccessful in following through with any plans to reduce stress and is then in danger of feeling defeated and shamed.

I often find it helpful to talk to the client about the relationship between depression and stress, encouraging her to take a look at her daily life to determine if there are any ways that she might reduce the stress in her life. This becomes a more pressing issue for clients with recurrent depressions who appear to relapse in response to identifiable increases in stressors. When the client continues to resist making any changes, I am extremely careful to convey my respect for her decision while expressing my concern for her well-being, letting the client know I am "planting a seed" for her future consideration of this problem.

The client who remains in therapy for the transformational phase will inevitably address a stress-laden lifestyle once self-schemas become more flexible, open, and affirmative. Often, the client will reinitiate a discussion about reducing responsibilities at this point, but may still need the therapist to make suggestions. During this phase, the client may begin to revise assumptions related to gender roles that will impact her willingness to renegotiate domestic responsibilities with a partner. In the future orientation phase, the client will begin to address plans for relapse prevention that will inevitably lead to a discussion of further stress reduction activities, as discussed in chapter 12. Table 8.4 summarizes interventions for the therapist that facilitate problem solving aimed at reducing daily stress.

## A MOBILIZED AND HEALTHY BODY

Depression is a mind-body experience that can be physically as well as emotionally immobilizing. The desire to just curl up in a ball and disappear or sleep may be overwhelming. Recovery requires actively fighting against what can feel like dead weight or overwhelming inertia. Similarly, the anxiety that accompanies some depressive episodes can be overwhelming or unbearable. IRT encourages the client to mobilize her body in fighting depression by engaging in regular exercise, practic-

---

**TABLE 8.4  Interventions: Facilitating Problem Solving**

The therapist can maximize the client's success in problem solving aimed at reducing day-to-day stress by

1. Explaining the strong relationship between depression and stress.
2. Helping the client to identify energy-consuming and stressful tasks and responsibilities.
3. Being attuned to the client's readiness to engage in problem solving.
4. Engaging the client in brainstorming to elicit creative solutions to eliminate daily stressors.
5. Naming rigid or dysfunctional schemas that maintain a stress-laden lifestyle and impede problem solving.
6. When the client is unwilling to problem solve, conveying acceptance while communicating concern for the client's well-being and hope for a future revisitation of the problem.
7. Reintroducing problem solving to reduce stressors at later points in the therapy by being attuned to the client's readiness.

---

ing relaxation or meditation exercises, and making healthy lifestyle choices. Exercise, relaxation, and meditation promote feelings of mastery and well-being. The therapist works with the client to devise an individualized program that meets her needs. For those with acute symptoms of depression, the concentration required for relaxation exercises may not be available until such symptoms have abated. The therapist works with each client to help her mobilize her body in a way consistent with her unique needs.

Therapists who see women complaining of "depression" need to be aware of autoimmune disorders, chronic fatigue syndrome, and fibromyalgia. Because the traditional medical community has limited knowledge about the diagnosis and treatment of these problems, therapists want to be particularly supportive and well informed. I refer the reader to three excellent articles: Caplan, 2001; Chrisler, 2001; White, Lemkau, & Clasen, 2001.

## PHYSICAL EXERCISE

Regular physical exercise is physically energizing and emotionally empowering and has been shown to be effective in ameliorating symptoms of depression (Hays, 1999; Tkachuk & Martin, 1999) and appears to be effective in lowering relapse rates (Babyak et al., 2000). In addition to having physiologic benefits, exercise gives a woman something she can do that leads to feelings of well-being, however fleeting. Having something to do that changes her mood instills a sense of mastery and nurtures a sense of hope, encouraging the client to continue onward with the struggle to recover.

The client who has been inactive should first obtain medical clearance from her medical practitioner before undertaking an exercise program. I collaborate with the client to find an exercise plan that is realistic and will be success oriented; she does not need one more thing about which to feel inadequate or overwhelmed. Although the research suggests that longer and more frequent exercise sessions result in the greatest decrease in depression (Hays, 1999), it is important to develop a plan that maximizes the client's ongoing involvement. Sometimes the client may need to start with as little as five minutes a day or once a week. For those already exercising, it is important to help the client evaluate whether she is over-exercising and to develop a plan of moderation.

The therapist may need to be creative in making suggestions for exercise that are consistent with the client's ability level, life circumstances, and financial resources. When feasible, joining a health club or enrolling in an exercise class gives the client the opportunity to be with other people, as well as the added structure of a schedule. I try to be aware of the various facilities and classes in my community, particularly those that are low fee or free. I also try to find out about classes that are low pressure and noncompetitive for clients who are not particularly athletic or who are self-conscious about their physical skills. It is also helpful to be aware of parks and wildlife areas that are appropriate for walking or hiking. For clients with limited resources or limited time, there are options such as borrowing exercise videos from the public library.

In contrast to solitary activities like running or walking, classes or clubs provide the potential for increased socialization, which may be a goal. However, for some clients in the early stages of recovery, simply being in the presence of others may be comforting, and social contact may be a premature goal. When possible, having the client exercise with a friend has the advantage of decreasing isolation and increasing motivation. For example, after our second session Laura asked a friend to run with her two evenings per week while their husbands watched the children. She recognized that she not only needed the extra incentive of meeting her friend, but she craved being with another woman after spending all day with children in her day care center.

For individuals who have never been physically active, an exercise plan may be best left to the middle or late stage of therapy. Long-standing schemas concerning body image or body discomfort may stand in the way of physical exercise. Addressing such issues in the early stage of therapy may be overwhelming for the client and lead to discouragement. Once the client is ready to tackle exercise, she is encouraged to develop a program that she can realistically maintain over the long term. Exercise can ultimately lead to an improved relationship with the body, leading to self-efficacy, mastery, and self-esteem. A regular exercise program is a proactive element in a solid relapse prevention plan, not only by influencing mood, but also by reducing risk factors for illnesses such as coronary heart disease.

"Psychological footbinding" (Brown & Gilligan, 1992, p. 218) has its impact on a woman's body. Sitting like "good girls" with legs crossed can cause stress and tension in the body. Exercise that hardens the body (such as aerobics, weight-training, karate, and most competitive sports) should be balanced with exercise that softens, expands, and mobilizes the entire body, particularly the pelvic region. Gentle yoga, tai chi, chi gong, modern dance, and ethnic dances that mobilize the hips and pelvis (such as Brazilian and Afro-Carribean dances) are some good options. There is nothing that frees the body more than an energetic dancing session to good old rock and roll. I often suggest that clients dance at home to new musical selections because they are free from painful memories. See Appendix A for resources.


## FOOD AND NUTRITION

Another important consideration for a mobilized and healthy body is whether the client is getting sufficient nutrition and water. Symptoms of hunger, hypoglycemia, and dehydration can mimic or worsen symptoms of depression and anxiety. Many women have issues with food and eating which become exacerbated during times of stress and distress. The therapist can help de-pathologize such issues by giving the client permission to eat whatever comforts her during such times and educating her about the potential negative impact on mood and anxiety of caffeine, sugar, alcohol, and poor nutrition. During the stabilization phase, the therapist can gently help the client plan good self-care related to eating. This is not a time for dieting or extreme changes in diet. During the transformation and future orientation phases, the therapist can initiate the topic of healthier eating, giving the client the option of focusing on this topic, particularly if it has been one of struggle or destructive patterns. Addressing such issues will only be successful if the motivation for doing such work comes from the client. The therapist needs to tread delicately here, taking cues from the client once an initial suggestion to work on eating has been made. A referral to a nutritionist or topic-specific group may be a good adjunct to individual therapy.

I often teach clients mindful eating (Kabat-Zinn, 1990), since many women tend to eat in a trance-like state. By slowing down the process of eating, paying attention to each movement involved, noticing each element of sensory experience (such as taste, smell, and body experience), and bringing an exquisite sense of focus to the entire endeavor of eating, the client may increase her sense of control over eating while simultaneously becoming more satisfied with smaller portions and healthier foods. I have had success helping clients break the cycle of binging and purging with this approach. I usually invite the client to practice first in the office with me. Dried apples are a good food to try eating mindfully together, but anything will work. In fact, eating an unhealthy food like a potato chip may intensify its negative characteristics such as its oiliness and saltiness, thus waking up the client to make healthier choices.

## SLEEP

Sleep disruption often accompanies or exacerbates depression. The therapist can help the client develop a going-to-sleep ritual that begins with slowing down as bedtime approaches, perhaps having a cup of chamomile tea, and putting on soothing music or a relaxation tape. Educating the client about sleep hygiene is often helpful, sharing such information as:

1. Reduce caffeine intake, especially after 5 p.m.
2. Exercise regularly, but finish vigorous exercise at least 2 hours before bed.
3. Avoid alcohol (Simonds, 1995).

For a recent review of assessment and treatment of insomnia, see Pallesen, Nordus, Havik, and Nielsen (2001). Appendix A lists some further resources to facilitate restful sleep.

### RELAXATION AND MEDITATION TRAINING

Relaxation skills provide the client with an opportunity to experience mastery and empowerment. Furthermore, relaxation and meditation cultivate the positive emotion of contentment, which not only counters the negative affective state of a depressive episode, but also supports relapse prevention (Frederickson, 2000; Teasdale et al., 2000). While relaxation and meditation training will benefit all depressed persons, it is particularly important for those with comorbid symptoms of anxiety, which are more common among depressed women (Silverstein, 1999). For individuals with agitated depression or concentration difficulties, strategies that require active participation, such as muscle and breathing exercises, may be easier to follow than imagination or visualization exercises. For some clients, learning relaxation or meditation skills may need to wait until the middle-to-late phases of therapy when concentration is not a problem.

For the client who habitually spends an overabundance of time in her head analyzing, ruminating, worrying, or planning, everyday mindfulness (Kabat-Zinn, 1990, 1994) may be an important skill to quiet inner voices. Mindfulness is based on Buddhist principles that have been applied to behavioral psychology for use with pain management, stress management, and most recently, to prevent relapse from depression (Teasdale et al., 2000). Mindfulness teaches being fully engaged in the present moment, which can provide an alternative mental focus for the habitually ruminating client. It also involves active mental awareness, which teaches the client to observe her thoughts and, thus, provides a way for the client to distance herself from distressing thoughts of anxiety and depression or negative self-talk:

> Another way to look at meditation is to look at thinking itself as a waterfall, a continual cascading of thought. In cultivating mindfulness, we are going *beyond* or *behind* our thinking, much the way you might find a vantage point in a cave or depression in the rock behind a waterfall. We still see and hear the water, but we are out of the torrent. (Kabat-Zinn, 1994, p. 94)

Learning to get "out of the torrent" of one's thoughts can be particularly helpful for clients who have ruminating cognitive styles. For example, Maddy, a 38-year-old client, described being constantly preoccupied with worrying about her job, family, and friends, continually anticipating problems, planning her next activities, and mentally rehearsing expected interactions. Having grown up as a minister's daughter, she had an unrelenting need to please everyone and appear perfect, recognizing that the internalized voice of "my father's daughter" attempted to control her life. One result was that she seldom gave her full attention to what she was doing at a given moment, but was usually doing one thing and thinking about another. I taught Maddy to practice mindfulness as she went about her day, concentrating fully on her present experience and nonjudgmentally returning her attention to the task at hand when she found her attention wandering to ruminating thoughts. This was quite a challenge for her, as she had habitually engaged in rumination and worry for most of her life. However, she immediately noticed a positive shift in her mood state when she was fully focused on the present moment and made a point of practicing this form of mindfulness at least three times during her day, once each morning, noon, and night.

In addition to mindfulness, the client may be provided with brief samples of two or three different relaxation approaches, allowing her to choose her preferred type. The therapist may then guide the client through the chosen approach for 20 to 40 minutes, audiotaping so that the client may use the tape at home. The client may find great benefit from focusing on her breath for 5 minutes a day. It may be helpful for the client to have strategies not only to practice daily, but also to use in the moment when anxiety-provoking situations arise or anxiety symptoms interfere with functioning. Many individuals may find that attending to breathing at these times is beneficial.

As the therapy unfolds, ways of thinking that exacerbate anxiety symptoms will become more obvious and the client may incorporate cognitive strategies into relaxation activities. More elaborate cognitive activities are described in the next chapter. When planning for relapse prevention, as discussed in chapter 12, a referral to a stress reduction program that incorporates meditation or relaxation training may be of benefit to the client.

## SUMMARY

This chapter described activation, the third element of therapy. Activation encompasses an empowered and proactive attitude regarding mind, body, and spirit. First, recovery from depression encompasses developing an actively aware state of mind. Through critical consciousness the client develops the active capacity to analyze distressing interpersonal situations through a politicized lens and to take action to improve oppressive situations in her life. Some clients may be interested in working to improve the oppressive situations in others' lives, although this is usually a goal for the later stage of therapy or post-termination. Through critical consciousness, she develops the ability to use her "poop detector," attending to her own reactions in close personal relationships and addressing interpersonal problems, rather than ignoring or minimizing problems in order to maintain connections.

Becoming mobilized to improve her daily life is another important activation goal. The client is encouraged to become an active participant in her therapy and to be proactive in improving the circumstances of her life. Early in the therapy, the client learns to mobilize self-care skills to elicit more positive mood states and improve the quality of her day-to-day life. The client learns the value of distracting coping strategies and develops a repertoire of such skills that are consistent with her own interests and values. She may wish to make a written action plan that delineates specific self-care activities and soothing statements to help her through particularly dark moments. The seriously depressed client may also need more structure in becoming activated in her day-to-day life and, in some cases, the therapist may collaborate with the client to make a daily schedule of activities. The client is encouraged to proactively problem solve ways to reduce stress in her daily life. Another focus of activation is becoming mobilized on a body level. The client is encouraged to address physically debilitating symptoms of depression through exercise, relaxation or meditation training, and healthy lifestyle choices.

Activation tasks may be only partially successful until the middle-to-late phases of therapy, depending on the client's ability to challenge limiting self schemas, particularly those related to "goodness," control, and perfectionism. Activation is interrelated to the treatment themes of the four other elements of therapy in a reflexive, mutually influential manner. Each element contributes to and stimulates activation and, as activation increases, the client revisits each element from a more empowered position. The next chapter discusses the fourth element of therapy, connection.

# CHAPTER NINE

# Connection: Part I

"**I**'ve lost myself" are words I inevitably hear from countless depressed women during the first therapy appointment. Depression results in and is caused by disconnection from the self (Jack, 1991, 1999; Lerner, 1988; Miller & Stiver, 1997) and recovery from depression involves strengthening and reclaiming the self. A foundational concept in IRT is that the influences of family, society, and culture create an internal split within the individual, consisting of a false self and an authentic self (Hancock, 1989; Harter, 1999; Jack, 1991, 1999; Miller, 1981; Winnicott, 1965). This split is more conceptual than actual. The false self develops at a young age to please others, particularly parents. Through sex role socialization, a girl's false self is imbued with moral injunctions of goodness and femininity, which promote idealized images of the self such as "good girl," "good mother," "good daughter," and "good wife." Family and culture convey the message that in order to be loved, a woman must fulfill these idealizations of goodness. The internal dialogue of the false self is characterized by self-criticism and moral dictates that constrain authenticity and promote other-pleasing behaviors, invoking statements that command, "you should," "you should not," "you must," and "you must not."

The authentic self contains the individual's genuine feelings and thoughts. The authentic self is free of the constraints of culture and family that negate a woman's genuine feelings. The authentic self knows from a woman's own visceral experience (Jack, 1991). She is competent, playful, purposeful, and spirited:

> A woman does not easily gain access to this authentic inner realm, the realm that is free from the patriarchal construction of who and what a woman should be. She must break through a crust of negative evaluations of the feminine in order to reach it at all. These evaluations affect her self-concept in a profoundly damaging way, even if she is a woman of accomplishment. (Hancock, 1989, p. 228)

A woman's developmental path involves a struggle between the idealized feminine facade of the false self that is thrust upon her beginning in childhood and her authentic identity as a person. Whether the false self dominates or the authentic self is accessible depends on each individual's unique familial environment, social factors, personality characteristics, developmental phase, life circumstances, and the particular relationship at hand. A woman who is dominated by the false self is more vulnerable to depressions and a depressed woman may lose access to the authentic self. When women recognize an ever widening gap between their outward presentation of self (the false self) and their inward experience (the authentic self), they feel anguish, despair, and self-betrayal over their inauthenticity (Jack, 1991). The internal conversations of depressed women contain the self-condemning voice of the false self, while the voice of the authentic self is muted or silent.

Nan, a 43-year-old artist and poet, who suffered from chronic depression since adolescence, portrayed in the following poem an ongoing struggle between her false and authentic selves.

I versus Me

1. Critic
I exists in sharp, icy places
   speaking in bruised, somber tones
I wishes to shut off and suffocate
   the me in my
I pontificates in absoluteness
   I should not
   I must not
   I am not
   I cannot
   I dare not
I is rigid, stiff born
   out of addiction to perfection
I is shadow trying to keep
   dark the world of me
I preaches out of fear and depression
   I am stupid
   I am ugly
   I am lazy
   I am fat
   I am blue

2. Artist
Me wants to be free
  and light
Me dreams of riding on
  the back of a crow looking down
Me talks in glowing terms
  me believes
  me dreams
  me does
  me hopes
  me skips
Me longs to bring I out
  of grey shadows into yellow light
Me is smart and knows
  that light and shadows can co-exist
Me sings out
  me will
  me can
  me dares to exist
  me says yes
  me is fuschia

—Nan, 10/98

Nan's depiction of the false self as self-condemning and of the authentic self as creative and competent is remarkably consistent with Jack's (1991) findings in her research with depressed women. Nan's work in therapy focused on strengthening the authentic self using many of the approaches discussed in this chapter.

Connection, the fourth element of therapy, is discussed in two chapters. This chapter discusses connection between client and therapist and connection with the authentic self. Chapter 10 discusses connection with others. The treatment themes of the two connection chapters are interrelated and interdependent. In the initial phase of therapy they are prioritized in that the connection between client and therapist is a catalyst for increased connection with self and significant others. Table 9.1 summarizes treatment goals for this chapter.

**TABLE 9.1   Connection: Treatment Goals**

1. Authentic connection between client and therapist
2. Strengthening connection with the authentic self
3. Connection with authentic feelings

## CONNECTION BETWEEN CLIENT AND THERAPIST

A major foundation of IRT is establishing a therapeutic relationship that is mutually empathic and mutually empowering. The importance of the therapeutic relationship was discussed earlier in the book in chapters 4 and 7. In this chapter, the therapeutic connection is emphasized as it relates to the client's connection with herself and her own authentic experience. "The therapeutic encounter must offer a quality of relationship that hears the silenced 'I' of a depressed woman and brings it into dialogue. This means that therapists need to *be with* the woman's 'I' "(Jack, 1991, p. 202). Together client and therapist uncover and listen to the client's deep, heartfelt inner knowledge and experience, making the client the subject rather than the object of her experience.

As the client becomes able to express herself freely with the therapist, together client and therapist experience a different kind of relational encounter, one that is alive and mutually affirming, supporting the client in becoming more fully connected not only to her true self, but also more fully connected to the therapist:

> At these moments of interchange, a person moves into more connection based on her more real representation of her experience. Simultaneously, she comes to feel in greater connection with her inner experience, and to feel a *right* to that experience. She becomes more accurately aware of herself as she becomes more accurately aware of the other person's responsiveness to her. (Miller & Stiver, 1997, p. 133)

The therapist's empathy for the client is the starting point for significant therapy events. As the therapist feels a sense of connection with the client, the therapist experiences a deep, moving sense of empathy for her. Empathy signals the seriousness with which the therapist takes the client and her feelings; the therapist feels the client has made an impact on her and communicates this to the client. The client, however, may not be used to being taken seriously and she may feel tremendous ambivalence about whether to honor her own feelings. Many women unknowingly have developed strategies of disconnection from self in order to maintain connection with others. In other words, disconnection from one's own authentic feelings has been a protective strategy to ensure that the woman will be able to placate and accommodate to others, stemming from the belief that these compliant behaviors will ensure relational connection. The therapy experience challenges these protective strategies, providing new relational templates that restore and strengthen connection with the authentic self.

The client experiences the therapist's empathy for her and, seeing herself through the therapist's eyes, begins to acknowledge and accept all parts of herself. The therapist's empathy for the client thus promotes the client's authenticity, which fosters feelings of self-empathy within the client. The sense of empathic connection that the client feels with the therapist can lead to movement into action. Miller and Stiver (1997) noted that

> A therapist's engagement in mutual empathy with the patient is a key factor leading not just to understanding, but to active change. We have often seen that as a therapist truly engages with a woman who is depressed and stuck, for instance, and she believes her therapist is truly with her, she can move toward action. That action may be a small step at first . . . and it can be the start out of a depressive spiral. (p. 46)

Not only do relational therapists such as Miller and Stiver (1997) emphasize the importance of the therapist's empathy, but CBT therapists have demonstrated its influence in recovery from depression (Burns & Nolen-Hoeksema, 1992). Thus, the therapist's empathy is an essential ingredient for a successful therapeutic encounter with a depressed client.

The therapist experiences empathy for the client by being present and attuned to her in a moment-by-moment way, seeing, hearing, and viscerally experiencing the client in an alive and authentic manner. This kind of emotional connection between client and therapist, rather than nurturing the client's dependency, creates an exciting energy between client and therapist called "zest" (Miller & Stiver, 1997, p. 30). The feelings of harmony and resonance in such a therapeutic encounter allow the therapist to collaborate with the client to articulate her authentic feelings and to voice her true thoughts. When the therapist is truly present with the client she can help her communicate hard-to-express feelings and tentative ideas, increasing the client's sense of connection with the therapist and with her authentic self. Such an encounter requires energy, awareness, and commitment on the part of the therapist.

During a depressive episode, the critical voice of the false self may become quite dominant, causing a woman to lose sight of her self capacities. The depressed client may minimize her accomplishments and talents, feeling inadequate and incompetent. Through the process of mutual empathy the client can begin to restore a more positive sense of self. However, the therapist is cautioned to express acceptance and empathy with an affective level that matches the client's own comfort level with closeness and emotion. Through being attuned to the client, the therapist modulates emotional expressiveness so as not to over-whelm the client.

Table 9.2 describes interventions that increase the strength of the connection between client and therapist. The process of feeling authentically connected to the therapist facilitates the client's increased self-empathy and self-acceptance, leading to an increased connection with her authentic self.

## STRENGTHENING CONNECTION WITH SELF

The conditions of female development conspire to create a context in which women doubt themselves and their own experience:

> Women come to question whether what they have seen exists and whether what they know from their own experience is true. . . . Personal doubts . . . invade women's sense of themselves, compromising their ability to act on their own perceptions and thus their willingness to take responsibility for what they do. (Gilligan, 1982, p. 49)

A woman's recovery from depression entails developing trust and confidence in her own experience, as she reclaims the lost self. The therapist may facilitate renewed connection with self through several specific interventions that integrate cognition and affect. This transformative work on the self is probably most distinctive of IRT. It is work that delves deep into the inner life of the client, for the inner life is

**TABLE 9.2    Interventions: Authentic Connection Between Therapist and Client**

The therapist can increase feelings of connection between client and therapist by
1. Being present with the client in a moment-by-moment way.
2. Being *with* the client as she expresses painful or negative emotions.
3. Attentively seeing, hearing, and viscerally experiencing the client.
4. Expressing acceptance and empathy for the client, verbally and nonverbally.
5. Expressing accurate empathy by summarizing what the client is saying and feeling, using the client's words and choosing language that is attuned to the client.
6. Expressing accurate empathy by using metaphors and imagery that crystallize the client's experience.
7. Modulating the affective expression of acceptance and empathy to match the affective tolerance level of the client.

where authenticity resides. However, this work is not necessarily long term and may be completed in a brief number of sessions for the client with strong self capacities and good access to the authentic self. For the client with limited self capacities and poor access to the authentic self, this work is likely to take longer. Recovery of the self is a multidimensional process that proceeds through all phases of therapy, involves the client's experiences inside and outside of therapy, and interweaves intrapsychic, interpersonal, and systemic phenomena.

The therapist helps the client to disempower the voice of the false self and to strengthen the voice of the authentic self. Initially, the client learns to turn up the volume on her internal dialogue and bring her internal conversations into her awareness. Although this work is similar to cognitive therapy by bringing automatic negative thoughts into the client's awareness, it differs by its equal emphasis on bringing forward the thoughts of the authentic self.

The specific interventions for connecting with self are listed below in Table 9.3. Although interventions are discussed separately, they often will occur simultaneously or in an interrelated fashion during one therapy session.

## HEARING INTERNAL CONVERSATIONS

It is not unusual for depressed women to be unaware of the extent that their inner world is dominated by rules of femininity, niceness, and other-pleasing behaviors. Bringing the client's internal dialogue into

**TABLE 9.3  Interventions: Connection With the Authentic Self**

The therapist can facilitate the client's connection with her authentic, inner experience by

1. Asking the client about internal conversations.
2. Helping the client to hear automatic, negative thinking by repeating the client's self-critical comments.
3. Helping the client to hear her authentic self by repeating self-nurturing, positive, or assertive self-statements.
4. Asking the client to give names to negative and positive inner voices.
5. Encouraging the client to state her opinions and express her feelings in session.
6. Asking the client to notice and describe bodily sensations related to affect.
7. Teaching the client the strategy of "talking back" to negative inner voices.
8. Suggesting and encouraging creative activities that express the authentic self.

her awareness breaks the power of its automaticity, reveals distressing conflicts, and defines a problem that the client could not name but could only feel as depression or feeling "bad."

The work of hearing and naming internal conversations can begin as early as the first or second session. Often the voice of the self-critical false self is evident in the client's own verbalizations about herself, as was evident in the first session with Serena, age 34, a supervisor in a community service agency who came to therapy owing to symptoms of depression and anxiety. Nine months before, she had ended a relationship with Maria who had been emotionally abusive, including demeaning her in front of friends on several occasions. Since the breakup, Maria had repeatedly called Serena at work and sent her letters asking her to resume their relationship. Although Serena refused, she felt unable to cut off contact with Maria, feeling guilty about rejecting Maria and confused about these feelings. Serena admitted to feeling shame and embarrassment about not being able to totally end things with Maria. She repeatedly told me, "I shouldn't feel this way and I feel so awful that I do. I'm so stupid and weak." She admitted to becoming increasingly isolated and avoidant of friends because she did not want to tell them about Maria's abuse or about the frequency of Maria's calls. Serena stated that she felt stuck and miserable.

Serena's self-condemning inner dialogue was apparent in the first session when she described herself as "stupid" and "weak." The therapist can bring the voice of the false self more into the client's conscious awareness by (a) repeating the client's critical comments about herself by using the client's own words, and (b) making queries such as, "Do you have conversations going on in your head?" or "Do you sometimes feel that there is an inner critic talking to you in your head?"

The therapist helps the client to hear and identify inner voices of self-condemnation as well as of self-affirmation. For the depressed woman, the negative voices may be more apparent. The therapist may need to prompt the client to hear the voice of her authentic, inner experience, asking if she hears what may be a softer voice or what people often refer to as "a little voice inside me" that is more nurturing, reassuring, and positive. This voice often eggs the client on to try new things, to trust herself, or to disregard the negative, self-critical voice. This is the voice of the authentic self. Serena lit up when I asked her, "Do you hear another, perhaps quieter voice inside your head that is more supportive than the voice that tells you that you are stupid and weak." "Yes," she exclaimed. "There is this little voice that tells me I am smart and strong." Serena used the words "little voice" without any prompting from me.

The client is encouraged to describe her inner dialogue and share these thoughts with the therapist. It is not unusual for the client to be surprised by the negativity and vehemence of her negative self-talk when it is brought into her awareness. Serena remarked, "I can't believe I talk to myself like that—that I am saying such crummy things to myself and that I think so little of myself. It's embarrassing." There is a danger here that the therapist will join the self-condemnation of the client's internal negative voice by conveying to the client the idea that she should not be thinking this way about herself because she has so many strengths, talents, or positive qualities. Adding another "should" to the dialogue will only contribute to the client's sense of low self-worth and hopelessness. Although the therapist wants to bring strengths to the client's attention, the therapist needs to be carefully attuned to the client in order to be successful in this endeavor. Further, an eventual goal is for the client to hear her inner discourse, identify the moral dictates that her inner voices convey, and choose which values with which she wishes to align (Jack, 1999). This work is described in chapter 11 where core cognitive schemas are discussed.

Initially, simply bringing the voice of the false self into the client's awareness gives it less influence. When such self-denigrating comments are automatic, the client has no idea that they are impacting her feeling state and such comments seem to be real and true to her. When the client can begin to use her observing self to notice negative self-talk, the false self becomes more separate from herself. The result is that such internal discussions are no longer happening automatically and the client is more able to evaluate whether the self-critical sentiments expressed are actually truth.

## EXTERNALIZING THE FALSE SELF

Naming the negative voice will provide an additional tool for disempowering the false self. Clients who resonate with the idea of the two internal voices will sometimes inadvertently use language in their discussion that will lend itself to becoming labels for the two different inner voices. Thus, the therapist is particularly attuned to the client's language as she talks about her internal conversations. Naming internal voices is most effective when the client's own words are used and the naming occurs in a natural, organic manner. The client may pick up on the therapist's words or interject her own original words for naming internal voices. If no label spontaneously occurs in the midst of discussion, however, the therapist may ask the client if the negative voice has a name or if she would like to name it. Some clients will respond to this request with cynicism, label it as "hokey," or fail to resonate with it. Therapeutic work with inner voices can continue without specific names for each voice.

In our first conversation about the two voices, Serena used the words, "little voice" to refer to the authentic self. I then adopted that term and began to use it to describe the internal conversations of the authentic self. At that time, no label for the false self was apparent and Serena was not inclined to name the voice of self-condemnation. Several sessions later, Serena told me about an incident that occurred in the supermarket when she saw an old friend who appeared not to notice her. Serena described being overcome by self-critical thoughts such as "She never liked you because you are such a jerk and you're so boring." She told me,

> Now that I am telling you about what happened, I realize that it was "the tyranny" that was putting me down. I couldn't tell then, but now it seems so clear. I hope next time it happens I can hear it for what it is. I don't want to let "the tyranny" rule my life.

In previous sessions when Serena had described her negative self talk, I had commented that "you are being tyrannized by a part of you that is so self-denigrating and so critical." Serena had picked up on the word "tyrannized," translating it into the label "tyranny" for the false self.

The client may become aware that negative internal dialogue dominates and silences her only in certain relationships or in certain situations. For women, certain types of hierarchical relational contexts will invite self-silencing (Jack, 1999). Helping the client recognize a loss of self through the dominance of the internalized, self-critical voice of the false self in specific situations leads the way to questioning underlying schemas that govern beliefs about lovability and self-acceptance. While working with inner voices is a task usually undertaken in the end of the stabilization phase or beginning of the transformational phase of therapy, working with schemas is usually approached a bit later in the transformational phase. As core cognitive schemas (CCSs) are revealed through working with inner voices, the therapist can make a mental note of such schemas, addressing them through interventions described in chapter 11. The client with strong self capacities and manageable life stressors may be able to proceed to naming and challenging CCSs within a few sessions.

## TALKING BACK

One intervention that may be introduced early in the therapy is for the client to invoke the voice of the authentic self to "talk back" to the self-critical voice of the false self, providing comfort and reassurance. This intervention is effective for clients who have begun to question the accuracy of self-denigrating internal comments. Typically, a client might say, "I know it's irrational for me to think this way about myself, but I do." Clients with pre-existing strong self capacities may be able to succeed at this task relatively easily. Even a client with vulnerabilities in self capacities may be successful at talking reassuringly to herself, although the self-condemning voice of the false self will probably continue to dominate. Renata, a 50-year-old attorney who suffered from dysthymia surprised us both by coming into the fifth session and exclaiming excitedly:

> I did it. I was able to talk to myself on a drive to Seattle. I was going shopping and that old voice kept telling me that I didn't deserve to buy myself anything. I told that self-critical voice to "shut up" and kept telling myself that I don't have to listen to this stuff. That it's just old junk in my head.

Here Renata's language describing the false self is apparent through the words "old voice," "self-critical voice," and "old junk in my head." Renata's description of talking to herself in a reassuring manner is typical of many clients' descriptions of invoking the authentic self. While this is a relatively simple intervention, it is not unusual for clients to react when first hearing about it with surprise, making statements such as Renata's: "You mean all I have to do is talk to myself? Why that's so simple." However, this may not be a simple task for clients with deficits in self capacities, particularly those with a seriously damaged sense of self.

## HEARING THE AUTHENTIC SELF

Although the voice of the false self may be loud and is more likely to use the pronoun "you" in an accusatory tone with numerous "shoulds," the authentic self is often subdued yet persistent, using the pronoun "I" (Jack, 1991). While the false self usually is restricted to cognitions, the authentic self not only contains cognitions but also "gut" feelings. The goal is for the client to become more attuned to the inner experience of the authentic self and, as will be discussed later, to become more attuned to her feelings. Again, the therapist carefully attends to the client's words to arrive at a label for the authentic self. As just described, hearing the client refer to a "little voice" is not unusual as are labels such as the "real me" and "my self-nurturing voice." The emphasis on working with the authentic self is distinctly different from that of the false self. With the authentic self, the goal is for the client to own her authentic thoughts and feelings, whereas with the false self the goal is to become more separate. Thus, naming the false self is more important than labeling the authentic self and the work of connecting with the authentic self can be successful without using names if the client does not resonate with such an approach.

In connecting with the authentic self, the client wants to become the subject of her own experience rather than the object of her internal life. Socially dictated templates of feminine behavior have relegated her to being the object of her own thoughts as she is at the mercy of how others think she should be. As the object of her experience, she views herself as others view her, seeing herself through others' eyes. By becoming the subject of her own experience, she owns her thoughts and feelings, using statements that begin with "I am" and "I feel" and "I know," rather than "you should" or "you should not" or "you must" or "you must not." Thus, the client wants to be able to experience her deep inner knowledge, feel her feelings, and trust her experiences of self, acting on her own needs and wishes rather than being governed by what she believes will please others.

Depressed women "refrain from speech not only to avoid conflict but because they fear they may be wrong" (Jack, 1991, p. 33). The interventions of reflection, summarization, and clarification are particularly meaningful when the client feels disconnection from her authentic self and lacks confidence in her thoughts and feelings. When the client hears her own sentiments verbalized by the therapist, she can begin to take ownership over them, feeling more confident about what she thinks and feels. For example, with Laura, the client with three children and a childcare center, I summarized her underlying emotions that were overshadowed by self-criticism and shame that she could not cope well:

> So what you are saying is that you feel sad and lonely and disappointed in your husband for not being more of a help to you. You also feel angry and hurt.

By repeatedly capturing the essence of less vocal feelings, the therapist assists the client in trusting her "gut" and acknowledging parts of herself that she has denied or discounted. Not only does this type of intervention lead to the client's increased recognition of her true feelings, but it provides relief from unrelenting and unproductive self-blame, ultimately leading to potential solutions to problems that had seemed immobilizing and insoluble to the client. Laura, a client who had exceptionally strong self capacities, responded quickly to this intervention. Within a week she spoke to her husband about her feelings of loneliness and disappointment, asked him to do specific tasks to help her, and was able to engage him in ongoing discussions about the stresses of their lives.

Sometimes clients with deficits in self capacities, particularly those with difficulty in having a positive sense of self, will be unable to summon a self-assuring or self-nurturing inner voice. The therapist's voice can serve as an intermediate self-nurturing voice that can supplant the client's voice. Eventually, the client may internalize the therapist's voice and be able to call upon it at will. When summoning a nurturing or self-assuring inner voice is problematic, the therapist may make an audiotape for the client with agreed-upon soothing and reassuring phrases on it. The client then may play the tape regularly or at times of distress, hearing the therapist's actual voice until she has internalized it.

Another simple intervention that will strengthen the authentic self is for the therapist to ask the client questions that allow the client to express her thoughts and feelings as well as expand upon her experience. Inquiring of the client, "How do you feel about that?" and "Tell me more about that?" encourages her to honor her own true thoughts and feelings. Many women are so used to being unheard and minimized that being attended to and *truly* heard can be transformational, propelling them to trust themselves in new ways.

The tentative client may balk at being asked to talk about herself and share her inner thoughts and opinions. The therapist must be patient, gentle, yet persistent in eliciting the client's true self. When the client asks the therapist her opinion on matters, the therapist responds by seeking out the client's opinion first. Frequently, the client will have some ideas of her own but lack the confidence to voice them. By repeatedly using the simple interventions of reflection, summarization, and exploration, the therapist increases the client's confidence in herself, strengthening authenticity. These interventions are ones that therapists may take for granted; however, within the context of self silencing, they have enormous potential to empower the authentic self. The next section describes a number of specific interventions that increase the client's connection with her authentic, inner experience through connecting with her feelings.

## CONNECTION WITH AUTHENTIC FEELINGS

IRT views expression of affect as an important therapy experience. Evocation of affect has been related to improvement in therapy (Castonguay et al., 1996; Jones & Pulos, 1993) and it is a cornerstone of the

Stone Center's relational approach to therapy (Jordan, 1997; Jordan et al., 1991; Miller & Stiver, 1997). Many people have learned strategies of disengagement from feelings beginning in childhood by having parents who failed to express their own feelings and failed to respond to their children's feelings. Being disconnected from feelings is, thus, an "adaptive" strategy that has ensured survival within a certain kind of family environment. When the individual grows up and leaves the family, she continues to function as if the same emotional disconnection is necessary for her emotional survival. The result can be unsatisfying relationships and ineffective coping strategies, which contribute to vulnerability for depression. For women, sex role socialization further reinforces strategies of emotional disconnection: "Good" girls only feel "good" emotions and to do otherwise is selfish, shameful, bad, or otherwise unacceptable. (Men, from their own sex role socialization, also have particular pressures to disconnect from emotions.) Such a pejorative attitude toward negative emotions creates additional vulnerability to depression.

When the client is able to express all of her feelings, particularly negative feelings, in the presence of a caring, empathic therapist, she has a corrective emotional experience that promotes acceptance and integration of ALL parts of herself, giving rise to new templates of connection that have the capacity to mobilize the client into action, moving her out of her depressed state. In addition to leading to a corrective emotional experience, expression of affect has the potential to catalyze a number of interrelated and important change events:

1. The client develops deeper knowledge about how she authentically feels.
2. The client can let go of energy-consuming defenses that hide, obscure, or suppress feelings.
3. Expression of affect frees the client to move on.
4. Recognition of authentic feelings leads to more effective problem solving.
5. The client has a new experience of connection that includes all parts of herself.

There are several interventions that the therapist may use to elicit or heighten the client's affect and make expression of affect a meaningful and growth-enhancing experience. Table 9.4 lists interventions that the therapist can use to facilitate the client's connection with affect. When working with clients who have deficits in self capacities, therapists should approach with caution interventions that elicit or heighten af-

**TABLE 9.4   Interventions: Increasing Connection with Feelings**

The therapist can facilitate the client's connection with feelings by
1. Reflecting and summarizing the client's own affect-laden words.
2. Asking the client to verbalize feelings related to nonverbal reactions.
3. Naming underlying feelings.
4. Slowing down the action. ("Stay with that feeling.")
5. Asking the client to focus on visceral sensations she mentions in relation to emotions.
6. Asking the client to talk about her feelings.
7. Asking the client to expand on her experience. ("Tell me more"; "Say more about that.")
8. Sitting quietly while the client emotes.

fect. In such cases, affectively focused interventions are to be carefully paced and interspersed with more containing work that is likely to result in mastery. All clients should be stabilized and not in an acute depressive crisis when facilitating expression of affect.

By naming feelings and allowing the client to freely emote, the therapist is providing a holding environment, a healing place where she is free to be herself and connect with all parts of herself. The expression of difficult emotions often leads the client to take action when she had previously felt stuck or immobilized. The therapist must learn to be comfortable with strong affect and only to curtail expression of strong negative affect when it is in the client's best interest and not because the therapist is uncomfortable or overwhelmed. Simply being with the client while she is crying or feeling deeply, letting her know you are there, and telling her that it is all right to feel the way she is feeling can be an enormously powerful experience for the client.

It cannot be emphasized enough how effective it can be to name and reflect to the client feelings that appear tentative or under the surface. By being attuned to the client's verbal and nonverbal responses, the therapist can assist the client in naming and owning her feelings. Commenting on the client's nonverbal reactions may allow her to be with her feelings and give voice to feelings she was avoiding, suppressing, or minimizing. For instance, in our first session Serena spoke very quickly about all the things that were upsetting to her. When I noticed her eyes filling with tears, I remarked: "I'm noticing that your eyes are tearing. What is happening for you right now that brings tears to your eyes?" Serena was then able to become more attuned to her fear of hurting Maria. Beneath a general feeling of depression that felt numbing to her, was the emotion of fear. Once Serena began to experience and acknowledge her fear, she was less self-critical and more self-empathic.

Asking the client to "tell me more about that" or "stay with that for a moment" when feelings are mentioned, heightens the client's emotion and encourages her to stay with her own experience rather than discounting or avoiding it. At times the therapist may hear words that describe visceral sensations that are related to emotions. The therapist can slow down the client's experience by asking her to return to those visceral sensations and be with them in the session.

In the transformational phase of therapy, when a client is motivated to become more in touch with her feelings, the therapist may use a step-by-step approach described in Table 9.5, that I call, "Feeling feelings with the body-felt sense" (Simonds, 1994). This intervention may be particularly helpful for clients who have used intellectual defenses or otherwise been disconnected from feelings. Such interventions facilitate connection with self and with deep feelings that underlie an overall feeling of depression. Ultimately, the client may learn to more effectively access her emotions on her own outside of therapy, thus strengthening her connection with herself and empowering her to handle "bad moods" and "stucknesses" more effectively.

The therapist wants to help the client reach her most authentic, core emotions. For depressed women, feelings of shame or guilt may be more immediately accessible and may obscure feelings of sadness, fear, or anger. Depressed women often feel ashamed of being depressed, feel guilty for being unable to cope as they usually do, and feel humiliated for being sad, fearful, or angry (and they also may feel ashamed of feeling ashamed). The depressed woman often comes into therapy condemning herself either because she has no feelings or because she has too many feelings ("I shouldn't be feeling this way"). The therapist wants to help the depressed woman reach all of her feelings and to particularly facilitate expression of sadness and anger.

## SADNESS

Depressed women often deny their feelings of sadness because they consider such feelings selfish. To be sad implies that they are experiencing a loss which, in turn, would mean that the woman has needs and desires. A "good woman" is selfless and has no needs. When depressed women deny their sadness, they simultaneously deny the therapist's offer of help, leading to frustration, helplessness, or disempowerment

**TABLE 9.5   Interventions: Feeling Feelings With the Body-Felt Self©**

This technique builds awareness of feelings. This is a middle-phase task for clients with strong self capacities or demonstrated ability to tolerate strong emotions. It may be used when a client who has difficulty consistently connecting with feelings expresses some feelings. It may also be used when a client describes a potentially affect-laden event, issue, or situation with no affect. In that case, the client is to concentrate on the abdominal and chest area, noticing any changes or sensations, however mild.

1.   Paying attention

   • Have the client be still and focus on the sensations in her body that accompany feelings.

2.   Location

   • The client finds a location in her body where she feels the feelings.

3.   Clarification

   • The client concentrates on the location and describes sensations and feelings.
   • If sensations are in the hands, feet, head, or other distal parts of the body, ask the client if the feeling goes to any other place in the body.
   • Have the client describe the sensation in detail, using as many adjectives as possible.
   • If the client is unable to verbalize the sensation because it is too undefined, have her place her hands on the body directly above the location of the sensation and imagine breathing through her hands to the location. Have her describe any sensations.
   • If the client is unable to verbalize the sensation because it is undefined or because she cannot find the words, ask her to draw a picture of the feelings in her body (a good homework assignment). This may also give information as to how the feelings are blocked or covering other feelings.

4.   Exploration

   • The client associates to the sensations, the words, or the drawing.
   • If appropriate, the therapist may ask, "Have you felt this way any time in the past?"

5.   Learning

   • Process the experience with the client, having the client make any relevant connections with work she has been doing to strengthen connection with self.

*Note.* From *Bridging the Silence: Nonverbal Modalities in the Treatment of Adult Survivors of Childhood Sexual Abuse* by S. L. Simonds, 1994.

for both client and therapist (Stiver & Miller, 1997). The process of bearing together the client's deep, painful emotions, and identifying underlying feelings of sadness can be a powerful intervention that moves the client out of hopelessness and into connection.

> We believe a major task in therapy is to help our women patients who are depressed move from that nonfeeling and defensive state to an affective experience in which their sadness can be recognized and validated. We often ask patients who are diagnosed as depressed whether they are feeling sad or depressed. At first, they often look confused and indicate that they don't know the difference or that they feel both. Then we elaborate, "When I ask if you feel sad, I mean something close to tears, are the tears connected with sad images, losses of important people, do you feel a lump in your throat, does your heart feel like it's breaking sometimes, does it sometimes feel like unbearable grief? These feelings," we add, "may be different from feeling 'depressed'; that may be more like feeling in a black pit or a deep tunnel, bleak and heavy, with no sense of any hope or light at the other end, without many images other than doing away with oneself, seeing no way out of the muddle, and feeling that one is a bad person and that nothing can change that." (Stiver & Miller, 1997, p. 220)

Asking the client to differentiate feelings of sadness from depression or asking her to focus on the emotions evoked by viscerally descriptive words often brings her feelings of sadness to the surface. When intense feelings are expressed in the caring context of the therapy relationship, the client comes to value her experience and to develop new templates of relating, freeing up emotional energy and giving her hope for the future. Identifying sadness allows the client to mourn her losses and, ultimately, move through these feelings.

Because our culture denigrates strong emotions, a woman experiencing loss may feel pathologized or abnormal. The therapist can normalize grief and loss reactions, giving a woman permission to cry and feel sad.

## ANGER

While both men and women may restrain themselves from expressing anger for the sake of a relationship, sex role socialization creates a particular problem for women where anger is concerned. From a young age, girls learn gender-prescriptive behaviors that prohibit anger (Cox, Stabb, & Bruckner, 1999; Jack, 1991; Lerner, 1985; Miller, 1991a). In adolescence, when the pressure to conform to feminine sex roles is greatest, the development of the self may be compromised through the suppression of anger. Anger can signal a violation of the individual's rights and can support the development of healthy boundaries. Suppression of anger can lead not only to poorly developed boundaries but also to physical and psychological symptoms.

Harriet Goldner Lerner (1985) in her well-known book, *The Dance of Anger*, describes women's problem with anger:

> The more we are nice, the more we accumulate a storehouse of unconscious anger and rage. Anger is inevitable when our lives consist of giving in and going along; when we assume responsibility for other people's feelings and reactions; when we relinquish our primary responsibility to proceed with our own growth and ensure the quality of our lives; when we behave as if having a relationship is more important than having a self. Of course, we are forbidden from experiencing this anger directly since "nice ladies," by definition, are not "angry women." (p. 6)

Anger, then, is often a problem for all women, not just depressed women. The suppression of anger can lead to depression and the resulting depression can amplify a woman's problems with anger. The loss of self experienced by the depressed woman places her more squarely between a rock and a hard place where her anger is concerned. On the one hand, the pressure to hide her authentic self angers her. She resents not being able to be honest about how she thinks and feels. Believing she cannot reveal her miserable inner state, she is angry and resentful that she must be someone she is not. On the other hand, the worse the depressed woman feels, the more intense are self-condemning injunctions to be quiet and "good," making expression of anger increasingly unacceptable. To preserve important relationships, she must quiet or suppress strong negative emotions. Such moral dictates become more acute as depression worsens. The result may be that some women suppress all anger while others are angry all the time.

Initially, client and therapist can investigate the client's beliefs about anger. It is often helpful to take an "anger family history," in which the client describes how parents, caretakers, and significant others handled anger and the messages received about expression of anger. Sometimes such a discussion will reveal misassumptions the client made as a child, illuminating developmentally young ways of thinking that have prevailed into adulthood. For example, Renata, a 50-year-old attorney, explained that when she was a child, her older sister repeatedly told her that she was responsible for her own feelings. At the time, she understood this to mean that she should not feel *any* feelings, a belief that continued.

An important first step in helping a woman connect with anger toward movement out of depression is for the client to acknowledge and accept her feelings. A client may feel more accepting of her angry feelings if she understands that to *feel* anger does not mean she has to *act* on anger. Limited relational templates teach a woman that if she expresses negative emotions, she will be rejected and then alone. Teaching the client that she is capable of feeling her feelings and then deciding how to act on them, allays her fears of rejection and gives her more choices. Whenever a client comes to challenge a habitual way of being, she is in danger of responding with self blame because she was doing things "wrong." The therapist can help the client to view her defensive relational style with compassion rather than self blame. Together client and therapist can develop a narrative that explains the client's current dilemma about anger, incorporating information from cultural contexts, family history, the client's own experiences, and her belief system.

It is important to note that expression of anger in the middle-class Caucasian manner is not necessarily a goal for all clients and, when appropriate, cultural norms of anger expression are to be explored by client and therapist. Together client and therapist will develop a picture of the various ways to handle anger that devour less energy, exact less of an emotional toll, and are consistent with cultural norms of anger expression that continue to be important for the client.

The client may need help identifying her feelings of anger. In session, the client may gloss over or rush past descriptions of anger-invoking events. She may present the "nice" facade to the therapist when she is probably feeling not-so-nice inside. The therapist can help the client become more attuned to her anger by asking her to stay with these feelings through noticing and describing her visceral sensations. Muscle tension, breathing patterns, and body temperature are specific types of sensations that the client is likely to feel. The goal is for the client to develop the skills to recognize her own angry reactions outside of session and to be more comfortable with the fact that she has these feelings rather than trying to deny, minimize, or rationalize them. Staying with angry feelings in sessions and truly feeling anger in the safe, holding environment of the therapy may assist the client in becoming more comfortable with these feelings and may reduce anger suppression or anger explosiveness outside of session.

For many clients, owning feelings of anger may be a powerful experience. Simply saying "I feel angry" may be frightening and anxiety provoking. When the client has tentatively or ambivalently acknowledged feelings of anger, asking her to say the statement, "I feel angry" or "I am angry at _____," may be a significant change event. When the client describes situations in which the therapist believes anger is an appropriate response but the client does acknowledge anger, the therapist is careful not to impose her own anger ideas on the client. In these situations, the therapist can ask if the client feels several different emotions, anger among them, giving the client a chance to identify feelings on her own.

There are a variety of activities that the therapist may introduce that facilitate expression of anger. The purpose of these activities is for the client to gain more comfort with feeling anger and to take more ownership over the emotion of anger. Physical anger release activities can be empowering for the client who has been disconnected from her anger or felt intimidated or afraid of her own anger. Physical anger release activities such as those using a punching bag or batacas may provide the client with a means to be truly in touch with feelings of anger, but require specialized training and are beyond the scope of this book. It should be noted that these kinds of activities have been found to exacerbate anger rather than to provide a cathartic release (Bushman, Baumeister, & Stack, 1999). Although I have found that these types of exercises can be particularly empowering in the context of a women's therapy group, they do not usually lend themselves well to the dynamics of individual psychotherapy. When a client wants to explore being more connected to her aggression or physical strength, I might recommend an aikido or judo class rather than an in-session activity.

Some clients may express a need to *do something* when feeling angry. This is often the case for clients who are newly discovering feelings of anger and have historically suppressed or avoided such feelings. At home, the client may try anger release activities such as screaming, punching a pillow, or tearing up phone books, with the client monitoring herself in order to discover if such activities provide a helpful outlet. These activities are for clients who are developmentally ready to be more in touch with anger and are not usually helpful for those who have a history of violence or explosive anger.

For some clients, creative projects about anger may be productive such as drawing anger, writing poetry, journalling, or selecting, listening to, or writing angry music. For the client who has been out of touch with anger, such activities provide an avenue for greater self-discovery. Sometimes a client may get enormous benefit from writing a letter or journal entry directed at the person at whom she is angry with the only intention of using such writing as a therapeutic activity—in other words, the client does not plan to actually send the writing to anyone. Particularly for the client who has avoided or suppressed anger in an effort to please others, writing is a safe way to begin to connect more with anger.

Developing an exercise plan that provides physical release may also help with chronic anger or newly discovered, intense feelings of anger. In addition, the chronically angry client may often benefit from learning to identify feelings of anger as soon as they arise and utilizing affect regulation activities to help her become calm enough to make healthy decisions about how to handle her anger. The therapist wants to convey to the client that not only are her authentic feelings important, but handling her feelings in an empowered way is also important. The chronically angry woman may also discover that while anger may be her first line of defense against interpersonally distressing situations, beneath the anger are feelings of hurt, fear, or sadness. Connecting with these more poignant, vulnerable feelings ultimately helps a woman move from self-loathing and alienation to self-empathy and connection.

Reconnecting with anger may be a difficult task for some women. Suppression of anger supports the status quo. Once a woman connects with her anger, she may have to take action to change untenable situations. One client told me, "I am afraid to feel my anger, because then I will probably have to change my life in ways that I don't want to think about." Feeling anger may mean taking responsibility for one's life and giving up passivity (see Table 9.6).

## CLIENT ACTIVITIES THAT STRENGTHEN THE AUTHENTIC SELF

Depression smothers creativity. By undertaking creative activities, the client nurtures the authentic self and brings herself into closer connection with her own deep knowledge. To be creative is to give voice to the authentic self. Furthermore, activities that engage the client in play are revitalizing and mobilizing, nurturing self-efficacy and eliciting positive emotions.

It has been my observation that many clients naturally express interest in exploring creative outlets as they progress in their recovery. In the middle-to-late phases of therapy, activities such as writing, artmaking, and crafting provide the client with the opportunity to voice and celebrate her authentic self, to nurture and revitalize herself, and to expand her horizons. Although the least structured and most free-form of these activities bring the client closest to her authentic experience, clients who are uncomfortable being spontaneous or independently undertaking creative activities may start with more structured activities such as dance classes or music lessons.

By doing the work of accessing and honoring the authentic self in therapy, the client may discover unfulfilled longings, such as Serena's

**TABLE 9.6   Interventions: Working With Anger**

The therapist can assist the client in connecting with anger and having healthier responses to anger by

1. Explaining that feelings of anger are distinct from behaviors that express anger.
2. Exploring a family history of anger, the client's history with anger, her beliefs about anger expression, and cultural norms of anger expression.
3. Asking the client to describe body-centered feelings related to anger.
4. Naming anger when the client's verbalizations, body postures, or gestures appear to reflect anger, but the client is not fully aware of her anger.
5. When the client is tentative in expressing or owning anger, exploring her tentativeness and asking her to make definitive statements, such as "I feel angry at _____."
6. When the client does not acknowledge anger in anger-invoking situations, asking her to explore a range of feelings.
7. Exploring more poignant, vulnerable feelings that chronic or explosive anger may be obscuring.
8. Being careful not to impose the therapist's own feelings on the client.
9. Suggesting anger expression activities such as drawing or journalling.
10. Helping the client to identify anger release activities for use at home when the client expresses a need to "do something" with her anger.
11. Identifying a range of ways to express and communicate anger to others.

discovery that, "I always wanted to write." While some clients may discover such specific longings, others will simply rejoice in the opportunity to be creative. Depending on the interest of the client, the therapist may suggest that she try some of the following creative tasks outside of therapy. Table 9.7 lists some creative activities that may draw out, nurture, or strengthen the authentic self. The client may complete creative projects outside of therapy and then may wish to discuss them in therapy as they relate to her growing self-confidence and self-acceptance. (For more details about using art tasks with the client, see Simonds, 1994.)

For some clients, the opportunity to play will be invigorating and inspiring, leading to a renewed connection with self. Often, such activities lead to more practical realizations about being authentic in work and relationships, catalyzing significant life changes as the client gains the confidence to pursue long silenced dreams and wishes. By making a commitment to ongoing involvement with creative endeavors that keep the client in contact with her authenticity, she is increasing her resilience against relapse. As will be discussed further in chapters 11 and 12, creativity expands the client's access to positive emotions, which is an important element in relapse prevention (Frederickson, 2000).

**TABLE 9.7   Creative Tasks for Nurturing the Authentic Self**

Journalling activities
   Free writing
   Poetry
   Writing about the authentic self: likes, dislikes, characteristics, and so forth
   Narrative history of the authentic self
Writing classes
Art projects
   Drawings or collages representing the false self and the authentic self
   Free drawings
   Art and craft classes such as photography, pottery, or ceramics
Dance classes, particularly improvisational dance
Music, voice, or acting lessons

## SUMMARY

Through the influence of family of origin, sex role socialization, and sociocultural context many women develop a dual self in order to please others and are vulnerable to losing connection with their authentic thoughts and feelings. Women whose authentic self is silenced are vulnerable to depression and depressed women lose access to the authentic self. This chapter has discussed therapeutic interventions that assist the client in reclaiming and strengthening her connection with the authentic self. A mutually empathic therapeutic connection between client and therapist will enable the client to integrate all parts of herself into the therapeutic encounter, thus creating a unique opportunity for connecting with the authentic self. Several specific interventions that disempower the false self and strengthen the authentic self are described, including hearing internal conversations, naming internal voices, talking back to the false self, and creative self-expression.

   IRT stresses the importance that expression of affect has on the client's recovery and on her future resilience. Through connection with the therapist, the client feels freer to express all parts of herself, including her negative emotions. By becoming more attuned to herself and *all* of her feelings, the client is mobilized to take action and move out of the stuckness of depression. There are a number of interventions that the therapist may utilize to heighten and access important emotions. Of particular importance to depressed women is expressing feelings of sadness and anger. As the client increases her connection with herself and her authentic feelings, she sets in motion change processes that impact her relationships with others, which are discussed in the next chapter.

# CHAPTER TEN

# Connection: Part II

Trish, a 38-year-old elementary school teacher, was coming out of her second depressive episode when she entered therapy. Looking back at her darkest hour, she realized that she had attempted to maintain a facade with her friends, eventually withdrawing because it was too much effort to pretend she felt good. "I want to be able to be more honest," explained Trish.

As depressed women become healthier and more in touch with their authenticity, they long for more honest connections. They begin to challenge and resolve the central relational paradox (Miller & Stiver, 1997) that governed relational behaviors and prohibited them from sharing important parts of themselves in order to maintain connection. Connection with one's authentic, inner experience in the context of a healing, therapeutic relationship catalyzes a series of changes that propel women to attend to important relationships in their lives, acknowledging disconnections, reclaiming lost connections, resolving disconnections, and seeking new connections. Greater connection with self and others inevitably leads the client to revisit and make even further progress on treatment goals related to the other elements of therapy. Most significantly, greater connection with self and others sets in motion shifts in the client's perspective that lead her to reconstruct important meaning structures, described in detail in chapter 11.

A depressed woman may feel afraid to be honest with others and herself about the dissatisfactions she feels regarding important relationships. Femininity training teaches women to feel responsible for maintaining harmony in relationships and provides few options for handling conflict. A woman may come to believe that she has an either/or choice in handling relational dissatisfaction: either to give up her sense of self to maintain harmony or to give up the relationship entirely (Jack, 1999). This limiting, dichotomous perspective heightens a woman's anxiety and hopelessness about relational problems. The prospect of being alone can cause her to feel scared and immobilized. Thus, subordination appears to be her only safe solution, yet to follow that route increases her alienation, hopelessness, and resentment. This may be the point at which a woman enters therapy, feeling stuck and hopeless about her most important relationships and feeling responsible for this impossible state of her life.

For some women, simply admitting to dissatisfactions with important relationships is threatening. The therapist may find that reflections and summarizations of a woman's complaints about her significant relationship are met with retractions, denials, or rationalizations for her partner's behaviors. At this point, to admit that the problem is serious exacerbates her despair and anxiety. Often, a woman will not be ready to admit to relational problems or to work on resolving disconnections until she has become more solid in her sense of self. As a woman feels more accepting of all parts of herself, she begins to question her assumptions and verbalize her longing for new ways to connect with others.

IRT stresses the importance of relationships in women's lives and recognizes that a woman makes changes only in ways that makes sense given her sociocultural context, life stressors, self capacities, level of depression, and stage of recovery. Because relationships are so central to women's lives, therapy must help a woman maximize affirmative, healthy relational connections that are characterized by authenticity and mutuality. The therapist, through empathic attunement and accurate assessment, collaborates with a woman to evaluate the important relationships in her life and to help her articulate appropriate goals regarding relationships. Having a supportive network of friends is seen as an important goal for all clients. Improving relational connections and resolving disconnections not only helps a woman recover from depression, but also increases her resilience against relapse. The treatment goals of this chapter are summarized in Table 10.1 and are aimed at facilitating healthier, more authentic connections with others.

**TABLE 10.1   Connection With Others: Treatment Goals**

1. More authentic and mutually supportive relationships with significant others
2. Improved boundaries
3. Healthy parenting
4. Greater awareness of relational behaviors
5. Wider range of relational behaviors
6. Stronger and broader network of supportive friends

The therapist can conceptualize the work of increasing relational authenticity as following the themes of each of the three therapy phases. Initially, in the stabilization phase, the client may be so debilitated by acute symptoms of depression that she is only able to address relationship concerns to garner help from potentially supportive others in fulfilling day-to-day responsibilities, minimizing isolation, and maximizing safety from self-harm. The client with solid self capacities and a sense of self-efficacy may be able to begin transformational phase work that focuses on improving relational connections and resolving disconnections relatively early in the therapy. However, the client with a negative sense of self or rigid and disempowering relational schemas may not be able to directly address relational disconnections for some time. Future orientation phase work is aimed at helping the client identify long-term goals and strategies related to strengthening and expanding positive relational connections to maximize resilience against relapse.

## STABILIZATION PHASE TASKS

Table 10.2 summarizes interventions that will assist the client in maximizing relational capacities in the stabilization phase of therapy. Initially, the therapist helps the client identify potentially healthy and supportive relationships and encourages the client to explore how those

**TABLE 10.2  Interventions: Stabilization Phase**

The therapist helps the client maximize her relational capacities in the stabilization phase of therapy by

1. Asking the client to describe the important relationships in her life.
2. Asking the client to identify potentially supportive people in her life.
3. Encouraging the client to restore connections with supportive others
4. Helping the client to decide with whom and how she wants to disclose information about her current depressive episode.
5. Helping the client to decide how others can be involved in her recovery.
6. Helping the client to set limits with unsupportive others.
7. Helping the client to name unhealthy relationships.
8. Collaborating with the client to identify goals regarding relationships that are consistent with the client's sociocultural context, life stressors, self capacities, and level of depression.
9. Helping the client understand if and how her depression has impacted her parenting and collaborating on strategies and supports for optimal care of children.

individuals may be involved in her recovery. While limiting relational schemas may be clarified at this point, the client may be too depressed to address such schemas and may simply need help managing her day-to-day life. The client is reminded that she has the right to privacy and can choose with whom she shares information about herself, how much information she wishes to share, and when she wishes to share it. The therapist encourages the client to restore previously healthy connections that were compromised due to stressors that precipitated the depressive episode or due to the client's depressive withdrawal. Likewise, the therapist urges the client to set limits with those who are energy-draining or unsupportive.

It is not unusual for a woman to hide her depression from significant people in her life. As a woman discusses her hesitations about involving significant others in her recovery, her limiting assumptions about relationships can be discerned, often revealing disempowering schemas of lovability and control, such as "I'm not entitled to have needs" and "If I am not happy, no one will love me." For example, Laura had been terrified to let her husband know she was depressed, telling him that she had a meeting about her childcare business when she actually was coming to her first therapy appointment. She was afraid he would reject her if he knew "how bad off I was," and this deception increased her feelings of aloneness and alienation. After our second therapy session, she got up the courage to talk with him, revealing her depression and her plan to go to therapy. She felt relieved and, ultimately, gained his support. Laura no longer felt like she was all alone in her troubles. She not only had a therapist helping her, but her husband was also behind her.

The safety of the therapeutic relationship encourages a woman to begin to evaluate her relationships and to be honest about relational dissatisfactions. IRT recognizes that the realities of women's lives do not necessarily allow for immediate amelioration, resolution, or dissolution of unhealthy relationships and, thus, stresses the importance of supportive friendships and kinships that may buffer clients who have unhealthy significant relationships. The therapist must be attuned to the client in matching the intervention to her level of readiness to approach relational problems. Although the ultimate goal for a woman is to have healthier, more authentic, mutual connections, her work on relationships will need to proceed in a way that honors her individual needs and capacities at a given time. Initially, a client may only be able to name a relational dissatisfaction, but feel unwilling to address this problem or take any action outside of therapy. As the client becomes less depressed and she becomes more attuned to her needs and genuine feelings, she may find that she is no longer as tolerant of others' behaviors toward her. However, the client may initially discount her feelings, labeling herself a "bitch" for being displeased with others. The therapist can help the client understand that this is a normal reaction to becoming newly attuned to her own needs.

Another important consideration in the early phase of therapy is helping the depressed mother to parent effectively. The reality of a depressed mother is that her parenting may be compromised, particularly when her symptoms are more severe. She may more easily become frustrated, irritable, impulsive, inconsistent, avoidant, or lax in her parenting. In addition, some depressed parents may place a child in the position of being a confidant or caretaker. The therapist can assist the client in becoming aware of how her depression has impacted her parenting and collaborate with her to ensure optimal parenting. There are a number of relevant issues that the client may be asked to explore, depending on the age, maturity, and personality of the children involved and the resources and needs of the parent: (a) deciding if and how to explain mom's depression, (b) making arrangements to get extra child care or assistance with the children or household responsibilities, (c) planning "quality time" with children, (d) finding ways to give children extra attention during stressful times, not only from mom but from other adults, and (e) making a referral for therapy for a child. In addition, the therapist can help the client find an age-appropriate way to talk to the child about the child's own feelings and to maintain ongoing communication with the child.

## TRANSFORMATIONAL PHASE TASKS

Table 10.3 summarizes interventions that facilitate greater authenticity in relationships in the transformational phase of therapy. As many women become more connected to and accepting of their authentic, inner experiences, they will long to be more authentic with important others outside of therapy. Partnered women often come to recognize that their strategies of self-silencing for the sake of protecting their primary relationships actually robbed them of true closeness with their partners. This recognition often allows a woman to become more willing to take risks in relationships by speaking her feelings. She may become motivated to resolve conflicts with a partner and seek new ways to handle conflicts. The therapist is attuned to these shifts and helps the client name these emerging, not yet fully formed desires, bringing them into the client's awareness.

**TABLE 10.3   Interventions: Transformational Phase**

The therapist can facilitate the client's progress in developing more authentic and mutual relationships by

1. Naming the client's emerging, not yet fully formed desires for more authenticity and mutuality in relationships.
2. Helping the client to notice and celebrate more authentic relational behaviors.
3. Explaining the nature of change within systems.
4. Encouraging the client to persevere in making changes.
5. Reminding the client to use affect regulation and self-care skills when making relational changes.
6. Encouraging the client to come up with alternative relational behaviors.
7. Asking the client to weigh pros and cons of trying new relational behaviors.
8. Asking the client to list ways to stay in touch with her authentic self and signs that she may be losing herself as she becomes closer to others.
9. Participating in role playing and rehearsal to help the client try out potential changes.
10. Teaching the client negotiation and conflict resolution skills.
11. Asking the client to explore the impact of her relational behavior on her children.
12. Asking the client to examine her parents' relational patterns.
13. Making a referral for couples therapy.
14. Making a referral for group therapy.

While ideally, a woman wants to be able to ensure that all of her relationships are healthy, authentic, and mutually supportive, the realities of some women's lives limit their relational options. For example, women who cannot tolerate being alone, who lack financial resources, or who value the sanctity of their marital vows may be willing to go only so far in effecting changes in their significant relationships. Thus, some women will remain at high risk for relapse if they are unwilling to leave unsupportive relationships or to take steps to address problems with a partner. Because working with women clients who are unable to leave a bad relationship can be quite a challenge for the therapist, a special section is devoted to this problem.

For some clients, such as Laura, changes in relationships will occur spontaneously outside of therapy as the work of connection with self progresses within therapy sessions. A woman may naturally become closer to others as she is more willing to reveal previously undisclosed parts of herself, while, simultaneously, she may become increasingly intolerant of others who fail to nurture or support authenticity. Thus, the client may experience a redefinition of boundaries. As a result of these changes, a realignment of family and friends may occur. A woman may become closer to those who support authenticity and mutuality while distancing herself from those who do not. She may find herself able to avoid unhealthy interpersonal situations that she previously had felt powerless to escape. Having developed a critical consciousness, she may perceive interpersonal situations differently. With her "poop detector" operating, the client may be attuned to relational problems and be more willing to address them. Through her increased confidence in her authentic self she may be more willing to express her wants and needs with clarity. A client who had previously been ineffectually angry by being explosive or whiny, may become articulate, reasonable, and direct in her communication. Suddenly, a client may be ready to ask for the therapist's help in exploring new relational behaviors to try outside of therapy. The therapist makes these spontaneous changes more meaningful and conscious by naming them as they occur, by describing them within the context of the client's progress in her therapy, by encouraging the client to explore new relational behaviors, and by helping the client to notice and celebrate her successes. Furthermore, this may be a time when a client begins to examine her own parents' relationship, seeking clues to understand the source of her relational patterns. The therapist is attuned to the opportunity to explore old family relational templates as a means of helping the client understand her current relational dilemmas with a more self-empathic attitude.

As the client begins to behave differently in important relationships, these shifts may not be without difficulty, as significant others react, making "countermoves" (Lerner, 1985, p. 33) to restore a relationship back to its prior state when the client was passive, accommodating, or dependent. The therapist helps the client weather these transitions by explaining the nature of change within systems, encouraging the client to persevere in her efforts to change, and reminding her to use affect regulation and self-care strategies as she tries out new relational behaviors.

As clients express their desire to be more authentic in important relationships, therapists can help them explore a wider range of relational repertoires and to examine the possible consequences of undertaking new behaviors. Sometimes middle-phase work leads a partnered woman to recognize that her relational inhibitions are based on old fears or outdated templates and that her partner would actually tolerate a wider range of behaviors from her. In these situations, the therapist can help the client articulate her desired changes and decide how to act on them, encouraging the client to explore the pros and cons of trying out new behaviors.

Some clients may be clear that they want to handle interpersonal situations differently, but express confusion as to what to do. The therapist should resist telling the client what to do, instead helping the client to verbalize her own wishes for more closeness or distance and to identify possible alternative behaviors. Some clients, however, due to their emotionally impoverished family and relational histories, may truly have no idea as to what is appropriate behavior where limit-setting or handling conflict is concerned. They have been so de-selfed that they have no context for saying "no" or negotiating. While therapists may need to become teachers at times, every effort should be made for clients to gain knowledge through trusting their own experiences. For example, while some clients may not notice when their own limits have been crossed, they may well perceive boundary violations when asked to imagine someone close to them, such as a daughter or a close friend, in a comparable situation. Clients may also expand their repertoires of relational skills by observing women they admire or whom they see as having the desired skills. The client may "borrow" a friend's, mentor's, teacher's, or the therapist's assertiveness until she feels that such an attitude is genuinely her own. In addition, the client may benefit from learning negotiation skills and conflict resolution skills.

In this phase, a client who has children may begin to explore the impact of her inauthentic relatedness with a partner on her children, particularly on daughters for whom she is modeling relational behavior. Sometimes a client's concerns about the possible impact of her marriage on her children will impel her to risk asking her partner to attend couples therapy with her. Exploring the client's childhood and her parents' relationship may help the client understand her own relational difficulties.

While a partnered woman may become more ready to take steps to increase closeness with a partner or begin the dissolution of an unhealthy relationship, a single or divorced woman may begin to address ambivalences about her relationship status. Some single women may feel extremely ambivalent about seeking closeness and have sought withdrawal from romantic possibilities and, sometimes, from most social contacts. This withdrawal, while feeling safe, contributes to the client's depression. Superficially, she expresses contentment with her single life, but under the surface she feels anxiety and deep sadness. The woman may rationalize her withdrawal by becoming overly busy with work or by telling herself that there are "no good ones out there—I'm better off alone." However, at her core, the woman longs for connection.

Her dilemma is that to admit she wants closeness opens her up to hurt and disappointment, yet if she is not able to recognize her longing, she remains closed off to new connections. The therapist can help a woman name this dilemma, connect with her longings and her fears, and learn alternative ways to protect herself from hurts that do not limit her relational possibilities. Simultaneously, the woman also can be encouraged to feel more satisfied with her single life, increasing her repertoire of meaning-making activities as well as expanding her social activities, not with the purpose of finding a romantic partner but with the aim of increasing aliveness and connection. The goal is for the client to build a satisfying single life that leaves her receptive to finding a partner yet not dependent on becoming partnered as her only vision of fulfillment.

Natalie, a 50-year-old psychotherapist, had been experiencing intermittent symptoms of mild depression, overeating, and lethargy since the breakup of a long-term relationship 4 years earlier. Initially, therapy focused on the overeating because this was Natalie's presenting problem. After tracking the incidents of overeating over a few weeks, it became apparent that eating represented a way for her to "fill herself up" to compensate for the dissatisfaction she felt in her life. However, Natalie resisted the idea of expanding her social contacts, insisting that her work and household chores took up all her time. She asserted that she was better off without a man and that she planned to spend the rest of her life alone. Eventually, Natalie began to recognize that she had literally "gone into a cave" after the breakup, shutting herself down emotionally, closing herself off from all people, and limiting her receptiveness to new experiences. Through the transformational phase work of connecting with authentic feelings and genuine inner experience, Natalie reached the realization that she truly wanted to find a partner, but was afraid that she would repeat her past mistakes of making a poor choice. I asked her to make a list of things she could do to maintain connection with her authentic feelings and keep her "poop detector" fully operational as she explored new social contacts. Natalie then began a period of expansiveness during which she joined a local political action group and began to look for new friends. When she left therapy, Natalie had not found a partner, but her life was more fulfilling, she was no longer overeating, and her mood was quite optimistic.

## REFERRAL FOR COUPLES THERAPY

The depressed woman is oftentimes unwilling to participate in couples therapy with her partner, particularly early in her recovery. A woman may feel that she cannot trust her thoughts and feelings, that she may be wrong about what is wrong in the relationship or that she is the problem. Even when a woman is no longer plagued by self-doubt, she may be afraid of expressing her true thoughts and feelings to her partner either because she fears that she will erupt with explosive anger or that her efforts to communicate will be futile. In other words, she is fearful either of being too effectual or ineffectual. Only when she has become more confident in her authenticity, gained some sense of mastery over her feelings, and expanded her view of relational images may she feel ready for couples therapy.

The individual therapist should make a referral to another therapist for couples therapy. When the woman client's therapist attempts to be the couple therapist, both therapies are compromised. The client may feel betrayed by the therapist in sessions with a partner when the therapist fails to blame her partner or undertakes such seemingly neutral therapy interventions as reflection and summarization of her partner's words. To hear her therapist voice the sentiments of the partner may be more than some women clients can tolerate. Alternatively, the partner may feel ganged-up upon by having the therapy conducted by the depressed woman's therapist, and it may not be possible for the partner to perceive the therapist as neutral regardless of the therapist's actual behavior. Couples therapy, however, can be an important part of a depressed woman's recovery. Therapists are advised to make referrals to couples therapists who understand gender issues. Emotionally focused couples therapy (Greenberg & Johnson, 1988; Johnson, 1996) is particularly compatible with IRT due to its similar roots in relational theory and its emphasis on expression of authentic feelings.

When authenticity and mutuality are not realistic goals for a relationship because a partner is authoritarian, a male partner holds rigid expectations of gender roles, or a partner refuses to change, the client is faced with a much more complex agenda with no immediate or easy resolution. A woman may be stuck in an unhealthy relationship that has no hope of improvement.

## WHEN THE CLIENT IS STUCK IN AN UNHEALTHY RELATIONSHIP

Perhaps one of the biggest challenges for the therapist is the client who is unable to leave an unhealthy romantic relationship, despite mounting evidence that the relationship is emotionally harmful or physically dangerous and has contributed to the client's current depressive episode. Clients may stay "stuck" for months or years in a relationship that has no hope of change. It is particularly important in these situations for the therapist to help the client come to her own conclusion about the relationship and for the therapist not only to resist telling the client what to do, but to refrain from expressing disapproval. In the first place, the client may feel even more shamed and immobilized if she feels the therapist's disapproval for her inaction. In the second place, advising the client to leave when the client is not ready to do so can backfire, eliciting further feelings of inadequacy, hopelessness, and immobility in the client. Finally, a therapist's failure to be empathically attuned to the client's readiness to make changes may result in premature termination.

A number of separate but related issues may impede a client's ability to take decisive action to terminate an unhealthy relationship. A therapist may be more able to maintain empathy and a client may be more willing to stay in therapy when together therapist and client can develop an empathic conceptual understanding of the client's stuckness and such conceptualization leads to a specific treatment plan.

Some possible factors that may impede the client from leaving a bad relationship are deficits in self capacities, financial dependence, parenting concerns, and cultural restrictions. While women who fear abandonment are sometimes labeled as "borderline," many women who are unable to leave a bad relationship do not have such severe deficits in self capacities to qualify for that diagnosis. Sex role socialization, culture, and economics can conspire to limit a woman's options. The term, "codependent," was coined to describe individuals who persist in remaining in unhealthy relationships, suggesting the widespread nature of this phenomenon. Whatever the reason for the client's failure to take action, the therapist can encourage the client to continue to increase her own emotional and physical resilience, to improve her financial autonomy, to build a strong support network, and to find positive meaning in her life. Additionally, when external barriers such as finances, children, or culture impede the client's ability to leave a bad relationship, the therapist can not only help the client evaluate all of her options but also assist her in working through accompanying feelings. I will briefly discuss some possible interventions for working with the client who is stuck in a bad relationship due to deficits in self capacities.

## Deficits in Self Capacities

Clients who are unable to leave a bad relationship due solely to deficits in self capacities and not due to financial, religious, or other cultural constraints, have the potential to elicit negative countertransference in the therapist. The therapist may become impatient and frustrated by the client's inability to make positive changes when it has long been evident that the client is being emotionally harmed by staying or that her depressive symptoms appear intertwined with her unhappiness in the relationship. Often, the client may be terrified of being alone. This issue may be addressed not only by exploring the client's beliefs about what it means for her to be alone, but also by helping the client increase her tolerance for strong affect.

Some women, due to their low self-worth and need to please others, view their partner's love as proof as their lovableness. Women with a negative sense of self may be obsessed with whether their partner finds them desirable, attractive, or interesting. While they are overfocused on their partner's acceptance, they seldom ask themselves if they find their partner acceptable. In fact, they may become so absorbed by the fear that their partner will reject them that they seldom consider whether they actually find their partner acceptable. They may disregard rude, cruel, disloyal, or abusive behavior toward them. The client may be unable to integrate good and bad qualities about her partner, alternating between idealization and devaluation. At times, the anxiety about leaving such a relationship may elicit idealized images of the relationship. The therapist may support the client in developing less dichotomous thinking, repeating the client's own verbalizations about the relationship, at times reminding the client of her own words about her partner. Also, the therapist may suggest that the client make a list of her partner's strengths and weaknesses, referring to it frequently in order to sustain a realistic, balanced perspective. Additionally, I have sometimes helped a client begin to develop more of a critical consciousness about her relationship by posing such questions as, "Last week you told me that your boyfriend refused to pay the rent and you found out that he set up two fraudulent credit cards, is this the kind of person you want as the father of your children?" This intervention has the potential to be successful when the therapist is careful to use only the client's descriptions of her partner, is genuinely interested in the client's opinion, refrains from any judgmental statements regardless of how the client responds, and does not overutilize these kinds of queries. The goal is for the client to see the unhealthy partner through her own alert and awake adult eyes, rather than only seeing herself through her partner's eyes.

Both client and therapist may become wearied or disheartened by the repetitiveness of the client's complaints. When the therapy seems stalemated in this way, the therapist can try to direct the client away from the relationship dilemma toward improving the quality of the client's life in other ways. Another tactic that may be fruitful is asking the client to notice her dreams and bring them into the therapy. In addition to shifting the focus from an insolvable situation, working on dreams may provide the client with new metaphors about her dilemma that offer new insights or new solutions. Simultaneously, exploring family-of-origin issues may provide the client with yet another perspective to understand herself and her problems. All of these approaches capitalize on using the therapeutic relationship as a holding environment within which the client can develop new internalizations and skills. Yet another approach is to ask the client to imagine how many years she needs before she leaves the relationship (S. Lyons, personal communication, March, 1999). This strategy shocked one particularly stuck client into recognizing how much of her life she was planning to waste in a bad relationship, propelling her to risk leaving.

Leanne, a 35-year-old chemist and mother of two, was hopelessly frustrated by her husband's lack of involvement in family life. She felt discounted, unheard, and overworked, yet was terrified of expressing her anger at her husband. Despite his refusal to be at home for dinner or to join her and their two daughters for activities on weekends, she constantly tried to please him, believing if she only asked him correctly, cooked the right meal, or planned the right activity, he would be impelled to change. When she planned weekend outings, her husband often refused to make a commitment to participate and she inevitably spent hours hanging around the house waiting for him to be ready to join her and her daughters. Jack (1991) calls this kind of behavior "compliant relatedness" (p. 40):

> Compliant relatedness, characterized by restriction of initiative and freedom of expression within a relationship, looks like an anxious attachment behavior and stems from an underlying fear that the loved one will not be available unless one hovers close and tries to please. (p. 40)

Compliant relatedness is a relational style that women with deficits in self capacities may rely on to protect them from their fear of being alone and their inability to tolerate their own negative feelings, which were problem areas for Leanne. As her therapy progressed, she came to be more accepting of her own feelings of anger at her husband and more able to tolerate them. Although she came to long for more enjoyable family time, she continued to fear being more honest with her husband about her feelings. However, she was tired of constantly giving up planned activities because her husband was not willing to make a commitment. Through discussing possible alternative behaviors, Leanne decided to try being more independent, planning activities that she and her daughters enjoyed regardless of her husband's interest. She stopped begging him to join them, instead telling him her schedule and letting him know that she hoped he would like to join them, leaving at the appointed time regardless of his whereabouts or commitment to attend. Very quickly, she discovered that she was happier getting out of the house and, most surprising to her, her husband began to come along, appearing ready to depart at the appointed time. These successes led Leanne to risk being more honest with her husband and she was ultimately successful in getting him to agree to attend couples therapy with her.

The client who has been dependent and compliant, without the desired attentive response of her partner, may find that as she develops more self-confidence through connection with her authentic thoughts and feelings she will feel ready to risk being more autonomous. Together client and therapist can identify more autonomous activities that may increase the client's pleasurable experiences or expand her social connections, starting with relatively "low-risk" changes. Because the client's ultimate goal is for more closeness with her partner, simultaneously she can be helped to find direct, nonblaming ways to communicate to her partner her desire for closeness.

When the client's inability to leave a bad relationship is due to deficits in self capacities, client and therapist can be forewarned that the client will need to do major reparative inner work before she is able to leave and therapy may be long term (or the client may be in therapy intermittently over an extended period of time). Group therapy, discussed below, may be helpful for the stuck client, providing her with examples of others who are able to take risks in their lives and expanding her support network.

## REFERRAL FOR GROUP THERAPY

Group therapy can be enormously empowering, particularly a group with other women, in the middle-to-late stages of therapy when the woman is ready to interact more with others. In fact, a women's therapy group can provide a wonderful arena for the recovering client to experience being authentically herself, trying out new perceptions and understandings of herself and her world:

> Group work offers community support for a woman to form new interpretations and evaluations of interpersonal events. In groups, women can gain

strength and support from one another through identifying, sharing, and reinterpreting (renaming) events together. Groups also allow women to break the destructive forms of relating they have learned. (Jack, 1991, p. 204)

Change can be confusing and isolating, as well as exciting. The support of a therapy group, particularly a group of women, provides the client with many "companions on the journey," who can provide not only affirmation, support, and comfort, but also new challenges and perspectives. Because some women find that by becoming more authentic their old friendships no longer work for them, a referral to a therapy group may be an especially needed support. In addition, group therapy can be an invaluable form of maintenance therapy, significantly contributing to relapse prevention.

## FUTURE ORIENTATION PHASE

In the middle-to-late stages of therapy, the client is encouraged to continue to strengthen and expand her network of supportive relationships, seeking out those that are characterized by mutuality and authenticity. Table 10.4 summarizes interventions that support the client's continued relational growth in the future-orientation phase of therapy. Together client and therapist can identify self-assessment strategies that the client can utilize in order to notice and honor her authentic thoughts and feelings in relationships over the long term. A client who has been working to strengthen a significant relationship may want to identify strategies that will encourage continued growth or will help

**TABLE 10.4  Interventions: Future Orientation Phase**

The therapist can assist the client to maintain her gains and to continue developing authentic, mutual connections by

1. Asking the client to identify ways to stay in touch with her feelings.
2. Encouraging the client to strengthen and expand her network of women friends.
3. Asking the client to identify long-term goals aimed at improving current relationships or finding new relationships.
4. Suggesting the client return to therapy to support her maintaining connection with self while entering into a new romantic relationship or dating.
5. Referring the client to group therapy or a support group.
6. Teaching the client social skills for making new friends.

sustain gains. Some clients may wish to make a list of "danger signs" that indicate that she may be sliding back into old relational patterns.

When a client is leaving therapy with the future wish to find a new romantic partner, I encourage her to return to therapy when she has begun a new relationship in order to help her stay in touch with herself. A woman who has historically sacrificed or lost herself for the sake of a relationship can usually benefit from the extra support of individual or group therapy as she navigates a new relationship.

The client is particularly encouraged to develop a solid group of women friends with whom she can be authentically herself. She may extend her social network by joining various community, educational, political, or enrichment groups. The experience of reclaiming the self often mobilizes clients into expanding their worlds through new activities and new communities, thus paving the way for an expanded network of friends that supports the client in authentically being herself. When the client reaches this stage, the therapist may be a coach or a guide, helping her to rehearse her new relational skills and choose new contexts and activities that support her newfound sense of self. Depending on the resources and motivation of the client, some women will stay in therapy as they expand their network and enrich their lives. Other clients may only be able to articulate these changes as future goals that they plan to pursue after therapy. It is important for the therapist to help the client understand the value of building a supportive network of friends in increasing her resilience against relapse. Apter and Josselson (1998) have written a good resource for understanding the complexity of women's friendships.

## SUMMARY

This chapter discussed connection with others, encompassing early-, middle-, and late-phase therapy tasks. IRT emphasizes the importance of relationships in women's lives and therapy must help a woman maximize affirmative, healthy relational connections that are characterized by authenticity and mutuality. However, IRT recognizes that a woman can only make changes in ways that make sense, given the realities of her life. Initially, the depressed client may need help deciding how and with whom to communicate about her depression. She may need the therapist's support to set limits with unsupportive others. Depressed mothers may need help with parenting.

In the middle-to-late stages of therapy, with a newly strengthened sense of self, the client may be ready to change the way she relates to others, nurturing those relationships that promote authenticity and mutuality while limiting those that do not. Couples therapy may be an important adjunct to the client's individual therapy. Group therapy provides the client with additional opportunities for growth and support while presenting an option for long-term, ongoing maintenance therapy. In the future-orientation phase of therapy, the client identifies strategies and supports that will help her maintain her gains and continue to strengthen and increase healthy relationships. The next chapter discusses the final element of therapy, meaning.

# CHAPTER ELEVEN

# Meaning

Connie, Laura, Renata, and Serena are clients who have been discussed in this book who were all suffering from depression. They each presented distinctly different identities, life circumstances, developmental stages, risk factors, strengths, and vulnerabilities. Yet, for each of these women, a transformation of meaning was an essential element in her recovery from depression. These women transformed their vision of their sense of self through empowering and positive meaning-making structures.

Social constructivism, one of the organizing theories underlying IRT, explains the fluid nature of reality and of the meaning-making structures that make up an individual's reality:

> The constructivist perspective is founded on the idea that humans actively create and construe their personal realities. The basic assertion of constructivism is that each individual creates his or her own representational model of the world. This experiential scaffolding of structural relations in turn becomes a framework from which the individual orders and assigns meaning to new experience. Central to the constructivist formulations is the idea that, rather than being a sort of template through which ongoing experience is filtered, the representational model actively creates and constrains new experience and thus determines what the individual will perceive as "reality." (Mahoney & Lyddon, 1988, p. 200)

Such a framework of "structural relations" is formed through interactions with others and the accompanying influences of language, family, and culture (Gergen, 1985). The individual's representational model of the world is made up of a number of meaning-making structures that contribute to an individual's sense of self and affective state. Meaning, the fifth element of therapy, addresses a number of key treatment tasks related to the transformation of important meaning-making structures that contribute to a more optimistic, self-efficacious, receptive, flexible, and resilient sense of self. The treatment goals related to meaning are listed in Table 11.1.

These treatment tasks unfold from the stabilization phase of therapy, continuing through termination. Meaning treatment tasks are interrelated and mutually reinforcing. An early, significant therapy task is the instillation of hope. The individual's ability to have hope is related to central aspects of the self, including worldview and core cognitive schemas. The instillation of hope is related to positive outcome in therapy (Yalom, 1975) and is particularly important for depressed individuals. A key task that proceeds throughout the therapy is the deconstruction and reconstruction of core cognitive schemas, the major meaning-making structures that contribute to an individual's beliefs about herself and the world. Such schemas will be apparent from the first session of therapy as the client describes her reality. The goal is for the client to reconstruct more flexible and empowering schemas. A related meaning task is developing an affirmative and integrated identity, which is usually addressed in the middle-to-late phases of therapy and is particularly important for women and minorities as they must reconcile multiple roles and identities within the larger social context of a Caucasian, male-dominated, heterosexual, Christian, dominant culture. As the client garners more hope and develops more empowering schemas, she constructs a new narrative, another important meaning task. The work of therapy leads to increased activation and a broadened perspective that engender a more empowering, multidimensional story about the client and her depression. A final meaning task, based on the concepts of positive psychology (Seligman & Csikscentmihalyi, 2000), is the development of an expansive sense of meaning that embraces an optimistic and self-efficacious worldview, nurtures more open, receptive, and creative cognitive styles, and fosters positive affects. The individual extends her sense of meaning through spiritual, altruistic, or creative activities, which increase avenues for contentment, connection, and resilience. As with all of the five elements of therapy, meaning tasks are interrelated to the four other elements and are only

**TABLE 11.1  Meaning: Treatment Goals**

1. Instillation of hope
2. Deconstruction and reconstruction of core cognitive schemas
3. Affirmative, integrated identity
4. Construction of a new narrative
5. Expansive sense of meaning

addressed to the extent that they are identified as relevant for a particular client. Meaning tasks are also interrelated to each other; while at a particular time in the therapy, one of the above-listed therapy tasks may be the focus, a shift in one meaning-making element usually leads to a shift in another meaning-making element.

## INSTILLATION OF HOPE

The depressed client comes to therapy feeling hopeless, helpless, stuck, or pessimistic. Through the instillation of hope, the client develops the energy, perspective, and encouragement to stay in therapy and to move forward in her recovery. The evocation of hope can be "one of the most important and central elements of healing" (Yahne & Miller, 1999, p. 229). Hope, an integral aspect of worldview, is related to positive expectancies, self-efficacy, and optimism (Magaletta & Oliver, 1999; Yahne & Miller, 1999). Hope is also related to the individual's view of the future and schemas concerning hope are tied to all other schemas (McCann & Pearlman, 1990). A normally self-efficacious client may temporarily lose hope due to adverse life events and the accompanying symptoms of depression, while a client with pre-existing disruptions in hope-related meaning-making structures may find hopelessness all too easily triggered by such. Laura was an action-oriented person who, prior to her depressive episode, was a real "go-getter," a self-efficacious, task-oriented person who believed that with effort and intelligence, she could solve any problem. Her depressive episode defied these expectations: she was unable to figure out how to "snap out of it." However, once she consulted with a therapist whom she felt understood her problems and resonated with her action-oriented approach, her usual positive outlook was restored. Laura said to me at the beginning of our second therapy session: "I felt much better as soon as I left last time. Knowing we had a treatment plan gave me hope." For a person like Laura who typically has positive expectations, self-efficacy, and optimism, the therapist may only need to convey a sense of caring, empathy, and competency combined with action-oriented suggestions in order to instill hope. When a mutually empathic therapeutic connection occurs between client and therapist, the self-efficacious person may feel her hope restored relatively quickly.

On the other hand, individuals with more disempowering worldviews than Laura may present more of a challenge regarding the instillation of hope. For example, Mallory had suffered from depression since adolescence and had several negative experiences with mental health professionals. At the age of 45, she sought therapy at the insistence of her best friend who felt overwhelmed by Mallory's most recent depressive episode. Mallory entered therapy feeling skeptical, untrusting, and hopeless. Clients such as Mallory present particular challenges to the therapist when it comes to the instillation of hope. With such clients, therapists are in danger of giving false hope or becoming hopeless themselves. An accurate understanding of the meaning of hope will assist therapists not only in being successful in instilling hope within the client, but also in maintaining hope within themselves. Hope is best understood as not a promise of a cure, but as encompassing a broader conceptualization that enriches and broadens the client's ways of being, doing, and seeing. Three practical ways that the therapist can foster the client's hope are educating, eliciting, and lending (Yahne & Miller, 1999). Table 11.2 summarizes treatment interventions that may instill hope in the depressed client.

Through educating the client about depression, about depression treatment, and about the external and internal factors related to her depression, the client potentially can begin to move from stable, internal, and generalized explanations of her depression to more multidimensional understandings of her symptoms, giving rise to hope. Reframing, recontextualizing, and educating are important tools in helping the client change her perspective (Yahne & Miller, 1999). Additionally, being able to remind the client that she has not always

**TABLE 11.2   Interventions: Instillation of Hope**

The therapist may help the client feel more hope by
1. Educating the client about depression.
2. Reframing the client's perspective to have a more multidimensional view of her depression.
3. Reminding the client about past recoveries from previous episodes.
4. Co-creating a treatment plan.
5. Offering the client your presence and support throughout her dark times.
6. Referring the client to group therapy where she will learn that others can overcome obstacles.
7. Expanding the client's options for ways to cope with depression.
8. Reminding the client of her dreams, aspirations, and successes.
9. Bringing forward metaphors and imagery presenting positive possibilities that are either coming from the client or are accurately reflective of aspects of the client's experience.
10. Letting the client know you have confidence in her.

been depressed and that depressive episodes usually pass, can give her hope that she will not be feeling miserable indefinitely.

Through educating, the therapist can also present the client with new visions and options of how she might handle her depression. Mallory, who suffered from depression since adolescence, had recently become increasingly isolated and was reluctant to make a commitment to therapy. I presented her with an alternative vision of coping with depression. I told her, "You know, you can choose to deal with this alone or you can allow me to be there with you. Sometimes it can help to have someone you can talk to, particularly someone who understands depression." As Martha Manning (1994) discovered, sometimes having a companion on the journey is an enormous comfort while struggling with the pain and suffering of a depressive episode. While not offering Mallory false hope of a recovery, I suggested that there may be ways that her depression might be less lonely and there may be ways that I could help her reduce the intensity of her misery.

Eliciting is a means of drawing out internal resources of hope from within the client, particularly resources of which the client is unaware. By empathically listening and reflecting the client's strengths, dreams, and wishes, the therapist brings the client's hope into the light of day, eliciting optimism and nurturing action. Mallory dreamed of buying her own house with a large garden. This vision portrayed her ability to be future oriented and have positive aspirations for herself. While Mallory mentioned this dream briefly, I was able to point out its importance to her, engage her in a discussion of her future hopes for herself, and encourage her to pursue her goals. In the midst of countless disappointments and hurts she was able to sustain a dream for herself that suggested more optimism than she realized.

"Evoking hope has to do with helping clients discover that there is more to them than they currently realize" (Yahne & Miller, 1999, p. 226). The depressed individual often sees only her current misery, losing any sense of perspective concerning past and future. The therapist can remind the client of past successes and positive experiences, recalling previous episodes that remitted, a particularly effective intervention when client and therapist weathered past episodes or difficulties together.

The therapist can lend the client a vision of hope and optimism when she is unable to do so for herself. Again, this does not mean holding out hope for a "cure," but having hope that the client will be, act, and see in more empowering ways. One example of lending is for the therapist to convey to the stuck client her confidence that she will take action when she is ready with statements such as, "I have confidence that when you are truly ready to make the changes that you would like to make, you will." Similarly, when a client seems uncertain or tentative about what to do and wants the therapist's opinion, the therapist may let the client know that the therapist believes the client has the capacity to figure out solutions, encouraging her to give voice to her opinions. By letting the client know that the therapist has confidence in her, the therapist is eliciting hope.

Instilling hope is a task that is important in the beginning of therapy for all clients and is especially crucial throughout the therapy for clients with persistent and chronic depressions. There is an interrelationship between the client's ability to experience hope and the remaining tasks related to meaning.

## A MORE AFFIRMATIVE, INTEGRATED IDENTITY

> If we accept the relational theorists' premise that making and maintaining relationships are primary motivations throughout life, then analysis of cognitive schemas about the self-in-relation becomes vital to the understanding and treatment of depression. The cognitive schemas most potent for a woman's depression are *beliefs about the self in intimate relationships*, specifically her understanding about what it means to be "good enough" to be loved. (Jack, 1991, p. 197)

Schemas provide a template from which the individual organizes and categorizes her knowledge and experiences, guiding her perceptions and behaviors, providing maps from which to navigate her world. Schemas have long been recognized as a key element in depressive thinking and as a vital part of cognitive therapy for depression (Beck et al., 1980; Lewis, 1994). A woman has grown up with a litany of schemas of how she is supposed to act and be in order to be loved. Such schemas have their source in sex role socialization from the client's family-of-origin and in larger cultural forces. These dual influences of family and culture dictate "feminine" ideals of goodness that limit and constrict a woman's sense of self. Such schemas are infused with idealizations related to roles and aspects of identity, such as "good girl," "good woman," "good daughter," "good wife," "good mother," "good sister," "good Catholic girl," "good homegirl," and "good student."

A woman must stifle her authentic self in order to fulfill these schemas of goodness. When a woman must deny her authenticity in order to satisfy injunctions of goodness, the result is often a series of negative emotions that contribute to depression, including self-condemnation and guilt for failing to live up to impossible standards, a loss of self in an effort to fulfill such schemas, plus concomitant self-silencing, anger, and resentment (Jack, 1991). Some women may enter therapy in a crisis when core cognitive schemas, which have long guided their lives, no longer make sense.

Because the larger culture trains women to please men, heterosexual relationships have the greatest potential for reinforcing limiting schemas of lovability (Jack, 1991). For example, Laura's beliefs about being a "good wife" kept her from talking to her husband about her depression, further alienating and isolating her. However, all women are vulnerable to disempowerment through such schemas. The multiple pieces of a woman's identity interact with such schemas, creating complex internalizations and conflicts. Gender, roles, ethno-cultural membership, sexual orientation, religion, age, able-bodied status, and developmental phase all form a part of a woman's identity. The more identities a woman has, the more idealizations of goodness a woman must accommodate. The multiple facets of a woman's identity have led specialists in women's identity development to compare a normal woman's identity process as similar to that experienced by someone with multiple personality disorder (Apter, 1995; Josselson, 1996). Thus, an important goal in a woman's identity development is the achievement of a positive, integrated identity. Such a goal involves helping a woman embrace more empowering, flexible schemas and resolve conflicts among disparate aspects of her identity.

Although all women face the challenge of balancing myriad roles, women of color, lesbians, disabled women, and women who are members of any minority group may face more complex challenges. Women who are members of nondominant groups must counter the negative messages of the dominant culture that denigrate difference and lead to negative internalizations of their womanhood. The road to an affirmative, integrated identity for the minority woman may be quite a challenge. She must simultaneously resolve idealizations of feminine goodness from the dominant culture (i.e., templates of idealized goodness for White, heterosexual, middle-class women), idealizations of goodness from her own minority culture (i.e., templates of idealized goodness as a member of her minority group), and idealizations of feminine goodness from her minority culture (i.e., templates of idealized goodness for a woman of her minority). This is further complicated for the biracial or bicultural client who must also integrate idealizations related to each of her racial or cultural identities (Comas-Diaz, 1994; Root, 1990). A client with multiple identities may focus on one identity at a time, developing an affirmative identity for one or more identities in a separate manner before synthesizing identification with all aspects of identity.

The process of coming to terms with these often conflicting and complex aspects of identity has been delineated in models of identity development that follow similar phases, beginning with a lack of awareness and acceptance of the status quo, progressing to an integrated, affirmative, and aware identity. An individual may not necessarily navigate these phases in a linear way nor pass through each phase. Such models have been explicated for racial and cultural identity (Cross, 1971; Helms, 1990; Jackson, 1975; Sue & Sue, 1990), feminist identity (Downing & Roush, 1985), gender identity (Ossana, Helms, & Leonard, 1992), and gay and lesbian identity (Cass, 1979; McCarn & Fassinger, 1996). While the therapist is advised to become familiar with specific models that are relevant for a given client's identity issues, here I outline a general process that may facilitate a woman's movement toward a more affirmative, integrated identity and more empowering cognitive schemas.

The length of time that the transition of meaning-making structures requires is dependent on a number of variables, including the rigidity of CCSs, the degree of ongoing stress in a woman's life, the availability of social supports, the flexibility of her sociocultural milieu, the complexity of identity conflicts, and the client's self capacities. While deconstructing and reconstructing CCSs is middle-phase work, a client with strong self capacities may get to these tasks relatively quickly. The tenacity of CCSs will determine the length of time a client may need to address these issues. Clients with histories of childhood abuse or neglect may have particularly tenacious CCSs that they are unlovable or undeserving of love. Such schemas of "badness" seriously impact an individual's self capacities, suggesting a longer course of treatment.

To truly recover from depression, a woman must let go of rigid moral frameworks that have guided her existence. "A woman must create new ways of valuing herself, new ways of perceiving, and new ways of interacting" (Jack, 1991, p. 196). A woman must learn to trust her own authentic inner wisdom, letting go of absolutes that have dictated other-pleasing behaviors so that she is able to decide how to behave in each situation based on its own context. "Women must 'jump outside' of frames and systems authorities provide and create their own frame" (Belenky et al., 1986, p. 134). A woman achieves this shift in perspective by becoming aware of the frameworks that have guided her, realizing that her experience does not fit with these guiding principles, and questioning these rules as they no longer make sense (Jack, 1991; Schreiber, 1996). This shift may occur rather dramatically and suddenly as a woman simultaneously experiences both cognitive and affective knowing (Belenky et al., 1986; Jack, 1991; Schreiber, 1996) recognizing that her own inner knowledge of what feels right for her does not fit within the moral framework of what she had believed was right.

Schreiber (1996) called this process, "clueing in" (p. 484), during which a woman begins to examine information in a new way, often "seeing" her experience from a new perspective of self-acceptance. As a woman comes to challenge old limiting schemas, she becomes more accepting of her humanness and fallibility. She lets go of rigid standards that she has required for herself but seldom required of others. Often, a woman reclaims lost parts of herself, reaching back to an earlier time of her life when she was more "authentic, real, and true to who and what she was" (Hancock, 1989, p. 232). During this process, a woman may be propelled into action to seek new solutions to old problems, to reach out to new people, and to otherwise expand her world. The ultimate goal is for a woman to progress from having automatic, rigid, disempowering schemas to more aware, flexible, contextual, and empowering ways of knowing. Thus, a woman progresses from an unaware sense of self to an aware and integrated self. A therapist may facilitate this process through a number of interventions that help the client deconstruct and reconstruct CCSs and her sense of self. Table 11.3

**TABLE 11.3   Interventions: Affirmative, Integrated Identity**

The therapist facilitates an affirmative, integrated identity by

1. Naming CCSs and related identities and roles.
2. Naming the client's emerging confusion or disillusionment with moral injunctions of goodness or perfectionism.
3. Asking the client deconstructing questions that operationalize CCSs.
4. Asking the client to consider if limiting CCSs would hold true for a friend or loved one.
5. Eliciting pivotal stories related to the development of CCSs that foster self-empathy. ("Where does that belief come from?")
6. Encouraging the client to generate "third solutions."
7. Encouraging the client to try out and experiment with new ways of being, seeing, and relating.
8. Suggesting sources of knowledge that may reveal more empowering ways of being (e.g., books, support groups, role models, etc.)
9. Helping the client to mourn losses related to letting go of idealizations.
10. Helping the client to notice and celebrate changes that reflect a more affirmative identity or more empowering CCSs.

summarizes these interventions, which are discussed in the following section.

## Deconstructing Core Cognitive Schemas

The therapist helps the client deconstruct CCSs by collaborating with the client to name them, identifying limiting behaviors that have been guided by them, and exploring alternative ways of seeing, being, and interacting. By empathically listening and reflecting the assumptions the client has made about herself, her roles, and her identities, the therapist guides the client in the collaborative process of uncovering her core assumptions. For some clients, hearing the secret moral imperatives that have guided their behaviors spoken aloud may be a powerful, integrative experience, invoking both cognitive and affective knowing. As Laura explained, "On some level I knew how important it was for me not to let my husband know how I was feeling, but until I heard you say my own words, I did not realize how afraid I was that he wouldn't love me if I told him how depressed I really felt." Laura and I immediately uncovered the assumption that in order to be loved by her husband she had to be the "perfect wife and mother" and to admit she was having trouble coping was to risk her husband's rejection. When Laura heard me name these schemas of goodness, she immediately recognized that they no longer made sense nor fit her own emerging awareness that keeping problems secret from her husband only made her feel worse.

In addition to naming CCSs, the therapist can help the client name schemas and related aspects of identities and roles that are governed by such schemas. Once Connie was able to name the conflicting pulls of being both a "good daughter" and a "good graduate student," she was not as likely to become immobilized by feelings of guilt and inadequacy. By naming both the conflicting roles of daughter and student and her long-held CCSs related to being a "good" daughter ("Everyone's needs are more important than mine"; "I should not have any problems"), she came to understand why she felt so stuck and hopeless. Naming CCSs and identity issues may quickly dislodge the hold that rigid injunctions have had over the client, propelling her to take action that had in the past seemed impossible. Naming sometimes has a synergistic effect, leading to new, exciting insights such that the client comes to let go of disempowering assumptions to develop more expansive and flexible meaning-making structures. Although the act of naming led Laura to be able to change by the second therapy session, Connie and other clients will require more continuous and active intervention by the therapist.

As early as the first session, the therapist may begin to name the assumptions and conflicts that underlie a woman's description of herself and her problems. Over time, as the client comes to reveal more of herself, naming may become more intricate as it includes increasingly complex relationships among pieces of the case conceptualization including CCSs, identities and roles, life stressors, and developmental transitions. For example, one client, Sandy, a 51-year-old administrative assistant, came to understand her long-standing depression and began to question her perfectionistic schemas through naming:

> I grew up with a critical father who was a retired marine and a depressed mother who was barely there for me. I was raised Catholic in the South in the 1950s and realized I was gay, which was an absolute no-no. I believed that if I were perfect then I would be accepted by my father. Now I realize no matter how perfect I am, he will never accept who I really am. I have to let go of perfectionism and figure out how to be myself. It is really hard because I have withdrawn from people for so long because I could not bear to let them see me.

As Sandy began to acknowledge the role that internalized oppression had played in her depression and in her drive for perfectionism, she became more willing to join a lesbian support group and to read books about lesbian identity. As is often the case for those with perfectionistic schemas (Blatt, 1995; Blatt et al., 1995), challenging perfectionism was a long, slow process for Sandy, but a process that began to move more quickly as Sandy put together more and more pieces of her identity that were related to perfectionism. Naming CCSs of perfectionism, internalized oppression, and identity issues may facilitate the integrative process of "cluing in" that leads a woman to begin to construct a more accepting and affirmative sense of self.

Once schemas have been identified, they can be further deconstructed by examining and operationalizing them. Asking Laura what it meant to her to be a "good wife" led her to exclaim, "Gee, it seems like I believe I should be this 'Stepford wife' who always has it together. You know—is cool, calm, and perfect. Do I really want to be like that?" Simultaneously, by asking what it meant to her on a day-to-day basis to be a "good mother," we began to deconstruct the meaning of her core schemas related to mothering. Laura actually believed she should be cleaning up her children's mess of toys repeatedly throughout the day so that the house was *always* neat, leaving her hypervigilant, exhausted, and constantly dissatisfied with herself as a mother. Laura's schemas that governed good mothering provided an either-or template of behavior: either you were totally neat at all times or you were a "bad" mother. Likewise, for Connie, being a "good daughter" meant going home *every* weekend. Dysfunctional schemas are dichotomous and absolute, blocking the client's ability to be flexible in decision making or creative in generating solutions to problems. As the client comes to question long-held rigid schemas, she becomes more open to finding so-called "third choices" (Austin, 2000, p. 12), which offer her ways to balance her need to please others with her own needs.

Sometimes the therapist can gently challenge the client's beliefs by asking "what if" kinds of questions. So, for example, I asked Laura, "What would happen if you told your husband you were struggling with depression?" and "What would happen if you cleaned up once at the end of the day? Would that mean you were a 'bad' mother?" While Laura felt unsure of the result from revealing her troubles to her husband, her immediate response to my question about cleaning was to laugh: She suddenly saw her expectations of being the perfect mother as silly. Occasionally, as with Laura, having the client "operationalize" a disruptive core schema by describing specific behaviors that it mandates may be enough to dislodge the tenacity of the schema.

The therapist needs to be careful not to sound judgmental or condescending when asking deconstructing questions. The goal is for the client to challenge the automaticity and dominance of rigid ways of thinking, exploring other perspectives and possibilities. In fact, asking Laura to envision talking to her husband led her to do just that after our first therapy session with positive results. Although she was initially unsure that changing her assumptions and behavior would have a positive outcome, naming and challenging broke the power of rigid schemas about being good enough to be loved by her husband, leading to new relational possibilities. Often the client discovers through being more authentic that the actual outcome of disregarding a moral injunction of "goodness" does not result in the devastating rejection she anticipates.

Another intervention that may disempower a dysfunctional schema is to ask the client if she would judge a loved one by the same rigid standard. For example, Connie had made a friend, Marta, who was in the final stages of completing her dissertation, applying for teaching jobs, and teaching a class. I asked Connie if she would judge Marta to be a "bad" daughter if she did not go home every weekend to help her family as Connie was doing. This intervention led Connie to risk telling Marta about her struggles, which she had previously revealed to no one except myself and her advisor. Marta was able to tell Connie how she had handled similar conflicts over family obligations and school. Helping the client to de-center and evaluate her assumptions from another perspective may broaden the client's vision of what is acceptable for herself. As her vision broadens, she may be emboldened to seek support and find new role models who help her redefine her sense of self.

As the client comes to question schemas that have ruled her life, she becomes open to new possibilities and constructions of the self. The client recognizes that she no longer needs to be dominated by the need to please others and can begin to set new boundaries and pursue her own needs. As the client negotiates these changes in core schemas, the therapist names them and helps the client to notice and celebrate her triumphs over resisting old, disempowering beliefs.

## Eliciting Self-Empathy Through Pivotal Stories

Sometimes a client will become stuck in the process of dislodging disempowering CCSs, saying something such as: "I get it up here (pointing to her head), but I don't get it down here (pointing to her chest or stomach)." The client is demonstrating that while she cognitively understands that a dysfunctional CCS no longer makes sense, affectively she is blocked and to disobey the injunction *feels* untenable. An intervention that may facilitate *both* cognitive and affective knowing is to ask the client, "Where do you think that belief comes from?" which elicits what I call, pivotal stories, leading to new perspectives on the self that are less critical and more compassionate, allowing the client to act on more flexible ways of thinking.

Frequently, the client will recall incidents from childhood. The therapist can help the client recontextualize the meaning of childhood events that defined important self-schemas by eliciting self-empathy. Through self-empathy, the client may have an "ah-hah" kind of experience that integrates cognitive and affective knowing. When the client comes to have a new perspective over the meanings of emotionally laden childhood experiences, the hold of rigid, dichotomous schemas is loosened, opening the way for the construction of more flexible, empowering schemas. Such a pivotal story is illustrated here:

> Serena came into a session, explaining that she had not had a chance to eat lunch or even go to the bathroom all day—she had been constantly bombarded by demands at her job. Suddenly, she burst into tears, exclaiming, "I know I should know how to do everything, but I just *can't!*" "You 'should know how to do everything.' Where did that idea come from?" I asked. Spontaneously Serena recalled an event that occurred when she was 12 years

old: In seventh grade—in the locker room after gym class I noticed that most of the girls were wearing bras. So I went home and told my mother that I needed a bra. The next day after school my mother gave me a twenty-dollar bill and told me to go to Woolworth's downtown to buy a bra. My friend Mary was with me and we got on our bicycles—I remember I had pigtails at the time—and we rode to Woolworth's. We got there and didn't really know what we were doing, but we bought this bra. You know, the kind with pointy cups. What did I know? The next day I wore it to school and everyone laughed at me. I was devastated. And now when I think of that, I realize that my mother expected me to know how to do everything. And she shouldn't have. I was only 12 years old! I didn't know anything about buying a bra! But she always expected me to know how to do everything.

At this point, Serena began sobbing, as she stated, "I was only 12 years old. She shouldn't have made me go alone. She should have helped me."

Relating this story as an adult, Serena realized that she was expected to know how to do everything as a child and had longed for her mother's help and attention at the time. This shift in perspective—of recognizing the formation of her assumptions about being "good" and the accompanying feelings of empathy for herself as a child—discredited the CCS that she should know how to do everything. From this session forth, she caught herself if she started to make a self-denigrating comment about herself, seeing herself with more compassion and holding herself to more flexible and benevolent standards. This type of experience of self-empathy that reintegrates cognition and affect through a memory is described by Jordan (1991):

[Self-empathy] could occur in the form of having a memory of oneself in which the inner state at that time has not been fully integrated because it was not acceptable. To be able to observe and tolerate the affect of that state in a context of understanding becomes a kind of intrapsychic empathy that actually can lead to lasting structural change in self-representations. (p. 77)

After the previously described session, Serena's sense of self shifted from being self-effacing and self-denigrating to being more assertive and self-accepting. She was catalyzed to take action at work to set limits on others' demands and be more in control of her work assignments. The transformation of self that self-empathy evokes can lead to establishing healthier boundaries and taking action in other self-actualizing ways. Self-empathy changes the meanings that the client has made of important life events and introduces new templates of the self.

In addition to eliciting pivotal stories, the therapist can facilitate the client's increased self-empathy through her own empathic attunement.

As has been discussed in chapters 4, 7, and 9, the therapist's empathy for the client allows the client to see herself through the therapist's accepting eyes, circumventing the critical hypervigilance of the internalized false self. When the therapist offers the client a kinder, more benevolent reframing of her distress, the client glimpses a different view of herself that challenges internalized moral injunctions which have been guiding and judging her behavior.

## *Reconstructing Core Cognitive Schemas*

As a woman comes to unearth her authentic self through the work of connection as described in chapter 9, limiting and disruptive schemas no longer make sense and a woman may be thrown into confusion, self-doubt, or immobility. "A depressed woman needs courage to leave ideas and pain that have become familiar and leap, like a spider held only with an invisible silken thread, into the unknown where she must spin her own meanings" (Jack, 1991, p. 193).

A woman may enter a tumultuous time of questioning major aspects of her life, feeling indecisive, confused, and distressed. Some clients may need to mourn losses over giving up old idealizations. Other clients may become excited by new possibilities, asking for reading recommendations, engaging in discussions about these issues with friends, and seeking out alternative models of womanhood. For example, when she no longer felt compelled to be "the perfect wife and mother," Laura consulted with her women friends to find out how they managed domestic responsibilities, getting affirmation for her ideas to hire a housecleaner and buy take-out food for dinner more often. A woman is often propelled into action as she begins to form new constructions of who she wants to be.

Sometimes, the therapist may need to suggest new solutions that support a more flexible perspective that allows the client to balance her own needs with those of others. I repeatedly find that I might offer what seem to be obvious "new" solutions, only to have the client respond with enthusiasm and excitement, "I never thought of that!" When the client no longer is under the power of old schemas, she is more open to solutions that in the past may have seemed intolerable. When introducing suggestions, the therapist must be careful to allow the client to come to her own conclusions as to which "third solution" is right for her, refraining from foisting the therapist's ideas on the client. Reminding a woman to "try out" some new behaviors and ways of being and to "just experiment," gives her permission to be patient with herself as she discovers who she truly wants to be and act. Ultimately, the goal is for the client to be more conscious of the guiding principles of her day-to-day interactions with important people in her life, becoming more flexible in the standards she sets for herself. The client may experience discomfort or anxiety when facing situations that previously would have been governed by old schemas. The therapist can help the client to be patient with herself and offer suggestions for managing anxiety.

As the client is awakened to embrace more empowering schemas, she may enter a phase of intense positive identification with members with the same identity. So, for example, a woman may become interested in feminism, an ethnic minority client may develop greater pride in her minority identity, and a lesbian client may join a gay rights organization. These transformational experiences may lead the client to adopt dichotomous and absolute schemas related to group identity. Hence, the newly feminist client may feel all men are bad and all women are good, the ethnic minority client may feel all Whites are bad and all minority group members are good, and the lesbian may feel all heterosexuals are bad and all lesbians and gay men are good. The therapist can sensitively guide the client toward a more integrated identity with more flexible schemas by encouraging her to continue to critically analyze her options and explore all possibilities.

The therapist addresses the work of naming, deconstructing, and reconstructing core cognitive schemas by being attuned to the client, recognizing when the client is ready to challenge and change her beliefs. The therapist carefully observes the client's shifts in perspective, watching and listening to cues that the client is ready to examine limiting beliefs. The therapist carefully tracks the client's experience in order to bring into the client's awareness the emerging but not yet fully formed changes in her beliefs. Work on CCSs is directly related to the construction of a new narrative.

## CONSTRUCTION OF A NEW NARRATIVE

The client enters therapy with a story about her self, her life, and her depression. This story line is constructed from the client's reality that has been informed by the dominant culture's stories about women, minorities, and psychiatric problems that are overwhelmingly pathologizing, blaming, and disempowering (White & Epston, 1990). The dominant story of a woman's depression, thus, often names the client as the culprit in her distress. This can be heard in the words of Connie who explained her difficulties with the statement, "I'm not smart enough to succeed in graduate school"; in the words of Laura who stated, "There's something wrong with me. I should be able to snap out of this"; and in the words of Sandy, who thought, "Because I am gay, the only way that I will be accepted is if I am perfect." Another client, Pamela, who had three serious depressive episodes by the time she entered therapy with me at the age of 47, described herself as "permanently damaged" and "mentally ill." These quotes illustrate the negative influence of the dominant culture on clients' disempowering narratives about their depressions.

The narrative metaphor has been described as an important development in cognitive behavioral therapy (Meichenbaum, 1993) and it is a fundamental ingredient in narrative therapies (Freedman & Combs, 1996; White & Epston, 1990). In IRT, therapy involves a process by which client and therapist are continually co-constructing a new story of the client's depression, one that incorporates the rich, multidimensional nature of the many factors related to her depression. "The client comes to rename experience, retell a narrative, in a way that no longer violates well-being, but rather, empowers and liberates" (Brown, 1994, p. 155). Throughout the therapy, the therapist uses reflective listening to bring forth the client's story. The process of therapy will challenge the client's meaning-making structures and guide her in the direction of more self-efficacious, empowered, optimistic, future-oriented perspectives.

Beginning in the first session, as the therapist gathers information about the client, the therapist tracks and summarizes the client's narrative and begins the process of reframing by developing a case conceptualization using the conceptual maps of IRT. The therapist offers a new story of the client's depression that interweaves biopsychosocial risk factors, strengths and vulnerabilities of aspects of the self, and an adaptational and relational view of depressive symptoms. As described above in the section on CCSs, Sandy's case conceptualization linking perfectionism with her upbringing and internalized homophobia was the beginning of a new narrative about her depression. The therapist collaborates with the client to refine and reformulate the narrative in a way that makes sense to the client, tracking changes in the client's perspective as the therapy progresses and altering the story accordingly. Throughout the therapy, client and therapist continually embark on a collaborative endeavor to coauthor a more empowering and comprehensive story of the client's distress and her movement toward change. As the client becomes more connected to her authentic self and her dysfunctional schemas are deconstructed, a new narrative emerges that mirrors more empowering templates of self. The therapist is especially attuned to the client's metaphors that describe herself and her problems, utilizing such metaphors not only to highlight the client's perspective but also to suggest new solutions to old problems.

Pamela's story provides an example of how the therapist can utilize the client's metaphors to heighten the client's recognition of her positive changes. Throughout therapy with Pamela, I invited her to challenge her view that she was "permanently damaged" and "mentally ill" by educating her about depression, helping her identify the multiple factors contributing to her depressive episodes, noticing and celebrating strengths and positive changes, and collaborating with her to choose and utilize numerous stress management and stress reduction strategies. By the end of one year of therapy, Pamela had made some major life changes aimed at leading a more fulfilling and less stressful life. She often reported quite vivid dreams and throughout much of her adult life, the theme of most of her dreams concerned battles and wars. At the end of the first year of therapy, she came to a session with a very different kind of dream.

In the dream there were two mothers and two babies. The first mother tried to teach her baby to walk down a flight of stairs and was unable to prevent her baby from falling on her head. The second mother, having learned by watching the first baby's fall, carefully guided her child down the steps backwards and very slowly, using her body to protect her baby from falling. The second baby made it down the stairs without mishap.

Pamela saw herself as represented by both the second mother and her baby, interpreting the dream to reflect the changes she was making to protect herself from "falling on her head" again—getting depressed again. I suggested that the dream offered a new metaphor for her depression: Her own mother had not known how to teach her to cope with life's difficulties, a topic she had discussed throughout her therapy. She was able to learn from her mother's mistakes and her own mistakes to parent her own children differently and also to "re-parent" herself to cope more effectively. I emphasized the fact that the dream reflected a shift in her own perceptions of herself: The "old" metaphor of "permanently damaged" and "mentally ill" no longer fit for her; she now saw herself as someone—like the second mother—who could learn and grow. In subsequent sessions, I referred to the dream, offering its new perspective as reflecting the self-efficacy and empowerment that Pamela had come to feel. The therapist can strengthen the power of a new narrative by reminding the client about it, pointing out new evidence that supports it, and suggesting that the client "re-vision" past experiences through her new eyes to reframe and normalize her reactions to stressors.

Pamela's "new" story demonstrates how a more empowering narrative embodies a more future-oriented relationship to time than the client's old story in which the problem was fixed in a stable time frame—as in Pamela's belief that she was "permanently damaged." The therapist may coax the client toward a more future-oriented perspective by offering stories in which situations changed or improved for others or for the client herself. Encouraging the client to have a more future-oriented perspective will help her cope with temporary disruptions in mood: Rather than seeing a bad mood as a sign that an interminable depression is returning, a thought which is likely to increase the client's anxiety, the client can soothingly remind herself that "this too shall pass." Furthermore, as the client becomes more adept at affect regulation skills (i.e., increased self capacities through activation skills), the therapist can help the client see how a more empowered approach to problems or symptoms will not necessarily lead to the same negative outcomes that she had experienced in the past, thus paving the way for hope and optimism (or at least, less pessimism). Table 11.4 summarizes ways the

**TABLE 11.4   Interventions: Creating a New Narrative**

The therapist can facilitate the co-creation of a new empowering narrative by
1. Creating a nurturing, accepting atmosphere that allows the client to tell her initial story and to co-create a new story.
2. Identifying strengths and internal resources.
3. Educating the client about depression, including incidence rates, risk factors, and symptoms.
4. Offering a case conceptualization based on biopsychosocial risk factors, an adaptational and relational view of symptoms, strengths and vulnerabilities of the self, and information about depressive disorders.
5. Helping the client to reframe and normalize her reactions to stressful events.
6. Collaborating with the client to coauthor a narrative that makes sense to the client.
7. Naming and celebrating each small success and movement forward and embroidering them into the narrative.
8. Tracking and integrating changes and shifts in the client's perspective to expand the narrative.
9. Noticing metaphors the client uses, utilizing such metaphors to create new solutions, and referring to such metaphors throughout the therapy.
10. Encouraging a future-orientation and including this shift in perspective into the narrative.
11. Recounting the ever-changing narrative throughout the therapy.

therapist can facilitate the co-creation of a more empowering personal narrative about the client's depression.

A careful reading of Table 11.4 reveals that it reflects many of the strategies already discussed in this book. In constructing a new narrative, however, the therapist purposefully draws the client's attention to changes in her behaviors, thoughts, and feelings, embroidering these changes into a story about who the client is, who she is becoming, and where she plans to go in the future. This new narrative not only refers to changes the woman is making to battle against depression and difficult life circumstances but also holds clues as to how to resist falling into the clutches of depression in the future. From the new narrative comes a relapse prevention plan that incorporates strategies for addressing the client's unique combination of strengths, competencies, and risk factors.

## DEVELOPMENT OF AN EXPANSIVE SENSE OF MEANING

To promote resilience against future depressions, IRT incorporates the concepts of positive psychology (Seligman & Csikscentmihalyi, 2000). Of particular importance is the development of skills and activities that engender an optimistic and self-efficacious worldview; nurture open, receptive, and creative cognitive styles; and foster positive affects. When the client has an expanded sense of meaning, seeing herself in the context of a larger, interconnected universe, she is more able to transcend her day-to-day experience, giving her a broader perspective about her troubles. It is particularly important for women to find meaning beyond their significant relationships and their children. When a woman is able to find positive meaning in life, she is more resilient against stresses and losses. The client is more likely to have fewer relapses and recover more quickly when she is attached to something greater than herself (Yapko, 2000).

IRT promotes the development of an expanded and positive sense of meaning by encouraging the client to approach life with passion, commitment, and involvement. Toward this end, the therapist can help the client identify interests, learn skills, and pursue activities within three realms: spiritual, altruistic, and creative. Such activities broaden and build the individual's capacity for positive emotions, which can strengthen an individual's enduring personal resources (Frederickson, 2000). The therapist's role is to assess the client's interest within the three realms and encourage skills and activities that support an expanded and positive sense of meaning. Each client will be unique in her interests, in the way she expands her sense of meaning and in the timing of undertaking such activities. Activities that facilitate an expanded sense of meaning are listed in Table 11.5.

The therapist works with the client to find tasks and activities that are uniquely suited to each individual person, being particularly respectful of cultural and religious affiliations. Therapists never impose their own biases, beliefs, or interests upon clients, but take their cues from clients in exploring particular avenues for developing an expanded and positive sense of meaning. An atmosphere of openness and acceptance combined with an empathically attuned therapeutic relationship is key in successfully identifying activities that expand the client's sense of meaning. In the early phase of therapy, the therapist may assist the client in reconnecting with spiritual, altruistic, or creative activities with which she has lost contact due to her depression or events leading up to her depression. New tasks which foster spirituality, altruism, or creativity are usually best left for the middle-to-late stages of therapy, maximizing the client's chances of success at a time when the client has sufficient energy and motivation. Often, as the client becomes engaged in transformational middle-phase work, she spontaneously becomes involved in spiritual, altruistic, or creative endeavors. As a woman becomes more authentic, she is frequently activated to enrich and expand her life. In some cases, particularly when there are a limited

---

**TABLE 11.5  Interventions: An Expansive Sense of Meaning**

The therapist can foster an expanded and positive sense of meaning by
1. Identifying spiritual, altruistic, or creative activities that the client already undertakes or previously undertook.
2. Explaining the value of activities that support an expanded and positive sense of meaning.
3. Encouraging the client to resume previously undertaken spiritual, altruistic, or creative activities (only if they are consistent with the client's current values).
4. Teaching the client the importance of "spiritual moments."
5. Teaching the client to meditate or do relaxation.
6. Discussing altruism and determining the client's interest.
7. Determining if the client is interested in joining a religious organization, spiritual community, or activist organization and strengthening any social skill deficits that participation may require.
8. Discussing creativity and determining the client's interest.
9. Suggesting creative projects or art classes.

---

*Note.* The therapist only suggests activities when they are attuned to the client's interests or beliefs.

number of therapy sessions available, the therapist can introduce the concept of having an expanded sense of meaning as a buffer against depression with the understanding that the client will identify specific activities after the completion of the therapy.

## SUMMARY

Through the fifth element of therapy, meaning, the client transforms meaning structures that support a positive and optimistic worldview, empowered and flexible core cognitive schemas, an affirmative and integrated identity, and an expansive sense of meaning. Fundamental to the success of all work that encompasses transforming meaning is a solid, empathically attuned therapeutic relationship. Challenging the client to expand and improve her reality requires the utmost respect and sensitivity for the therapist.

Meaning activities begin with the first session as the therapist attempts to elicit hope; continue throughout the process of therapy as the therapist draws out the client's story and co-creates a more empowering narrative, helping the client construct a more affirmative, integrative sense of self; and may extend beyond termination as the client engages in activities that expand her sense of meaning. Shifts in meaning-making structures are catalyzed by progress in therapy tasks related to the four other elements of therapy, and a client may revisit meaning tasks throughout her therapy. The next chapter discusses relapse prevention, one of the final tasks in a comprehensive treatment approach.

# CHAPTER TWELVE

# Relapse Prevention

"What if it happens to me again?" worried Pamela, a 47-year-old school counselor who entered therapy with me in the midst of her third major depressive episode. As she began to recover, Pamela was plagued with fear that depression would return. The recurrent nature of women's depressions (Coyne, Pepper, & Flynn, 1999; Mueller et al., 1999) behooves client and therapist to make relapse prevention an integral part of treatment (McGrath et al., 1990; Nezu et al., 1998). Although developing a relapse prevention plan is part of the final stage of therapy, the first two phases of therapy lay the groundwork to expand the client's repertoire of coping skills and to transform her sense of self to become more resilient. Treatment needs to be sufficiently lengthy and far-reaching to allow for the fullest possible recovery, as recent research has found that incomplete recovery predicts a more severe, chronic, relapsing future course (Judd et al., 2000).

Research on relapse prevention is limited and lacking (Nezu et al., 1998). Most studies have followed up on participants in brief therapy trials (i.e., 12 weeks) and there are few actual relapse prevention studies. Longitudinal studies that have followed individuals with major depression for more than 3 years have failed to track psychosocial treatments (e.g., see Kupfer et al., 1992; Mueller et al., 1999). While the research shows that stress is clearly linked to depression, thus far, few studies have explored whether reducing stressors through transforming negative life circumstances and improving stress management skills actually prevent relapse. I have observed in my own clinical practice that clients who make major affirmative changes in lifestyle and identity, resolve troubling life circumstances, expand their coping skills, and are committed to their long-term well-being have longer periods between episodes and less severe depressions. For clients with recurrent or chronic depressions, an acceptance of the recurrent nature of depression and of the importance of sustaining positive changes seems essential. However, the reality is that there are no guarantees that people will remain well, despite everyone's best efforts. The vicissitudes of life are unpredictable. Life is not fair.

The IRT approach to relapse prevention is to develop a comprehensive, individualized plan that considers each person's unique personality, risk factors, life circumstances, and course of depression. As the case discussions below will illustrate, a relapse prevention plan is based on the unique needs of each individual woman. First, the therapist educates the client about depression and the potential for relapse. This is particularly crucial for individuals who have had two or more episodes. For all clients, however, termination activities should include a discussion of relapse prevention. Although the client who has a history of recurrent episodes will usually introduce this topic due to her fear of recurrence, the client having a first or second episode may not be aware of the potential for recurrence. The therapist does not want to unnecessarily alarm the client about the potential for recurrence, but wants the client to be prepared and empowered through knowledge.

The co-creation of a new narrative about the reasons for the client's depression sets the stage for the formulation of a relapse plan: Once the client no longer blames herself for her depression and has a more multidimensional understanding of its causes, she can identify vulnerable circumstances, risk factors, potential signs of relapse, and possible preventative actions. As therapy progresses, client and therapist build a knowledge base that will assist in the development of the relapse prevention plan, incorporating relevant knowledge. Sleep disruption, changes in eating patterns, and increased rumination are examples of potential signs of relapse. When the client is aware of possible precursors of depressive symptoms and is armed with coping strategies, she can feel prepared and empowered to take action. Long-term goals that may reduce risk factors as well as short-term goals that provide symptom relief are identified and reviewed. Some clients may make a written relapse prevention plan to remind themselves of potential early warning signs and prevention tasks.

Together client and therapist assemble a clear picture of risk factors, identifying those which are changeable over the long term, such as job dissatisfaction or financial instability, and those which are immutable, such as having a disabled child or being a member of an oppressed group. Such a characterization of risk factors not only gives the client a picture of her risk for relapse, but suggests the benefit of continuing to work on life changes and stress reduction techniques.

In addition to addressing risk factors, the client is encouraged to maintain those activities that support self-assessment, safety, activation, connection, and meaning in her life. Table 12.1 summarizes key activities related to each of the five elements of therapy that are considered to be significant in increasing resilience against relapse. Together, client and therapist review the significant accomplishments the client has made in her therapy as related to the five therapy elements and also identify those areas still to be addressed after termination. By specifically naming the tasks and activities that have strengthened the client in each of the five elements, she has a blueprint from which to sustain a proactive, empowered life direction. Feeling that she can *do something* adds to the woman's sense of empowerment and agency. A proactive

**TABLE 12.1   Relapse Prevention Plan**

Assessment
    Identification of early warning signs and vulnerable situations
    Activities for self-monitoring
        Journalling
        Self-reflection
        Checklist
        Discussion with close friend, family member, or partner
        Regular maintenance appointment with therapist
Safety
    Crisis plan for the client with a history of suicide attempts or suicidal ideation
    Goals related to personal safety and financial security
    Long-term plans to address risk factors
Activation
    Commitment to ongoing well-being and personal growth
    Commitment to critical consciousness and using the "poop detector"
    Specific symptom reduction strategies using self capacities
    Ongoing exercise program
    Stress management and stress reduction activities
    Healthy diet and lifestyle
Connection
    Activities that support authenticity
    Self-reflective activities to monitor connection with self
    List of people who can be helpful in times of difficulty
    Activities that nurture increased authentic connection with others
    Goals to expand support network or affirmative contact with others
Meaning
    Attention to ways of thinking, particularly in stressful situations
    Spiritual, altruistic, or creative activities
    Hobbies
    Pets

stance is at the heart of relapse prevention. IRT encourages women to make a commitment to their ongoing personal growth.

For those with a history of recurrent depressions, the limited research on maintenance therapy suggests that monthly psychotherapy may extend the time until relapse even if it does not forestall recurrence indefinitely (Frank et al., 1990). Such monthly sessions not only give the client an external source of assessment, but also maintain a sense of connection between client and therapist, which for some individuals may provide a buffer against isolation or stagnation. When ongoing maintenance psychotherapy is not chosen, the client may benefit from follow-up sessions with increasing duration between sessions, such as in 2 months, 3 months, 6 months, and so on. Together, client and therapist determine a plan that makes sense given the unique needs and resources of each woman.

## ASSESSMENT

The client is urged to independently and regularly assess herself and her life circumstances. Those clients for whom connecting with authenticity was a major task of recovery may benefit from identifying specific self-assessment activities that can be used in an ongoing manner after termination. Some may wish to make a checklist that delineates indications of well-being and warning signs that they can periodically review. While the client does not want to become overly self-absorbed, a commitment to regular self-reflection is desired. A client may choose introspective activities such as keeping a journal, having a weekly "self-check," or taking a regular meditative walk during which she monitors her mood, the quality of her important relationships, her life circumstances, her stress level, and her self-care. In short, she wants to make time to ask herself, "How am I doing?" Some women may identify a specific confidant—a close friend or partner—with whom they can discuss their ongoing well-being. However, the client wants to be empowered to be in charge of her own well-being neither solely depending on others to tell her how she is doing, nor cutting herself off from others' feedback.

Some clients may wish to include ongoing visits to the therapist as part of their assessment activities. A woman may feel that she needs the support of the therapist or she may feel insufficiently confident to rely solely on herself to monitor her progress.

When, through assessment activities, the client determines that she is exhibiting early warning signs of depression or increased stress, she can utilize an action plan based on the remaining four elements of therapy.

## SAFETY

The client with a history of suicide attempts or suicidal ideation develops a safety plan that will give her a course of action should suicidal impulses return after termination. Such a plan may include resources that the client can access immediately, such as a local crisis line or suicide hot line. Therapists need to decide to what extent they can realistically be available to clients after termination and what kind of ongoing contact is appropriate for a client who wants to access the therapist for crises after termination.

For example, Molly is a 52-year-old client who had a history of recurrent suicidal episodes and had been in and out of therapy for most of her adult life. She periodically returned to therapy during times of stress or when depressive symptoms returned. However, her suicidal episodes often occurred out of the blue, and she did not want to come to therapy weekly or even biweekly once she recovered from an episode. I started seeing Molly when she moved from out of state and confirmed with her previous therapist of 15 years that Molly was stable and high functioning for long intervals sometimes lasting for years, and that she responded well to phone interventions during crises. After 12 months of therapy during which we initially met weekly, eventually tapering to bimonthly, I agreed to be available to Molly for emergencies if she came to see me once every 2 months. In addition, we made a written copy of specific strategies that had proven helpful in the past to which we would refer in emergencies. I was also able to share this plan with colleagues who provided coverage for me while I was on vacation.

For clients who have not attained safety in their life circumstances and remain financially dependent, in an abusive relationship, working in an unsafe job, or living in an unsafe environment, client and therapist should develop a long-term plan aimed at improving these conditions after termination. Such a plan may be as specific and immediate as a referral to a career counselor or as general as returning to college once children have reached a certain age. The therapist wants to instill in the client the importance of continuing to reduce risk factors by building a life that is safe, meaningful, and life-affirming.

## ACTIVATION

The client is encouraged to continue to be actively committed to her well-being and growth. She is urged to continue to use activating coping strategies and to stay awake and alert in her life. Through the ongoing use of critical consciousness and her "poop detector" the client is empowered to address problems as they arise, proactively seeking creative solutions.

Given the relationship between stress and depression, the client is encouraged to engage in stress management and stress reduction activities. Depending on the client and the course of therapy, stress reduction and stress management may be embedded in therapeutic work. At the minimum, termination sessions should include a discussion of the importance of stress management and the value of regular exercise and a healthy lifestyle. Research is beginning to confirm the benefits of mindfulness-based stress reduction strategies (Teasdale et al., 2000) and exercise (Babyak et al., 2000) in relapse prevention. The client is informed of potential resources for increasing and maintaining such skills including books, videos, and seminars. Self-contained and time-limited stress reduction programs are often available in the community through local hospitals or medical centers.

The decision to take antidepressant medication during active treatment and as ongoing maintenance treatment will vary with each individual client. The client should be educated about medication: about possible contraindications, side effects, the lack of knowledge concerning the effects of long-term use, and the pros and cons of reducing dosage for maintenance treatment. The therapist assists the client in making a decision about maintenance medication that is practical, safe, and consistent with the client's values.

As part of a proactive stance, client and therapist map a clear picture of future areas for attention and growth, preparing the foundation for additional work if indicated. Based on life circumstances and available resources, some individuals will return to therapy intermittently throughout their lives. The therapist presents returning to therapy as a proactive, affirming, and empowering act, particularly when possible signs or symptoms of relapse appear.

## CONNECTION

The client is urged to incorporate strategies in her daily life that keep her connected to her authentic, inner experience, and she is encouraged to pursue activities that support her authentic self. A client may find it helpful to have a visual symbol of the authentic self, such as a photograph or a pendant.

Ongoing self-reflection is also key in maintaining connection with self. The client may be encouraged to periodically ask herself if she is being true to her authentic self in her relationships and in her work. Most importantly, she wants to stay attuned to her needs and to continually seek ways of getting those needs met. Some clients may decide that an ongoing therapy appointment, perhaps interspersed over weeks or months, may provide a vehicle to maintain connection with her authenticity. Creative outlets such as drawing, journalling, or dancing may provide some clients with ongoing access to their authenticity. The client is encouraged to seek activities and arenas in which she can be genuinely herself and be free to voice her opinions. Connection with self also goes hand-in-hand with self-reflective activities of assessment.

The client is instilled with the value of building and maintaining authentic, mutually empowering connections with others. Thus, the client is asked to identify whether expanding her current support network will be a goal post-termination. Some clients may identify a friend or acquaintance with whom they plan to build a closer friendship while others may have a more general plan to make more friends. Partnered women can be asked to identify activities that enhance closeness, authenticity, and mutuality in their significant relationship. For example, Laura made a commitment to get a baby-sitter and spend a night out with her husband at least once every month. She also asked him to regularly help her plan the division of domestic responsibilities on the weekend for each upcoming week. Another client asked her husband to continue their couples therapy as a monthly check-in to help keep them "on track and not fall into our old ways." Yet another client, Sonia, who was single when she ended therapy, planned to make an appointment to "check-in" if she found herself seriously involved with a new romantic partner.

Joining a support group or a psychotherapy group is one option for maintaining healthy connection with others and with oneself. The client may also benefit by joining groups in the community such as a book club, a baby-sitting coop, or a choir.

Together client and therapist identify specific activities that will not only support authenticity and connection but also will help the client pursue her own needs while maintaining healthy connections with others.

## MEANING

There are two important dimensions of meaning that are relevant for relapse prevention: core cognitive schemas and an expansive sense of meaning. The client who entered therapy with dysfunctional schemas may need to continually resist backsliding into old ways of thinking, particularly under stressful conditions.

One persistent schema that may impede a woman's ability to become proactive in dealing with recurrences is the belief that "I should be able to handle everything" or "It is weak to ask for help." One case in point is Joanna, a 39-year-old high school teacher who was married with two children. Joanna had been suffering from recurrent episodes of depression with symptoms of panic for about 7 years when she was referred to me by her physician. She believed that her episodes were biologically based and that she did not really need therapy. She had been off and on antidepressants throughout the past 7 years. During the first 6 months of therapy, Joanna had three episodes. It was apparent that Joanna's life was very stressful, particularly with her teaching and parenting demands. She resisted all suggestions to get more help with domestic responsibilities and child care, to develop an exercise program, or to plan more free time for herself. When she was having an episode, she refused to take time off from work or to take clonazepam, a minor tranquilizer that had been prescribed for acute anxiety symptoms. Eventually it became clear that Joanna held the belief that she should be able to handle anything and that to ask for or use help meant she was weak. The complexity and multitude of the demands on her life and her reluctance to come to therapy more than once a month initially made it difficult to identify a specific core schema that was limiting Joanne's effectiveness in coping with her episodes. Although we had identified several strategies to help Joanna through an episode, she had difficulty following through on them. Once we identified and deconstructed the schema, "I should be able to handle anything," Joanna recognized that therapy could help her make important changes that would assist her in handling her episodes differently. She also became aware that her tenacity in doing everything was guided by her beliefs about what a "good wife" and "good mother" should do. This perception led Joanna to question her assumptions and to consider being more flexible in her role expectations. Joanna actually headed off her last episode in late summer, which was triggered by the anticipation of the start of the school year, the most stressful time in Joanna's life. Not only did she have the rush of preparing her classroom, but this was the busiest time of year in her husband's job as well and he often did not get home until after the children were in bed. In July, Joanna and I collaborated on a relapse prevention plan to help her through this stressful time. Table 12.2 summarizes Joanna's plan.

Just before Labor Day, Joanna woke up with feelings of dread and worry that usually signalled the onset of an episode. Although she had planned to spend the day with her children, she called her mother-in-law and asked her if she would spend the day with the children at a local pool, a plan which they had discussed several months earlier. She then took the antianxiety medication and spent the day in bed resting. For dinner, she took the children to their favorite fast food restaurant and after they went to bed she called her best friend who helped her make arrangements for her children the next day. She then listened to a relaxation tape I had made for her and was asleep by the time her husband arrived home. The family had planned to spend Labor Day weekend at a lake with friends. Joanna had her husband leave with the

---

**TABLE 12.2  Joanna's Relapse Prevention Plan**

1. If I am feeling low:
   - Listen to what I am telling myself.
   - Remind myself that it is OK to ask for help and that I do not have to be perfect.

2. If I stop exercising, have trouble sleeping, or stop being social:
   - Pay extra attention to myself, be mindful, and do more self-care. Push myself to be active.

3. Spend time alone and ask myself "What do I need?" and "Am I getting my needs met? If not, what can I do?" (especially do this if I am stressed)
4. Hire a housecleaner to come every 2 weeks.
5. Talk to after-school childcare program to keep children for an additional half hour at the end of the day.
6. Ask Elizabeth to go to gym two mornings a week. Ask Glen to wake the kids up.
7. People I can turn to: my husband, my sister, Elizabeth.
8. If things are not getting better:
   - Take the day off from work.
   - Ask mother-in-law to take kids.
   - Ask Glen to handle dinner.
   - Listen to relaxation tape.
   - Call Elizabeth or my sister.
   - Take clonazepam.

9. If things are still not better: Call Susan for an appointment.

children while she spent the day at home by herself, driving up to meet them the next day. At the cabin, she took walks by herself while her husband and friends looked after her children and she took the antianxiety medication throughout the weekend. While Joanna was not able to completely prevent a recurrence, her coping strategies limited the intensity of symptoms and shortened their duration. As part of her relapse prevention plan, she recognized that she might be prone to returning to old ways of thinking (i.e., schemas of goodness and control), particularly in stressful situations. Hence, Joanna made a written plan to remind her to think more flexibly.

In addition to core cognitive schemas, the second element of meaning that is relevant to relapse prevention is having an expansive sense of meaning. Being connected to something greater than oneself may be a buffer against the bumps in the roads of a woman's life. Individuals who are attached to something greater than themselves seem to fare best (Yapko, 2000). Spirituality, altruism, and creativity provide opportunities to transcend everyday experience, expanding the potential for finding positive meaning in life and experiencing positive emotions. The client should be encouraged to broaden and build her capacity for positive emotions through activities that connect her with a larger sense of meaning and that cultivate positive emotions (Frederickson, 2000). For some clients, getting a pet or finding a hobby are also pathways that expand the client's sense of meaning and cultivate positive emotions. While momentary relief from sad or depressed mood is not sufficient to prevent depression, experiences of positive emotions can accumulate:

> The psychological broadening sparked by one positive emotion can increase an individual's receptiveness to subsequent pleasant or meaningful events, increasing the odds that the individual will find positive meaning in these subsequent events and experience additional positive emotions. This can turn into an "upward spiral" that might, over time, lessen depressive symptoms. (Frederickson, 2000, p. 16)

Over time, through repeated meaningful positive experiences that generate positive emotions, the individual may increase her psychological and physical resilience and interpersonal resources that, when taken together, enhance health and well-being (Frederickson, 2000).

While some clients may be able to nurture an expanded sense of meaning through specific activities during their therapies, others may only be able to identify finding such activities as a goal after therapy ends.

Relapse prevention often requires changes on multiple levels that incorporate goals related to all five elements of therapy. Although some clients will develop a more resilient sense of self relatively quickly, particularly those with strong self capacities, supportive environments, and financial resources (as the following case description illustrates), such changes sometimes require years in order to reduce risk factors, increase resilience, and transform identity.

## SARAH—A CASE OF LONG-TERM THERAPY

With Sarah, a client I saw in therapy for 6 years, I had the opportunity to work through the process of her acknowledging and naming the risk factors related to a lack of safety and security in her life and making major life changes that were ultimately transforming. Sarah entered therapy with me at a community agency 2 years after she had undergone inpatient treatment for polysubstance abuse. She was suffering from depression and struggling to learn to live life without substances for the first time since she was a young teenager. At the time she began therapy, she was 28 years old and a bank teller with a high school education who resided with her mother, sleeping on the couch in her mother's living room. She had several women friends with whom she had remained close since high school, but these friends inevitably socialized with heavy drinking. Sarah's car was constantly breaking down and she had overdue medical bills. She was engaged to an alcoholic and drug addict who was not interested in recovery. The first two years of therapy involved intermittent depressive symptoms and constant turmoil with her fiancé before she was able to leave the relationship. Despite having excellent social skills, Sarah's self-confidence was tenuous—particularly in new social situations—and it took almost 2 years before she worked up the courage to attend Narcotics Anonymous (N.A.) meetings.

Recognizing that she needed to have more financial security so she could have her own living space and a reliable car, Sarah gradually began to explore career options and decided to become an occupational therapy assistant. She became the first person in her family to attend college and surprised herself by doing extremely well in school, excelling in her clinical rotations, and immediately landing a well-paying job once she received an associate degree. She found a career she loved and which gave her a sense of self-efficacy and affirmed a positive identity.

Eventually, Sarah moved to another state so she could pursue a longtime dream of living near the ocean. Our therapy terminated 7 years ago and each Christmas she sends me a letter that updates me on her life. She now owns her own condominium and drives a new jeep. She enjoys her job and has become seriously involved with a man who seems solid. She has now been free from depression for 9 years, has remained sober, and has been actively involved in N.A., serving as a sponsor for a number of women over the years. For Sarah, developing safe and secure life circumstances was pivotal in her sustained recovery and increased resilience. In fact, this therapy task was pivotal for Sarah in that her identity as an occupational therapist led to a crucial transformation of meaning concerning her vision of self and her life goals. It is important to note that this work took many years on Sarah's part and that she stayed in therapy for a total of 9 years, 7 of them with me. While there are many benefits to short-term therapy, Sarah's story suggests that in order to reduce vulnerability to depression, it may be necessary to make major life changes.

Thus far, the research has shown that short-term treatment approaches have had limited success in preventing recurrences. We are badly in need of research that follows people over the long-term and explores the impact on recurrence of making long-term life changes such as those made by Sarah. Unfortunately, most health insurance only covers therapy if the client has a diagnosable condition and the work of developing safe and secure life circumstances often does not begin in earnest until the client no longer has symptoms. It is particularly important to help clients find resources in the community that can support ongoing growth.

## SUMMARY

This chapter has discussed a model for relapse prevention based on the five elements of therapy. The client's work in therapy lays the groundwork for developing a relapse prevention plan as one of the final tasks in the future orientation phase of therapy. The client is encouraged to maintain a proactive stance in her life and to regularly engage in self-assessment. When the client is familiar with her early warning signs of an episode or symptoms of stress, she can utilize specific action-oriented strategies that she and the therapist have identified. Relapse prevention includes coping strategies to improve mood and longer-term goals to improve the quality of the client's life, aimed at reducing risk factors and increasing resilience. IRT embraces the value of developing a life of ongoing commitment to empowerment and growth, authenticity, connection to others, and connection to an expansive sense of meaning. While the ideal situation is that all clients recover and go on to lead fulfilling, healthy lives, the reality is that some individuals may not respond as expected to therapy. The next chapter provides some suggestions for working with clients with persistent depressions.

# CHAPTER THIRTEEN

# When the Client Is Not Improving

**B**ecky just left my office and I am feeling tired and discouraged. A 35-year-old returning college student, married with a 13-year-old son, Becky is about to graduate with a degree in engineering and just returned from a job interview in Seattle. She is now more depressed than when she entered therapy 6 months ago. Furthermore, her insurance will cover only two more sessions.

In an ideal world, all our clients get well quickly and can afford as much therapy as they need. However, the reality is that we are all likely to face clinical dilemmas such as the one just described and, at times, we may have to grapple with far more challenging situations. This chapter provides suggestions for revising the treatment plan when the client does not appear to be improving.

In addressing my work with Becky, I had two areas that required my attention. First, I needed to decide how next to handle the therapeutic work with Becky. She was not getting better and I needed to decide if, how, and why to alter the treatment plan. Second, I needed to address my own feelings of exhaustion and frustration. Sometimes, coming to a new plan of action revives me. So my first order of business was to figure out what to do therapeutically. If, however, I was still feeling low even with a new plan of attack, I would require some extra attention for my own personal "treatment plan."

Sometimes, a course of action will immediately present itself when the therapy seems stalemated. With Becky, however, no obvious solution presented itself. Perhaps I was feeling too depleted to be creative or even to see clearly. Whatever the reasons, this was a time to methodically review all my possibilities. When the therapist feels stuck, it can be helpful to systematically reappraise several key factors. Table 13.1 lists the three areas to reassess: client factors, therapist factors, and therapy factors. These areas allow the therapist to review and revise the case conceptualization, to address potentially disruptive countertransference issues, and to make relevant changes in the treatment plan.

**TABLE 13.1   When the Client Is Not Improving**

Reassess client factors
   Expectations
   Risk factors
   Aspects of the self
   Comorbid diagnoses
   Transference issues
Reassess therapy factors
   Expectations
   Expertise
   Empathic attunement
   Other countertransference issues
Reassess treatment plan
   Assess for medication referral or reevaluation
   Increase frequency
   Change focus or modality
   Referral to another therapist
   Consult with colleagues

Client factors include the client's expectations, biopsychosocial risk factors, aspects of the self, comorbid diagnoses, and transference issues. Therapist factors include expectations, expertise, empathic attunement, and other countertransference issues. Therapy factors describe elements of the treatment plan such as frequency of therapy, type of modality, focus of treatment, medication, and number of sessions available.

An assessment of therapist or client factors may lead to a new understanding of the client's lack of improvement, leading to an adjustment in the therapy factors (i.e., a change in treatment plan). However, even when reassessment of therapist and client factors does not offer obvious new directions, a change in therapy factors is usually warranted. If, after a change in treatment approach, the client still does not show improvement, consultation with colleagues is definitely warranted. As the following discussion will illustrate, client factors and therapist factors are often intertwined.

## CLIENT FACTORS

An important area to assess is the client's expectations of treatment. Because I receive a large percentage of my referrals from medical practitioners, particularly in the rural environment in which I practice, clients may enter therapy without a clear idea of what therapy is and may have unrealistic expectations. Although I incorporate an explanation of therapy into the first few sessions and continually work to educate the client, some people may not be prepared to take responsibility for their own recovery or may not be motivated to work in therapy. Although lack of knowledge may be one contributing factor in such situations, if the therapist consistently seems to be working harder than the client, then appropriate avenues to explore in the therapy may be the meaning to the client of motivation, passivity, and responsibility. Another obstacle to recovery may be the meaning the client places on getting well. For example, a client may believe that if she is no longer depressed she will have to face a problem that she feels unable to handle. The therapist can help the client explore any worries she has about recovering and address obstacles to recovery.

Often the therapist's expectations may be overly optimistic due to an underestimation of biopsychosocial risk factors or vulnerabilities in aspects of the self. Consequently, reviewing possible risk factors and aspects of the self may yield a more accurate case conceptualization, leading, in turn, to a change in treatment plan or an adjustment in the therapist's expectations. A therapist may not necessarily have missed seeing these client factors, but the client may have left out important pieces of her story because she was not aware of their significance or because she was not feeling safe enough in the therapy. Sometimes, simply reviewing the client's risk factors and aspects of the self assists the therapist in revising expectations. For example, Becky had a history of recurrent depressions, had a seriously ill parent living with her, and held rigid schemas of perfectionism, seeing a grade of B+ as a sign of failure. When I mentally tallied up these risk factors and vulnerabilities of the self, I understood her reasons for relapse, which helped me realign my expectations and feel less overwhelmed by her worsening of symptoms.

In addition, the therapist wants to explore whether the client may have a serious comorbid diagnosis that has been obscured or hidden such as substance abuse, an eating disorder, or obsessive compulsive disorder. In such situations, the therapist may enlist the client in collaboratively investigating the possibility that there are "missing pieces" that may explain the persistence of her depression.

Sometimes the client's course of recovery proceeds in such a way that she shows great improvement over several weeks or months only then to reexperience symptoms of depression. Often, a stressor or "trigger" that reminds the client of a stressful event may arouse painful memories that then elicit negative affect. The therapist can help the client name this process, access coping skills to manage negative affect, and work through the issues related to the stressor. This type of bumpy recovery often seems to occur with clients whose depression was related to a painful relationship breakup, particularly when the woman felt betrayed or rejected by her partner. Frequently, the woman engages in an agitating rumination, repeatedly revisiting the hurtful events in her mind or repetitively trying to make sense of the partner's behavior. I have found it helpful to conceptualize this process as similar to posttraumatic reactions (e.g., see Gordon & Baucom, 1999) and utilizing trauma-based strategies may be helpful. For example, Eye Movement Desensitization and Reprocessing (EMDR) (Shapiro, 1995) may be a useful adjunct to the IRT approach in these kinds of clinical situations. The therapist should have the proper level of training to use EMDR, and the client needs to meet the appropriate criteria for the use of the modality, integrating EMDR into the therapy in a sensitive and informed manner.

Another client factor to assess is transference issues. Overly positive transferences, erotic transferences, or negative transferences may impede the progress of therapy. Transference issues based on differences in sociocultural factors such as gender, race, ethnicity, sexual orientation, or age may also have an impact on the efficacy of the therapy, particularly when these issues are not addressed. When the therapist determines that transference issues may be interfering with the client's recovery, the therapist decides whether to address the issue directly with the client, seeking consultation or supervision as needed.

## THERAPIST FACTORS

The research on therapy outcome suggests that particular therapist factors, which may also be conceptualized as countertransference issues, influence outcome. In particular, the research refers to the impact of therapist expectations (Blatt, Sanislow, et al., 1996) and empathy (Burns & Nolen-Hoeksema, 1992) as key in predicting positive outcome. Furthermore, research has shown that clinicians tend to respond negatively to depressed persons, making negative appraisals about depressed people and experiencing negative mood reactions (Ford & Elliott, 1999). Thus, attention to countertransference reactions is particularly crucial in working with depressed individuals.

Therapists should, therefore, reevaluate their expectations when clients are not making progress. Is the therapist expecting too much too soon, particularly given the unique risk factors and vulnerabilities of the client? In the NIMH treatment outcome study, a large number of participants were only partially remitted by the end of 16 sessions (Elkin et al., 1995), and those individuals with the best outcome saw therapists who expected treatment to last longer, were more psychologically minded, and eschewed biological interventions (Blatt, Sanislow, et al., 1996). Successful treatment may require longer-term psychotherapy for many depressed individuals.

It is difficult to make specific predictions as to how quickly a given client should recover. Depression is a heterogeneous disorder and each client brings her own unique life situation and personality factors to therapy.

When the client is not showing sufficient improvement, one possibility is that the client is actually improving slightly but she is not moving ahead at a rate that the therapist *recognizes* as sufficient improvement. For example, a client may not be as immobilized by the fifth session as she was when she entered therapy, but may still be suffering from moderate symptoms of depression. New therapists may find that their lack of expertise, particularly with chronic or severely depressed clients, may interact with expectations and create feelings of being overwhelmed or hopeless early in the therapy. Another factor that may impact the therapist's expectations is working from a short-term treatment or managed care model. While the model may expect rapid improvement, the reality may be quite different. As the research has shown, recovery from major depression often takes more than 16 sessions (Elkin et al., 1995).

As discussed throughout the book, a positive therapeutic alliance is a foundation of successful psychotherapy. Thus, empathic attunement is a vital ingredient of therapy. If empathic attunement is lacking, the therapist should be compelled to address this problem. I sometimes find that I am able to restore a sense of empathy with a client if I remind myself of her vulnerabilities and risk factors. Consultation or supervision are particularly warranted when empathic attunement is persistently a problem with a particular client, with the purpose of exploring possible sources of this problem and determining whether a realignment is possible. Therapists who find themselves repeatedly struggling to be empathic with more than one client should definitely seek professional help in sorting out the source of this problem.

Finally, the therapist should review all aspects of the countertransference. Any feelings—positive or negative—that the therapist may be having toward the client are fertile ground for exploration. For example, a therapist with strong positive feelings for the client may shy away from confrontation or see the client as less vulnerable than she is; whereas, a therapist with negative feelings may minimize complaints or refrain from interventions that will encourage the client to remain in therapy. As discussed in chapter 4, differences and similarities between client and therapist regarding sociocultural identities may have a positive impact on the therapy as well as a detrimental impact. Therapists are responsible for exploring how such differences affect them and the client. Having trusted colleagues with whom to explore possible counter-transference issues is invaluable.

## THERAPY FACTORS

When the client is not improving, there are a number of therapy factors that the therapist can reassess and adjust. As stated previously, regardless of whether a lack of improvement is explained by any of the aforementioned factors, a change in therapy factors may be warranted. For the client who is only coming to therapy for one session per week, an immediate increase in frequency to twice per week or more, if feasible, is an immediate adjustment that can be made in the treatment plan.

The therapist should also evaluate the focus of therapy and determine if another direction would be beneficial. For example, a depressed client may enter therapy wishing to decide whether to stay or leave a troubling relationship, but a focus on this issue may be unsuccessful while the client is having serious symptoms. Often this presents a kind of double bind in that the client feels she will be depressed until she resolves this issue but she really cannot resolve this issue until she is functioning more effectively and thinking more clearly. The therapist can help the client balance her need to focus on the relationship problem while encouraging her to engage in activities and strategies that decrease depressive symptoms and cultivate positive emotions.

For the client whose progress appears stymied, it is also appropriate to consider a referral for a medication evaluation or a reevaluation of current medications. For the client who has refused medication in the past, revisiting the issue may be warranted, with particular sensitivity to the client's beliefs and values about medication. As discussed in chapter 5, it is important not to overvalue or undervalue medication, viewing it as one of many treatment options that may be helpful given the client's unique characteristics, symptoms, beliefs, values, and resources.

With Becky, I made a number of changes in the therapy. First, I saw her for two, half-hour sessions over the course of a week. Second, I asked her to name all of the possible things in her life that were making her unhappy, which led to her sharing her frustration over her marriage, something she had not done before. (Sometimes, I find myself exclaiming to myself with exasperation, "Now you tell me!" when a client has neglected to mention an important detail of her life or minimized problems, as Becky had.) Although I had asked this question in the first session, I got a much richer answer this time, probably because Becky had been quite hesitant about trusting me after having an unsatisfactory experience with her last therapist. In the next session, Becky surprised me by reporting that upon leaving our session, she went home and met with her husband to "negotiate" for his help in being more involved around the house. She also went to play racketball daily, something she had claimed she was too tired to do when I had suggested it. While changing the frequency and the focus of therapy is never assured to have a positive result, in this case, it did make a difference.

For the client who is not improving despite changes in the treatment plan, referral to another therapist should be approached with extreme care and as a last resort unless the client has initiated such a request. The therapist needs to ensure that the client is not being abandoned and should work collaboratively with the client if such an option is chosen. It is important not to minimize the power of a supportive, therapeutic relationship and recognize that even when the client is not making progress, the client may wish to continue with the therapist. If a change of therapist is the mutually agreed upon course of action, the therapist needs to see the client through the transition, working with the new therapist and collaborating with the client to make this a safe and successful transfer.

Consultation with colleagues can be invaluable in generating new perspectives and renewed energy for clients who are not improving or who pose challenges. The therapist can discuss cases while maintaining confidentiality by not disclosing identifying information. Although consultation can be undertaken at any time, when progress still appears stalemated after reassessing all factors and making an adjustment in the treatment plan, then consultation with colleagues is essential. As a risk management measure, the therapist should document the consultation in the client's record.

Sometimes, having the client evaluated by a colleague may be helpful, particularly by a colleague who has expertise in the area of depression or who is particularly experienced with women's issues or issues that have special relevance for the client. If this route is taken, it is particularly important to establish a collaborative approach among all three parties.

## SUMMARY

When the client is not showing sufficient improvement, the therapist wants to reassess the case conceptualization (client factors), counter-transference issues (therapist factors) and the treatment plan (therapy factors). Consultation with colleagues may be helpful at any point, but is essential if, after a change in treatment plan, the client is still not improving. A referral to another therapist should be undertaken with the utmost care for the client's well-being and with attention to ethical concerns.

The stress of seeing depressed clients on a daily basis, particularly when the course of recovery is slow or progress is minimal, can take its toll on the therapist. IRT views the therapist's own self-care as equal in importance to providing effective, responsible treatment to clients. As just suggested, when the therapist is feeling exhausted, frustrated, or is in any way unable to give fully to the process of psychotherapy, then the client's well-being is in jeopardy. The next chapter describes a model for the therapist's own self-care and ongoing resilience.

# CHAPTER FOURTEEN

# Therapist Self-Care

I had just seen two extremely depressed clients, one after the other, at the end of a long day of seeing clients in my private practice. I was wearied and troubled by the intensity of both clients' misery. "It's time for a movie," I told myself as I left the office for the drive home. At the video store, I went to the "comedy" section, knowing I needed a good injection of optimism.

Therapists' self-care has a profound effect upon our clients. Whether we explicitly let clients know when we are stressed or energized, our mental state is often apparent. Furthermore, when we are tired, disheartened, frustrated, or overworked, we simply cannot be fully present for our clients. Not only are therapists faced with the stress of helping troubled people deal more effectively with life, but we are also under the pressures of working in the current professional environment that values short-term, medicalized solutions. As this book has demonstrated, depression is a recurrent disorder and recovery may involve a slow progression of internal and external changes that may require months or even years. The reality is that myriad elements in the mental health system undermine the kind of comprehensive, ongoing treatment that depressed individuals often need. It is not unusual for a therapist to regularly face difficult decisions due to the constraints of the current system. For example, in the last week I had to advocate for a client with an insurance company to get more sessions approved, decide what to do about a client who had utilized all of her benefits but still needed therapy, determine whether I could take on a new client for a lower fee in my private practice, and intervene with a supervisee who had been assigned a case that was beyond her expertise. These kinds of ethical and professional predicaments can be draining, frustrating, irritating, and disempowering, making the clinician vulnerable to burnout and compassion fatigue.

In addition to job stress, we all have our own lives to manage, with our unique personal circumstances, risk factors, and personality strengths and vulnerabilities. Furthermore, mental health professionals are at least as prone to depression as people in the general population with one study finding that 61% of psychologists had experienced at least one episode of depression (Pope & Tabachnick, 1994) and another study finding that 76% of women practitioners had suffered from some form of depression (Gilroy et al., 1998, cited in Carroll et al., 1999).

With these multiple stresses in mind, IRT emphasizes the importance of therapists' commitment to their own self-care and ongoing growth. The IRT five elements model provides a useful framework for creating a practical action plan for the therapist's own self-care and increased resilience. Table 14.1 summarizes the application of the five elements in the service of the therapist's own self-care.

## ASSESSMENT

First and foremost, therapists should evaluate their risk for burnout (Watson, 2000) and vicarious traumatization (Pearlman & Saakvitne, 1994). Activities that may be indicative of high risk are: seeing multiple clients consecutively without meal or bathroom breaks; seeing potentially dangerous clients without appropriate safety measures; seeing mostly clients who are survivors of trauma; seeing clients who are beyond one's expertise; working with chronic clients; seeing clients who show little improvement; feeling professionally isolated; putting clients' needs before one's own needs; not taking vacations or time off; working in unsupportive institutional environments; having unrealistic expectations; and being underpaid (Carroll et al., 1999; Kestnbaum, 1984; Maslach, 1978; Raquepaw & Miller, 1989; Watson, 2000). If risk for burnout appears high, suggestions for remedies are discussed later.

In addition to evaluating the risk for burnout, therapists can benefit from regularly evaluating their stress levels and overall well-being. It is important to become familiar with one's own behavioral, somatic, cognitive, and emotional signs of stress. For example, I know that when I am stressed, I tend to drink more caffeinated beverages, have neck and shoulder pain, sleep less, ruminate more about clients, increase my intake of sweets, drink more than my customary half glass of wine, and feel more easily overwhelmed. When therapists are aware of their own stress signs, such signs may act as a trigger, mobilizing self capacities in the service of stress reduction activities.

It can also be helpful to identify trusted friends or colleagues with whom therapists can regularly discuss their personal and professional well-being. In our group practice, we meet biweekly and begin each

**TABLE 14.1    Therapist's Action Plan for Self-Care**

Assessment
  1. Evaluate your risk for burnout.
  2. Become familiar with your personal signs of stress.
  3. Identify at least one way to regularly check in with yourself to evaluate your personal and professional well-being.
  4. Identify at least one person or group from whom you can elicit feedback about your personal and professional well-being.

Safety
  1. Identify unsafe situations in your work and personal life and make a commitment to improve these conditions.
  2. Evaluate your job security and make long-term goals to improve your economic security.

Activation
  1. Make a commitment to your own personal and professional self-care, competence, and growth.
  2. Make a commitment to critical consciousness in your personal and professional life.
  3. Be aware of your personal issues and how they impact your clinical work.
  4. When signs of stress appear, use stress reduction strategies.
  5. Develop an ongoing exercise program.
  6. Maintain a healthy diet and lifestyle.
  7. Arrange your daily work schedule to support physical, emotional, and spiritual well-being.
  8. Be proactive in developing long-term goals to attain a nurturing work life.
  9. Be proactive in seeking personal therapy, supervision, consultation, and continuing education.

Connection
  1. Engage in activities that keep you in connection with your authentic self (journalling, meditation, self-reflection, quiet time).
  2. Develop a professional life that supports your authenticity.
  3. Find like-minded colleagues and arrange regular contact.

Meaning
  1. Balance your personal and professional activities.
  2. Find and engage in professional activities that are meaningful for you.
  3. Remind yourself of the reasons that being a therapist is important to you.
  4. Periodically review successful cases and reminisce about favorite clients.
  5. Nurture an expanded sense of meaning about life through creativity, spirituality, or altruism.
  6. Ask yourself what you can learn from treatment failures or from challenging clients.
  7. Maintain a sense of humor and a sense of perspective.

meeting with a "check-in" during which each of us describes what is happening in our lives and how we are doing personally and professionally. This gives us the opportunity not only to contemplate our own well-being, but also to feel connected and supported.

## SAFETY

Safety is an important issue in therapist self-care, especially in working with depressed clients with suicidal ideation or histories of suicide attempts. Therapists want to ensure that they have sufficient training and access to professional support so as not to be working beyond their skills or in isolation when seeing high-risk clients. The therapist's own personal safety should not be minimized and safeguards should be made for working with dangerous clients.

When therapists do not have job security or when they are grossly underpaid, they are at risk for burnout and their effectiveness with clients may be compromised. In such situations, the therapist should make long-term goals to increase economic security, seeking professional help, such as career consultation, as needed. Money issues are often difficult for mental health professionals to confront, particularly for women therapists who may be prone to guilt for not being caring enough or for minority therapists who may feel that they need to give back to the community. As a therapist who relies on private practice for the majority of my income, I am continually challenged in my dealings with money. I have found it helpful to maintain an ongoing dialogue about money issues with other private practitioners.

Finally, therapists should address their own risk factors for depression. Those with a history of depression or other psychological problems should develop their own safety plans to ensure that their symptoms do not interfere with their ability to function ethically and effectively in their jobs. A therapist should not hesitate to seek personal therapy, despite the effort that may be required to locate a practitioner without dual relationships with the therapist.

## ACTIVATION

Activation tasks are probably the most salient for therapist self-care. Key is the need to make a commitment to one's personal and professional self-care and ongoing growth. Critical consciousness is equally important for the therapist as it is for the client. Critically conscious therapists recognize that self-care is part of personal and professional empowerment. Empowered therapists take responsibility for their own personal and professional competence (Brabeck & Brown, 1997). Further, critically conscious therapists not only are alert and awake to their own biases, but are committed to addressing oppressive situations in their own personal and professional lives. Therapists should advocate for daily work schedules that support optimal functioning and self-care. Therapists will not be able to be effective over the long term if they stay in oppressive situations for which they have given up hope of changing. When therapists find themselves in oppressive work situations, they must take steps to improve their work environment, establishing long-term goals as needed.

Stress should be recognized as a normal reaction to life, and stress management through proactive self-care should thus be a moral imperative for psychotherapists (Carroll et al., 1999). Regular physical exercise is particularly important, especially given the sedentary nature of doing psychotherapy. It is important to engage in frequent exercise in order to release tension that builds up in the body while listening to others' distress. Maintaining a healthy diet and lifestyle are also buffers against stress. I keep a supply of herbal tea, spring water, dried fruit, and energy bars in my office, frequently sharing these with clients. Taking regular vacations is yet another essential element of responsible self-care and proactive stress management. The therapist is actually modeling good self-care and healthy boundaries for clients by taking vacations.

Finally, empowered therapists are committed to their ongoing personal and professional growth. I believe that personal therapy is a prerequisite for anyone who strives to be a truly good therapist. An empowered therapist is one who engages in ongoing, continuing professional education, maintaining a sense of hunger and excitement for knowledge.

## CONNECTION

Self-care also involves staying connected with one's authenticity. Therapists want to stay connected with who they truly are. Activities that promote connection with ones' authenticity include quiet self-reflection, journalling, time with nature, arts, crafts, or sports. It is important to find activities that nurture and feed the essence of who one is as an individual. Having a life that allows no time for self-connection sets the stage for burnout.

The vicissitudes of working from a relational therapeutic approach often involve feeling intense emotion for and with clients. A truly empathic therapist *feels*. Furthermore, the process of forming deep, meaningful connections with clients who then terminate can leave therapists with feelings of loss and sadness. Being in connection with one's authentic, inner experience allows therapists to work through feelings and to activate self-care strategies that are healing and nurturing.

Finding a work environment that supports authenticity is part of self-care. Many years ago, I worked for a wonderful private psychiatric hospital that valued creativity and collaboration in its therapists. The hospital was bought out by a corporation that only valued the bottom line. It became clear that despite the good salary and great benefits, the environment demoralized and devalued me. I voluntarily left for another position elsewhere, but it took me several years to recreate an optimal work environment for myself. Self-care often requires a long-range view of improving one's circumstances.

Finally, it is important to find like-minded colleagues who provide a sense of connection and support. In addition to the biweekly consult group that I attend as part of a group practice, I have a monthly telephone consult with a good friend who is a psychologist in another city. We catch up on our personal lives and then each presents a case for discussion. I also do not hesitate to consult with local colleagues and have made it my business to seek phone consultation from regional experts as needed.

To counter the isolation of private practice, I schedule lunch with a friend or colleague once a week. When I move to a new area, I have made it a habit to initiate coffee or lunch meetings with potential friends and colleagues. Joining professional organizations is another means of maintaining connection. If there is no local organization to join, you can always create one. I have had the pleasure of cofounding two organizations for women therapists and have found these activities to be not only intellectually stimulating but also a source for new friendships and collegial relationships. Each of these groups has given me something different, but they both provided me with a sense of positive connection with others and kindled renewed excitement for my work.

## MEANING

It is important to feel passion, conviction, and love for your work as a psychotherapist. Without intense positive feelings about some aspect of your work, how can you possibly develop empathic, mutually empowering, healing relationships with clients? However, balance is key in regard to where a therapist finds meaning in life. Woe unto the person whose identity as a therapist is the sole source of positive meaning in life. It is vital not only to find work meaningful, but also to experience meaning in other aspects of life such as through family, spirituality, or creativity. An effective therapist wants to feel an overall sense of aliveness and excitement about life.

Sometimes when I have had a rough day at the office, I may ask myself, "Why am I doing this?" It can be helpful to recall the reasons why you decided to become a therapist (or psychologist, social worker, counselor, etc.). Reminiscing from time to time about your own journey to become a therapist may be an affirming touchstone that reconnects with core values and inspirational experiences. Likewise, remembering clients with whom I felt an exceptionally close connection or who triumphed against adversity can be uplifting. I keep a folder of "thank you" notes and letters from clients that I go through every few years to remind myself of what my help has meant to others. Even though I am not able to help every client, there are those for whom my help has been meaningful and significant. Reminding myself of those "special connections" with clients can be especially inspirational when I am having a particularly unrewarding stretch.

Finally, if your work seems to be without meaning, it is imperative to address this issue. A therapist who finds meaning in work and in life conveys a sense of enthusiasm and contentment that can be contagious to clients.

## SUMMARY

Self-care is a moral imperative for therapists (Carroll et al., 1999). The five elements may serve as a guide to develop an individual action plan for self-care and increased resilience. Assessment provides the means by which therapists can evaluate their vulnerability for burnout, become attuned to their signs of stress, and develop a personalized self-care plan. Safety refers to the need to ensure personal safety on the job, develop economic security, and address the therapist's own vulnerability to depression. Activation refers to the overall attitude of commitment to self-care and personal growth, encompassing mind, body, and spirit with particular attention to stress management. Connection concerns staying connected to one's authenticity and finding ways to maintain authentic connection with like-minded others. Meaning refers to the importance of finding meaning in one's work and in life. As one of my clients in a helping profession reminded me, when the well is dry, we have nothing to give. Self-care involves an ongoing commitment to keeping the well abundantly flowing.

## APPENDIX A

# Integrative Resources and Recommended Readings

## DEPRESSION AND ANXIETY

Boyd, J. A. (1998). *Can I get a witness? For sisters, when the blues is more than a song.* New York: Penguin Group.

Jack, D. C. (1991). *Silencing the self: Women and depression.* New York: HarperCollins.

Formanek, R., & Gurian, A. (1987). *Women and depression: A lifespan perspective.* New York: Springer Publishing.

Lark, S. (1996). *Overcoming chronic fatigue: Effective self-help options to relieve the fatigue associated with CFS, candida, allergies, PMS, menopause, anemia, low thyroid, and depression.* New Canaan, CT: Keats Publishing, Inc.

Lark, S. (2000). *Anxiety and stress self help book.* Berkeley, CA: Celestial Arts.

McGrath, E., Keita, G. P., Strickland, B. R., & Russo, N. F. (1990). *Women and depression: Risk factors and treatment issues.* Washington, DC: American Psychological Association.

Mitchell, A., Croom, G., & Herring, K. (1998). *What the blues is all about: Black women overcoming stress and depression.* New York: Berkeley.

## FOOD

Lark, S. (1996). *The woman's health companion: Self help nutrition guide & cookbook.* Berkeley, CA: Ten Speed Press.

Simonds, N. (1999). *A spoonful of ginger: Irresistible, health-giving recipes from Asian kitchens.* New York: Alfred A. Knopf, Inc.

## FEMINIST THERAPY ORGANIZATIONS

Association for Women in Psychology. A nonprofit scientific and educational organization committed to encouraging feminist research, theory, and activism. For further information, visit their website on the World Wide Web: http://www.awpsych.org.

Society for the Psychology of Women. Division 35 of the American Psychological Association. To join, contact Society for the Psychology of Women, Division 35 Administrative Office, American Psychological Association, 750 First Street, NE, Washington, DC 2002-4242, (202) 336-6013, email: div35apa@apa.org.

# MEDICATION

Hamilton, J. A., Jensvold, M. F., Rothblum, E. D., & Cole, E. (1995). *Psychopharmacology from a feminist perspective*. New York: Harrington Press.

Raskin, V. (1997). *When words are not enough: The women's prescription for depression and anxiety*. New York: Broadway Books.

# MIND/BODY

Alexander, J. (2000). *The energy secret: Practical techniques for understanding and directing vital energy*. Hammersmith, London: Thorsons.

Iyengar, G. S. (1991). *Yoga: A gem for women*. Spokane, WA: Timeless Books.

Kripalu Yoga Fellowship (1998). *Gentle yoga with Carolyn Lundeen*. [video]. Lenox, MA: Kripalu. Available on the World Wide Web: http://www.kripalu.org.

Kabat-Zinn, J. (1995). *Mindfulness meditation practice tapes: Guided body scan; Guided yoga 1*. [audiocassette]. Lexington, MA: Stress Reduction Tapes. Available on the World Wide Web: http://www.mindfulnesstapes.com. (Very easy yoga—good for beginners.)

Olsen, A. (1998). *BodyStories: A guide to experiential anatomy*. Barrytown, NY: Barrytown.

# MINDFULNESS

Bennett-Goleman, T. (2001). *Emotional alchemy: How the mind can heal the heart*. New York: Harmony Books.

Hanh, T. N. (1990). *Present moment, wonderful moment*. Berkeley, CA: Parallax Press.

Kabat-Zinn, J. (1990). *Full catastrophe living: Using the wisdom of your body and mind to face stress, pain, and illness*. New York: Delta.

Kabat-Zinn, J. (1994). *Wherever you go, there you are*. New York: Hyperion.

Kabat-Zinn, J. (1995). *Mindfulness meditation practice tapes: Guided body scan; Guided yoga 1*. [audiocassette]. Lexington, MA: Stress Reduction Tapes. Available on the World Wide Web: http://www.mindfulnesstapes.com.

Kabat-Zinn, J. (1995). *Mindfulness meditation practice tapes: Guided sitting meditation; Guided yoga 2*. [audiocassette] Lexington, MA: Stress Reduction Tapes. Available on the World Wide Web: http://www.mindfulnesstapes.com.

## MULTICULTURAL THERAPY

Blotzer, M. A., & Ruth, R. (1995). *Sometimes you just want to feel like a human being: Case studies of empowering psychotherapy with people with disabilities.* Baltimore: P. H. Brookes.

Comas-Diaz, L., & Greene, B. (1994). *Women of color: Integrating ethnic and gender identities in psychotherapy.* New York: Guilford.

Jackson, L. C., & Greene, B. (2000). *Psychotherapy with African American women.* New York: Guilford.

Perez, R. M., Debord, K. A., Bieschke, K. J., & Brown, L. S. (1999). *Handbook of counseling and psychotherapy with lesbian, gay, and bisexual clients.* Washington, DC: American Psychological Association.

Siegel, R. J., & Cole, E. (1991). *Jewish women in therapy: Seen but not heard.* New York: Harrington Park Press.

Sue, D. W., & Sue, D. (1990). *Counseling the culturally different: Theory and practice,* 2nd ed. New York: Wiley.

## MUSIC OF RESTORATION AND TRANSFORMATION (TAPES & CDs)

Bloom, Luka. (1992). *Acoustic motorbike.* Reprise. Available on the World Wide Web: http://www.lukabloom.com. (An evolved man.)

Das, Krishna. (1999). *Live on earth.* TriLoka. Available on the World Wide Web: http://www.krishnadas.com. (Energetic jazz-tinged chanting—great for yoga or cleaning the house.)

Lyman, B. J. (1996). *Do or die.* To order, email drbjlyman@home.com. (Straight-ahead rock and roll for transformation.)

Mitchell, J. (1998). *Taming the tiger.* Reprise. Available at most record stores and online music sources. (The master of women's self-reflective music.)

Khan, Nusrat Fateh Ali, & Brook, M. (1995). *Night song.* Real World. Available on the World Wide Web: http://www.realworld.on.net/index/flash.html. (The Pavarotti of Asia singing devotional music.)

Suonio, Sana Kurki (1988). *Musta.* Northside. Available on the World Wide Web: http://www.noside.com. (She sings haunting lyrical vocals old and new from Finland.)

Williamson, Cris (1975). *The changer and the changed.* Olivia. Available on the World Wide Web: http://www.cwilliamson.com. (Rousing women's music—good for feeling hopeful but may only work if it is new for you.)

*Women of Spirit* (1998). Putomayo World Music. Available at most record stores and online music sources. (A collection of lively songs from women around the world.)

## PSYCHOLOGY OF WOMEN

Apter, T. (1995). *Secret paths: Women in the new midlife.* New York: Norton.

Apter, T., & Josselson, R. (1998). *Best friends: The pleasures and perils of girls' and women's friendships.* New York: Three Rivers Press.

Brown, L. M., & Gilligan, C. (1992). *Meeting at the crossroads: Women's psychology and girls' development.* New York: Random House.

Brown, L. S., & Root, M. P. P. (1990). *Diversity and complexity in feminist therapy.* New York: Harrington Park.

Chrisler, J. C., Golden, C., & Rozee, P. D. (1999). *Lectures on the psychology of women.* Boston, MA: McGraw Hill.

*The Feminist Psychologist.* Newsletter of the Society for the Psychology of Women, Division 35 of the American Psychological Association. To subscribe, email: div35apa@apa.org.

Gilligan, C. (1982). *In a different voice.* Cambridge, MA: Harvard University Press.

Hancock, E. (1989). *The girl within.* New York: Fawcett Columbine.

Jordan, J. V., Kaplan, A. G., Miller, J. B., Stiver, I. P., & Surrey, J. L. (Eds.). *Women's growth in connection: Writings from the Stone Center.* New York: Guilford.

Jordan, J. V. (1997). *Women's growth in diversity: More writings from the Stone Center.* New York: Guilford.

Josselson, R. (1996). *Revising herself: The story of women's identity from college to midlife.* New York: Oxford University Press.

Kaschak, E. (1992). *Engendered lives: A new psychology of women's experience.* New York: Basic Books.

Lerner, H. G. (1985). *The dance of anger: A woman's guide to changing the patterns of intimate relationships.* New York: Harper & Row.

Lerner, H. G. (1988). *Women in therapy.* New York: Jason Aronson.

Lott, D. A. (1999). *In session: The bond between women and their therapists.* New York: Freeman.

*Psychology of Women Quarterly.* Journal of Division 35 of the American Psychological Association. To subscribe, email: div35@apa.org.

*Women and Therapy: A feminist quarterly.* To subscribe, visit their website on the World Wide Web: http://www.haworthpressinc.com.

Worrell, J., & Johnson, N. G. (1999). *Shaping the future of feminist psychology: Education, research, and practice.* Washington, DC: American Psychological Association.

Worrell, J., & Remer, P. (1992). *Feminist perspectives in therapy: An empowerment model.* New York: Wiley.

## RELAXATION

Gawain, S. *Creative Visualization.* [audiotape and CD]. Mill Valley, CA: Whatever Publishing, Inc. Available on the World Wide Web: http://www.shaktigawain.com.

Halpern, S. (1984). *Sleep soundly.* [CD]. Inner Peace Music. Available on the World Wide Web: http://www.stevenhalpern.com.

Miller, E. E., & Halpern, S. (1980). *Letting go of stress.* [audiotape and CD]. Belmont, CA: Halpern Sounds. Available on the World Wide Web: http://www.docmiller.com.

Simonds, S. L. (1995). *Sleep tips.* Counseling and Testing Services Self Help Website. Washington State University, Pullman, WA. On the World Wide Web: http://www.counsel.wsu.edu/csweb/sleep.htm.

Simonds, S. L. (1995). *Tips for relaxing.* Counseling and Testing Services Self Help Website. Washington State University, Pullman, WA. On the World Wide Web: http://www.counsel.wsu.edu/csweb/relax.htm.

## SEXUALITY

Friday, N. (1998). *My secret garden: Women's sexual fantasies.* New York: Pocket Books.

Heiman, J., & LoPiccolo, J. (1992). *Becoming orgasmic: A sexual and personal growth program for women.* New York: Simon & Schuster.

Maltz, W. (2001). *The sexual healing journey: A guide for survivors of sexual abuse.* New York: Quill.

Newman, E. (1999). *The whole lesbian sex book: A guide for all of us.* San Francisco: Cleis.

Schwartz, P., & Lever, J. (2000). *The great sex weekend: A 48-hour guide to rekindling sparks for bold, busy, or bored lovers, includes a 24-hour plan for the really busy.* New York: Perigee.

## TRADITIONAL CHINESE MEDICINE

Reid, D. (1994). *The complete book of Chinese health & healing.* Boston, MA: Shambhala Publications, Inc.

Tierra, M. (1998). *The way of Chinese herbs.* New York: Pocket Books.

*Traditional Chinese Medicine World.* A newsletter for practitioners and the general public. Its mission is to serve as the source for authentic information on health and healing with TCM. For further information, visit their website on the World Wide Web: http://www.tcmworld.org.

## WOMEN'S HEALTH

### GENERAL

Boston Women's Health Collective (1998). *Our bodies, ourselves for the new century: A book by and for women.* New York: Simon and Schuster.

Domar, A. D., & Dreher, H. (1997). *Healing mind, healthy woman: Using the mind-body connection to manage stress and take control of your life.* New York: HarperCollins. (Good sections on infertility, PMS, and menopause.)

*The Network News.* Newsletter of the National Women's Health Network. To subscribe, visit their website on the World Wide Web: http://www.womenshealthnetwork.org.

Northrup, C. (1998). *Women's bodies, women's wisdom: The complete guide to women's health and wellbeing.* New York: Bantam.

Sichel, D., & Driscoll, J. W. (1999). *Women's moods: What every woman must know about hormones, the brain, and emotional health.* New York: William Morrow.

## Abortion

De Puy, C., & Dovitch, D. (1997). *The healing choice: Your guide to emotional recovery after an abortion.* New York: Simon & Schuster Trade.

## Fertility, Pregnancy, and Postpartum

Kleinman, K. R., & Raskin, V. D. (1994). *This isn't what I expected: Overcoming postpartum depression.* New York: Bantam.

Kohn, I., Wilkins, I., & Perry-Moffit, L. (2000). *A silent sorrow: Pregnancy loss—guidance and support for you and your family.* New York: Routledge.

Paynbe, N. B., & Richardson, B. L. (1998). *The whole person fertility program: A revolutionary mind-body process to help you conceive.* New York: Three Rivers Press.

Placksin, S. (2000). *Mothering the new mother: Women's feelings and needs after childbirth a support and resource guide.* New York: Newmarket Press.

Wesson, N. (1997). *Natural mothering: A guide to holistic therapies for pregnancy, birth and early childhood.* Rochester, VT: Inner Traditions International, Limited.

Wesson, N. (1999). *Enhancing fertility naturally: Holistic therapies for a successful pregnancy.* Rochester, VT: Inner Traditions International, Limited.

## Menopause

Crawford, A. M. (1999). *The herbal menopause book.* Freedom, CA: The Crossing Press.

Lark, S. (1990). *The menopause self help book: A woman's guide to feeling wonderful for the second half of her life.* Berkeley, CA: Ten Speed Press.

Lark, S. (1995). *The estrogen decision self help book: A complete guide for relief of menopausal symptoms through hormonal replacement and therapy.* Berkeley, CA: Ten Speed Press.

Laux, M., & Conrad, C. (1997). *Natural woman, natural menopause.* New York: Harper Perennial.

Lieberman, S. (2000). *Get off the menopause roller coaster: Natural solutions for mood swings, hot flashes, fatigue, anxiety, depression & other symptoms.* New York: Avery.

National Women's Health Network (2000). *Taking hormones & women's health: Choices, risks, and benefits.* Washington, DC: National Women's Health Network. Available on the World Wide Web: http://www.womenshealthnetwork.org.

Northrup, C. (2001). *The wisdom of menopause: Creating physical and emotional health and healing during the change.* New York: Bantam Books.

## MENSTRUATION

Lark, S. (2000). *Fibroid tumors & endometriosis self help book.* Berkeley, CA: Celestial Arts. (Also good information about fertility issues.)

Lark, S. (1996). *Heavy menstrual flow and anemia self help book: Effective solutions for premenopause, bleeding due to fibroid tumors, hormonal imbalance.* Berkeley, CA: Ten Speed Press.

Lark, S. (1995). *Menstrual cramps self help book: Effective solutions for pain and discomfort due to menstrual cramps and PMS.* Berkeley, CA: Ten Speed Press.

Lark, S. (1997). *PMS Self Help Book.* Berkeley, CA: Celestial Arts.

Further resources and updates available at the author's website on the World Wide Web: http://www.susansimondsonline.com.

# References

Ablon, J. S., & Jones, E. E. (1999). Psychotherapy process in the National Institute of Mental Health Treatment of Depression Collaborative Research Process. *Journal of Consulting and Clinical Psychology, 67,* 64–74.

Abrahamson, D. J. (1999). Outcomes, guidelines, and manuals: On leading horses to water. *Clinical Psychology: Science and Practice, 6* (4), 467–471.

Abramson, L. Y., Metalsky, G. L., & Alloy, L. B. (1989). Hopelessness depression: A theory-based subtype of depression. *Psychological Review, 96,* 358–372.

Ackerman, R. J. (1999). An interactional approach for pharmacopsychologists and psychologists: Gender concerns. *Journal of Clinical Psychology in Medical Settings, 6* (1), 39–61.

Addis, M. E., Wade, W. A., & Hatgis, C. (1999). Barriers to dissemination of evidence-based practices: Addressing practitioners' concerns about manual-based psychotherapies. *Clinical Psychology: Science and Practice, 6* (4), 431–433.

Agency for Health Care Policy and Research (1993a). Clinical practice guideline: Depression in primary care. Vol. 1. *Detection and diagnosis* (AHCPR Publication 93-0550). Washington, DC: U.S. Government Printing Office.

Agency for Health Care Policy and Research (1993b). Clinical practice guideline: Depression in primary care. Vol. 2. *Treatment of Major Depression* (AHCPR Publication 93-0551). Washington, DC: U.S. Government Printing Office.

American Psychiatric Association (1994). *Diagnostic and statistical manual of mental disorders* (4th ed.). Washington, DC: American Psychiatric Press.

American Psychological Association (2000, August 21). *What you should know about women and depression.* Washington, DC: Author. Retrieved September 15, 2000, from the World Wide Web: http://www.apa.org/publicinfo/depress.html

Amsterdam, J., Garcia-Espana, F., Fawcett, J., Quitkin, F., Reimherr, F., Rosenbaum, J., & Beasley, C. (1999). Fluoxetine efficacy in menopausal women with and without estrogen replacement. *Journal of Affective Disorder, 55* (1), 11–17.

Angst, J. (1986). The course of affective disorders. *Psychopathology, 19,* 47–52.

Antonuccio, D. O., Danton, W. G., & DeNelsky, G. Y. (1995). Psychotherapy versus medication for depression: Challenging the conventional wisdom with data. *Professional Psychology: Research and Practice, 26* (6), 574–585.

Apter, T. (1995). *Secret paths: Women in the new midlife.* New York: Norton.

Apter, T., & Josselson, R. (1998). *Best friends: The pleasures and perils of girls' and women's friendships.* New York: Three Rivers Press.

Asay, T. P., & Lambert, M. J. (1999). The empirical case for the common factors in therapy. In M. A. Hubble, B. L. Duncan, & S. D. Miller (Eds.), *The heart and soul of change: What works in therapy* (pp. 23–55). Washington, DC: American Psychological Association.

Aube, J., Fichman, L., Saltaris, C., & Koestner, R. (2000). Gender differences in adolescent depressive symptomatology: Towards and integrated socio-developmental model. *Journal of Social & Clinical Psychology, 19* (3), 297–313.

Austin, L. (2000). *What's holding you back? 8 critical choices for women's success.* New York: Basic Books.

Babyak, M., Blumenthal, J. A., Herman, S., Khatri, P., Doraiswamy, M., Moore, K., Craighead, W. E., Baldewicz, T. T., & Krishan, K. R. (2000). Exercise treatment for major depression: Maintenance of therapeutic benefit at 10 months. *Psychosomatic Medicine, 62* (5), 633–638.

Bachelor, A., & Horvath, A. (1999). The therapeutic relationship. In M. A. Hubble, B. L. Duncan, & S. D. Miller (Eds.), *The heart and soul of change: What works in therapy* (pp. 133–178). Washington, DC: American Psychological Association.

Bancroft, J., Rennic, D., & Warner, P. (1994). Vulnerability to premenstrual mood change: The relevance of a past history of depressive disorder. *Psychosomatic Medicine, 56,* 225–231.

Barnett, R. C., Marshall, N. L., & Singer, J. D. (1992). Job experiences over time, multiple roles, and women's mental health: A longitudinal study. *Journal of Personality and Social Psychology, 62,* 634–644.

Beatty, C. A. (1996). The stress of managerial and professional women: Is the price too high? *Journal of Organizational Behavior, 17* (3), 233–251.

Beck, A. T., & Greenberg, R. L. (1974). Cognitive therapy with depressed women. In V. Franks & V. Burtle (Eds.), *Women in therapy: New psychotherapies for a changing society* (pp. 113–131). New York: Brunner Mazel.

Beck, A. T., Rush, A. J., Shaw, B. F., & Emery, G. (1980). *Cognitive therapy of depression.* New York: Guilford.

Belenky, M. F., Clinchy, B. M., Goldberger, N. R., & Tarule, J. M. (1986). *Women's ways of knowing: The development of self, voice, and mind.* New York: Basic Books, Inc.

Belle, D. (1982). The impact of poverty on social networks and supports. *Marriage and Family Review, 5,* 89–103.

Beutler, L. E., Machado, P. P. P., & Neufeldt, S. A. (1994). Therapist variables. In A. E. Bergin & S. L. Garfield (Eds.), *Handbook of psychotherapy and behavior change* (4th ed., pp. 229–269). New York: Wiley.

Bifulco, A., & Moran, P. (1998). *Wednesday's child: Research into women's experience of neglect and abuse in childhood and adult depression.* New York: Routledge.

Biggs, M. M., & Rush, A. J. (1999). Cognitive and behavioral therapies alone or combined with antidepressant medication in the treatment of depression. In D. S. Janowsky (Ed.), *Psychotherapy indications and outcomes* (pp. 121–172). Washington, DC: American Psychiatric Press.

Bird, C. (1999). Gender, household labor, and psychological distress: The impact of the amount and division of housework. *Journal of Health & Social Behavior, 40,* 32–45.

Blackburn, I. M., Eunson, K. M., & Bishop, S. (1986). A two-year naturalistic follow-up of depressed patients treated with cognitive therapy, pharmacology, and a combination of both. *Journal of Affective Disorders, 10,* 67–75.

Blackburn, I. M., & Moore, R. G. (1997). Controlled acute and follow-up trial of cognitive therapy and pharmacotherapy in out-patients with recurrent depression. *British Journal of Psychiatry, 171,* 328–334.

Blatt, S. J. (1995). The destructiveness of perfectionism: Implications for the treatment of depression. *American Psychologist, 50,* 1003–1020.

Blatt, S. J., Quinlan, D. M., Pilkonis, P. A., & Shea, M. T. (1995). Impact of perfectionism and need for approval on the brief treatment of depression. *Journal of Consulting and Clinical Psychology, 63,* 125–132.

Blatt, S. J., Sanislow, C. A., Zuroff, D. C., & Pilkonis, P. A. (1996). Characteristics of effective therapists: Further analyses of data from the National Institute of Mental Health Treatment of Depression Collaborative Research Program. *Journal of Consulting and Clinical Psychology, 64,* 1276–1284.

Blatt, S. J., Zuroff, D. C., Quinlan, D. M., & Pilkonis, P. A. (1996). Interpersonal factors in brief treatment of depression: Further analysis of the National Institute of Mental Health Treatment of Depression Collaborative Research Program. *Journal of Consulting and Clinical Psychology, 64,* 162–171.

Blazer, D. G. (1994). Epidemiology of late life depression. In L. S. Schneider, C. F. Reynolds III, B. D. Lebowitz, & A. J. Friedhoff (Eds.), *Diagnosis and treatment of depression in late life* (pp. 9–19). Washington, DC: American Psychiatric Press.

Blazer, D., George, L. K., Landerman, R., Pennybacker, M., Melville, M. L., Woodbury, M., Manton, K. G., Jordan, K., & Locke, B. (1985). Psychiatric disorders: A rural/urban comparison. *Archives of General Psychiatry, 42,* 651–656.

Blazer, D. G., Kessler, R. C., McGonagle, K. A., & Swartz, M. S. (1994). The prevalence and distribution of major depression in a national community sample: The national comorbidity survey. *American Journal of Psychiatry, 151,* 979–986.

Brabeck, M., & Brown, L. (1997). Feminist theory and psychological practice. In J. Worrell & N. G. Johnson (Eds.), *Shaping the future of feminist psychology: Education, research, and practice* (pp. 15–36). Washington, DC: American Psychological Association.

Bradford, J., Ryan, C., & Rothblum, E. D. (1994). National Lesbian Health Care Survey: Implications for mental health care. *Journal of Consulting and Clinical Psychology, 62,* 228–242.

Brems, C. (1995). Women and depression: A comprehensive analysis. In E. E. Beckham & W. R. Leber (Eds.), *Handbook of depression* (pp. 539–568). New York: Guilford.

Briere, J. (1989). *Therapy for adults molested as children: Beyond survival.* New York: Springer Publishing.

Bromberger, J. T., & Matthews, K. A. (1996a). A "feminine" model of vulnerability to depressive symptoms: A longitudinal investigation of middle-aged women. *Journal of Personality and Social Psychology, 70* (3), 591–598.

Bromberger, J. T., & Matthews, K. A. (1996b). A longitudinal study of the effects of pessimism, trait anxiety, and life stress on depressive symptoms in middle-aged women. *Psychology & Aging, 11* (2), 207–213.

Brown, G. W., & Moran, P. M. (1997). Single mothers, poverty, and depression. *Psychological Medicine, 27,* 21–33.

Brown, L. M., & Gilligan, C. (1992). *Meeting at the crossroads: Women's psychology and girls' development.* New York: Random House.

Brown, L. S. (1994). *Subversive dialogues: Theory in feminist practice.* New York: Basic Books.

Bruce, M. L., Takeuchi, D. T., & Leaf, P. J. (1991). Poverty and psychiatric status: Longitudinal evidence from the New Haven Epidemiological Catchment Area Study. *Archives of General Psychiatry, 48,* 470–474.

Burns, D. D., & Nolen-Hoeksema, S. (1992). Therapeutic empathy and recovery from depression in cognitive-behavioral therapy: A structural equation model. *Journal of Consulting and Clinical Psychology, 60* (3), 441–449.

Burt, V. K., Altshuler, L. L., & Rasgon, N. (1998). Depressive symptoms in the perimenopause: Prevalence, assessment, and guidelines for treatment. *Harvard Review of Psychiatry, 6* (3), 121–132.

Bushman, B. J., Baumeister, R. F., & Stack, A. D. (1999). Catharsis, aggression, and persuasive influence: Self-fulfilling or self-defeating prophecies. *Journal of Personality and Social Psychology, 76* (3), 367–376.

Butler, L. D., & Nolen-Hoeksema, S. (1994). Gender differences in responses to depressed mood in a college sample. *Sex Roles, 30,* 331–346.

Byrne, C. A., Resnick, H. S., Kilpatrick, D. G., Best, C. L., & Saunders, B. E. (1999). The socioeconomic impact of interpersonal violence on women. *Journal of Consulting and Clinical Psychology, 67,* 362–366.

Canetto, S. S. (1995). Suicidal women: Prevention and intervention strategies. In S. S. Canetto & D. Lester (Eds.), *Women and suicidal behavior* (pp. 237–255). New York: Springer Publishing.

Canetto, S. S., & Lester, D. (1995). The epidemiology of women's suicidal behavior. In S. S. Canetto & D. Lester (Eds.), *Women and suicidal behavior* (pp. 35–57). New York: Springer Publishing.

Caplan, P. J. (2001). Chronic fatigue syndrome: A first-person story. *Women & Therapy, 23,* 23–43.

Caplan, P. J., McCurdy-Meyers, J., & Gans, M. (1992). Should "premenstrual syndrome" be called a psychiatric abnormality? *Feminism & Psychology, 2* (1), 27–44.

Carr, D. (1997). The fulfillment of career dreams at midlife: Does it matter for women's mental health? *Journal of Health & Social Behavior, 38* (4), 331–344.

Carroll, L., Gilroy, P. J., & Murra, J. (1999). The moral imperative: Self-care for women psychotherapists. *Women and Therapy, 22* (2), 133–143.

Cass, V. C. (1979). Homosexual identity formation: A theoretical model. *Journal of Homosexuality, 4,* 219–235.

Castonguay, L. G., Goldfried, M. R., Wiser, S., Raue, P. J., & Hayes, A. B. (1996). Predicting the effect of cognitive therapy for depression: A study of unique and common factors. *Journal of Consulting and Clinical Psychology, 64* (3), 497–504.

Chin, J. L. (1994). Psychodynamic approaches. In L. Comas-Diaz & B. Greene (Eds.), *Women of color: Integrating ethnic and gender identities in psychotherapy* (pp. 94–122). New York: Guilford.

Chodorow, N. J. (1978). *The reproduction of mothering: Psychoanalysis and the sociology of gender.* Berkeley, CA: University of California Press.

Chrisler, J. C. (2001). How can feminist therapies support women with autoimmune disorders? *Women & Therapy, 23,* 7–22.

Clark, R., Anderson, N. B., Clark, V. R., & Williams, D. R. (1999). Racism as a stressor for African Americans: A biopsychosocial model. *American Psychologist, 54* (1), 805–816.

Comas-Diaz, L. (1994). An integrative approach. In L. Comas-Diaz & B. Greene (Eds.), *Women of color: Integrating ethnic and gender identities in psychotherapy* (pp. 287–318). New York: Guilford.

Comas-Diaz, L., & Greene, B. (1994). Overview: Gender and ethnicity in the healing process. In L. Comas-Diaz & B. Greene (Eds.), *Women of color: Integrating ethnic and gender identities in psychotherapy* (pp. 85–112). New York: Guilford.

Comas-Diaz, L., & Jacobsen, F. M. (1995). Psychopharmacology for women of color: An empowering approach. In J. A. Hamilton, M. F. Jensvold, E. D. Rothblum, & E. Cole (Eds.), *Psychopharmacology from a feminist perspective* (pp. 85–112). New York: Harrington Press.

Conte, H. R., Plutchik, R., Wild, K. V., & Karasu, T. B. (1986). Combined psychotherapy and pharmacotherapy for depression: A systematic analysis of the evidence. *Archives of General Psychiatry, 43* (5), 471–479.

Cooper-Hilbert, B. (1998). *Infertility and involuntary childlessness: Helping couples cope.* New York: Norton.

Courtois, C. A. (1988). *Healing the incest wound: Adult survivors in therapy.* New York: Norton.

Courtois, C. A. (1999). *Recollections of sexual abuse: Treatment principles and guidelines.* New York: Norton.

Cox, D. L., Stabb, S. D., & Bruckner, K. H. (1999). *Women's anger: Clinical and developmental perspectives.* New York: Brunner Mazel.

Coyne, J. C., Pepper, C. M., & Flynn, H. (1999). Significance of prior episodes of depression in two patient populations. *Journal of Consulting and Clinical Psychology, 67,* 76–81.

Craig, A., & Pitts, F. (1968). Suicide by physicians. *Diseases of the Nervous System, 29,* 763–772.

Craighead, W. E., Craighead, L. W., & Ilardi, S. S. (1998). Psychosocial treatments for major depressive disorder. In P. E. Nathan, & J. M. Gorman (Eds.), *A guide to treatments that work,* (pp. 226–239). New York: Oxford University Press.

Cross, W. E., Jr. (1971). The Negro-to-Black conversion experience: Towards a psychology of Black liberation. *Black World, 20,* 13–27.

Cross-National Collaborative Group. (1992). The changing rate of major depression: Cross-national comparisons. *Journal of the American Medical Association, 268,* 3098–3105.

Culbertson, F. M. (1997). Depression and gender: An international review. *American Psychologist, 52,* 25–31.

Danquah, M. N. (1998). *Willow weep for me: A Black woman's journey through depression.* New York: Norton.

Davis, L., & Yonkers, K. A. (1997). Diagnosis and treatment of premenstrual dysphoric disorder. *International Journal of Psychiatry in Clinical Practice, 1,* 149–156.

DeBarona, M. S., & Dutton, M. A. (1997). Feminist perspectives on assessment. In J. Worrell & N. G. Johnson (Eds.), *Shaping the future of feminist psychology: Education, research, and practice* (pp. 37–56). Washington, DC: American Psychological Association.

DeBattista, C., Smith, D. L., & Schatzberg, A. F. (1999). Modulation of monoamine neurotransmitters by estrogen: Clinical implications. In E. Leibenluft (Ed.), *Gender differences in mood and anxiety disorders: From bench to bedside* (pp. 137–160). Washington, DC: American Psychiatric Press.

DeRubeis, R. J., Gelfand, L. A., Tang, T. Z., & Simons, A. D. (1999). Medications versus cognitive behavior therapy for severely depressed outpatients: Mega-analysis of four randomized comparisons. *American Journal of Psychiatry, 156,* 1007–1013.

Domar, A. D., & Dreher, H. (1997). *Healing mind, healthy woman: Using the mind-body connection to manage stress and take control of your life.* New York: HarperCollins.

Downing, N. E., & Roush, K. L. (1985). From passive acceptance to active commitment: A model of feminist identity development. *The Counseling Psychologist, 13* (4), 695–709.

Duncan, B., Miller, S., & Sparks, J. (2000a, March/April). Exposing the mythmakers. *The Family Therapy Networker,* pp. 24–34.

Duncan, B., Miller, S., & Sparks, J. (2000b, November/December). SSRIs: Client's choice—Author's response. *The Family Therapy Networker,* p. 9.

Dunner, D. L., Schmaling, K. B., Hendrickson, H., Becker, J., Lehman, A., & Bea, C. (1996). Cognitive therapy versus fluoxetine in the treatment of dysthymic disorder. *Depression, 4,* 34–41.

Earle, J. R., Smith, M. H., Harris, C. T., & Longino, C. F. (1998). Women, marital status, and symptoms of depression in a midlife national sample. *Journal of Women & Aging, 10* (1), 41.

Eichenbaum, L., & Orbach, S. (1989). *Between women.* New York: Penguin Books.

Elkin, I., Gibbons, R. D., Shea, M. T., Sotsky, S. M., Watkins, J. T., Pilkonis, P. A., & Hedeker, D. (1995). Initial severity and differential treatment outcome in the National Institute of Mental Health Treatment of Depression Collaborative Research Program. *Journal of Consulting and Clinical Psychology, 63,* 841–847.

Elkin, I., Shea, T., Watkins, J. T., Imber, S. D., Sotsky, S. M., Collins, J. F., Glass, D. R., Pilkonis, P. A., Leber, W. R., Docherty, J. P., Fiester, S. J., & Parloff, M. B. (1989). National Institute of Mental Health Treatment of Depression Collaborative Research Program. *Archives of General Psychiatry, 46,* 971–982.

Fava, G. A., Grandi, S., Zielezny, M., Rafanelli, C., & Canestari, R. (1996). Four-year outcome for cognitive behavioral treatment of residual symptoms of major depression. *American Journal of Psychiatry, 153* (7), 945–947.

Figert, A. E. (1996). *Women and the ownership of PMS: The structuring of a psychiatric disorder.* New York: Aldine De Gruyter.

Fitzgerald, L. (1993). Sexual harassment: Violence against women in the workplace. *American Psychologist, 48,* 1070–1076.

Fletcher, J. K. (1999). *Disappearing acts.* Cambridge, MA: MIT Press.

Fodor, I. G. (1988). Cognitive behavior therapy: Evaluation of theory and practice for addressing women's issues. In M. A. Dutton-Douglas & L. E. Walker (Eds.), *Feminist psychotherapies: Integration of therapeutic and feminist systems* (pp. 91–117). Norwood, NJ: Ablex.

Fopma-Loy, J. (1988). The prevalence and phenomenology of depression in elderly women: A review of the literature. *Archives of Psychiatric Nursing, 2,* 74–80.

Ford, G. R., & Elliott, T. R. (1999). Clinicians' reactions to depressive behavior and ill health. *Professional Psychology: Research and Practice, 30* (3), 269–274.

Frank, E., & Dingle, A. D. (1999). Self-reported depression and suicide attempts among U.S. women physicians. *American Journal of Psychiatry, 156* (12), 1887–1894.

Frank, E., Kupfer, D. J., Perel, J. M., Cornes, C., Jarrett, D. B., Mallinger, A. G., Thase, M. E., McEachran, A. B., & Grochocinski, V. J. (1990). Three-year outcomes for maintenance therapies in recurrent depression. *American Journal of Psychiatry, 47,* 1093–1099.

Frank, E., Kupfer, D. J., Wagner, E. F., McEachran, A. B., & Cornes, C. (1991). Efficacy of interpersonal psychotherapy as maintenance treatment of recurrent depression. *Archives of General Psychiatry, 48,* 1053–1059.

Frederickson, B. L. (2000). Cultivating positive emotions to optimize health and well-being. *Prevention and Treatment, 3,* 1–28.

Freedman, J., & Combs, G. (1996). *Narrative therapy: The social construction of preferred realities.* New York: Norton.

Galinsky, E., & Bond, J. (1996). The experiences of mothers and fathers in the U.S. labor force. In C. Costello & B. Krimgold (Eds.), *The American woman 1996–1997: Where we stand* (pp. 102–127). New York: Norton.

Gatz, M. (2000). Variations in depression in late life. In S. H. Qualls & N. Abeles (Eds.), *Psychology and the aging revolution: How we adapt to longer life* (pp. 239–254). Washington, DC: American Psychological Association.

Gergen, K. (1985). The social constructivist movement in modern psychology. *American Psychologist, 40,* 266–275.

Gilbert, L. A., & Scher, M. (1999). *Gender and sex in counseling and psychotherapy.* Boston: Allyn and Bacon.

Gilligan, C. (1982). *In a different voice: Psychological theory and women's development.* Cambridge, MA: Harvard University Press.

Gilroy, P., Carroll, L., & Murra, J. (1998). Does depression affect clinical practice: A national survey of women psychotherapists. Poster session presented at the annual meeting of the American Psychiatric Association, San Francisco, CA.

Godfried, M. R. (1999). The pursuit of consensus in psychotherapy research and practice. *Clinical Psychology: Science and Practice, 6,* (4), 462–466.

Gonzalez, L., Lewinsohn, P. M., & Clarke, G. (1985). Longitudinal follow-up of unipolar depressives: An investigation of predictors of relapse. *Journal of Consulting and Clinical Psychology, 53,* 461–467.

Gordon, K. C., & Baucom, D. H. (1999). A multitheoretical intervention for promoting recovery from extramarital affairs. *Clinical Psychology: Science & Practice, 6* (4), 382–399.

Gottman, J. M. (1999). *The marriage clinic: A scientifically based marital therapy*. New York: Norton.

Greenberg, L. S., & Johnson, S. M. (1988). *Emotionally focused therapy for couples*. New York: Guilford.

Greene, B. (1994). Ethnic-minority lesbians and gay men: Mental health and treatment issues. *Journal of Consulting and Clinical Psychology, 62*, 243–251.

Greene, B. (1996). African-American women: Considering diverse identities and societal barriers in psychotherapy. *Annals of the New York Academy of Sciences, 789*, 191–209.

Halbreich, U., & Lumley, L. A. (1993). The multiple interactional biological processes that might lead to depression and gender differences in its appearance. *Journal of Affective Disorders, 29*, 129–173.

Hamilton, J., Alagna, S., King, L., & Lloyd, C. (1987). The emotional consequences of gender-based abuse in the workplace: New counseling programs for sex discriminations. *Women and Therapy, 6*, 155–182.

Hamilton, J. A., & Gallant, S. J. (1990). Debate on late luteal phase dysphoric disorder. *American Journal of Psychiatry, 147* (8), 1106.

Hamilton, J. A., Grant, M., & Jensvold, M. F. (1996). Sex and treatment of depressions: When does it matter. In M. F. Jensvold, U. Halbreich, & J. A. Hamilton (Eds.), *Psychopharmacology and women: Sex, gender, and hormones* (pp. 241–260). Washington, DC: American Psychiatric Press.

Hamilton, J. A., & Jensvold, M. F. (1995). Sex and gender as critical variables in feminist psychopharmacology research and pharmacology. In J. A. Hamilton, M. F. Jensvold, E. D. Rothblum, & E. Cole (Eds.), *Psychopharmacology from a feminist perspective* (pp. 9–30). New York: Harrington Press.

Hamilton, J. A., & Yonkers, K. A. (1996). Sex differences in pharmacokinetics of psychotropic medications, Part I: Physiological basis for effects. In M. F. Jensvold, U. Halbreich, & J. A. Hamilton (Eds.), *Psychopharmacology and women: Sex, gender, and hormones* (pp. 11–42). Washington, DC: American Psychiatric Press.

Hammen, C. (1997). *Depression*. East Sussex, UK: Taylor & Francis.

Hammen, C., Risha, H., & Daley, S. E. (2000). Depression and sensitization to stressors among young women as a function of childhood adversity. *Journal of Consulting & Clinical Psychology, 68* (5), 782–787.

Hancock, E. (1989). *The girl within*. New York: Fawcett Columbine.

Harter, S. (1999). *The construction of the self: A developmental perspective*. New York: Guilford.

Hauerstein, E. J., & Boyd, M. R. (1994). Depressive symptoms in young women of the Piedmont: Prevalence in rural women. *Women and Health, 21* (2/3), 105–123.

Hays, K. F. (1991). *Working it out: Using exercise in psychotherapy*. Washington, DC: American Psychological Association.

Helgeson, V. S., & Fritz, H. L. (1998). A theory of unmitigated communion. *Personality and Social Psychology Review, 2*, 173–183.

Helms, J. E. (1990). *Black and white racial identity: Theory, research, and practice*. Westport, CT: Greenwood.

Herman, J. L. (1992). *Trauma and recovery*. New York: Basic Books.

Hertzberg, J. F. (1990). Feminist psychotherapy and diversity: Treatment considerations from a self psychology perspective. In L. S. Brown & M. P. P. Root (Eds.), *Diversity and complexity in feminist therapy* (pp. 275–298). New York: Harrington Park.

Hirsch, S. R., Walsh, C., & Draper, R. (1983). The concept and efficacy of the treatment of parasuicide. *British Journal of Clinical Pharmacology, 15,* 189S–194S.

Hollon, S. D., & Beck, A. T. (1979). Cognitive therapy of depression. In C. P. Kendall & S. D. Hollon (Eds.), *Cognitive-behavioral interventions: Theory, research, and procedures* (pp. 153–204). New York: Academic Press.

Hooley, J. M., & Teasdale, J. D. (1989). Predictors of relapse in unipolar depressives: Expressed emotion, marital distress, and perceived criticism. *Journal of Abnormal Psychology, 98* (3), 229–235.

Ilardi, S. S., & Craighead, W. E. (1999). Rapid early response, cognitive modification, and nonspecific factors in cognitive behavior therapy for depression: A reply to Tang and DeRubeis. *Clinical Psychology: Science and Practice, 6* (3), 295–299.

Imber, S. D., Pilkonis, P. A., Sotsky, S. M., Elkin, I., Watkins, J. T., Collins, J. F., Shea, M. T., Leber, W. R., & Glass, D. R. (1990). Mode specific effects among three treatments for depression. *Journal of Consulting and Clinical Psychology, 58* (3), 352–359.

Iwamasa, G. Y., & Hilliard, K. M. (1999). Depression and anxiety among Asian American elders: A review of the literature. *Clinical Psychology Review, 19* (3), 343–357.

Jack, D. C. (1987). Silencing the self: The power of social imperatives. In R. Formanek & A. Gurian (Eds.), *Women and depression: A lifespan perspective* (pp. 161–181). New York: Springer Publishing.

Jack, D. C. (1991). *Silencing the self: Women and depression.* New York: HarperCollins.

Jack, D. C. (1999). Silencing the self: Inner dialogues and outer realities. In T. Joiner & J. C. Coyne (Eds.), *The interactional nature of depression* (pp. 221–246). Washington, DC: American Psychological Association.

Jackson, B. (1975). Black identity development. *Journal of Education Diversity, 2,* 19–25.

Janowsky, D. S., Halbreich, U., & Rausch, J. (1996). Association among ovarian hormones, other hormones, emotional disorders, and neurotransmitters. In M. F. Jensvold, U. Halbreich, & J. A. Hamilton (Eds.), *Psychopharmacology and women: Sex, gender, and hormones* (pp. 85–106). Washington, DC: American Psychiatric Press.

Jensvold, M. F. (1996). Nonpregnant reproductive-age women, Part I: The menstrual cycle and psychopharmacology. In M. F. Jensvold, U. Halbreich, & J. A. Hamilton (Eds.), *Psychopharmacology and women: Sex, gender, and hormones* (pp. 139–169). Washington, DC: American Psychiatric Press.

Jensvold, M. F., Halbreich, U., & Hamilton, J. A. (1996). Gender sensitive pharmacology: An overview. In M. F. Jensvold, U. Halbreich, & J. A. Hamilton (Eds.), *Psychopharmacology and women: Sex, gender, and hormones* (pp. 1–10). Washington, DC: American Psychiatric Press.

Johnson, S. M. (1996). *The practice of emotionally focused couples therapy: Creating connection.* New York: Brunner Mazel.

Joiner, T. E., Wonderlich, S. A., Metalsky, G. I., & Schmidt, N. B. (1995). Body dissatisfaction: A feature of bulimia, depression, or both? *Journal of Social and Clinical Psychology, 14,* 339–355.

Jones, E. E., & Pulos, S. M. (1993). Comparing the process in psychodynamic and cognitive-behavioral therapies. *Journal of Consulting and Clinical Psychology, 61,* 306–316.

Jordan, J. V. (1991). Empathy and self boundaries. In J. V. Jordan, A. G. Kaplan, J. B. Miller, I. P. Stiver, & J. L. Surrey (Eds.), *Women's growth in connection: Writings from the Stone Center* (pp. 67–80). New York: Guilford.

Jordan, J. V. (1997). *Women's growth in diversity: More writings from the Stone Center.* New York: Guilford.

Josselson, R. (1996). *Revising herself: The story of women's identity from college to midlife.* New York: Oxford University Press.

Judd, L. L., Paulus, M. J., Schettler, P. J., Akiskal, H. S., Endicott, J., Leon, A. C., Maser, J. D., Mueller, T., Solomon, D. A., & Keller, M. B. (2000). Does incomplete recovery from first lifetime major depressive episode herald a chronic course of illness? *American Journal of Psychiatry, 157* (9), 1501–1504.

Kabat-Zinn, J. (1990). *Full catastrophe living: Using the wisdom of your body and mind to face stress, pain, and illness.* New York: Delta.

Kabat-Zinn, J. (1994). *Wherever you go, there you are.* New York: Hyperion.

Kaplan, A. G. (1991a). Empathic communication in the psychotherapy relationship. In J. V. Jordan, A. G. Kaplan, J. B. Miller, I. P. Stiver, & J. L. Surrey (Eds.), *Women's growth in connection: Writings from the Stone Center* (pp. 44–50). New York: Guilford.

Kaplan, A. G. (1991b). The "self in relation": Implications for depression in women. In J. V. Jordan, A. G. Kaplan, J. B. Miller, I. P. Stiver, & J. L. Surrey (Eds.), *Women's growth in connection: Writings from the Stone Center* (pp. 206–222). New York: Guilford.

Kaplan, G., Roberts, R., Camacho, T., & Coyne, J. (1987). Psychosocial predictors of depression: Prospective evidence from the Human Population Laboratory Studies. *American Journal of Epidemiology, 125,* 206–220.

Karasu, T. B. (1990). *Psychotherapy of depression.* Northvale, NJ: Jason Aronson.

Karp, J. F., & Frank, E. (1995). Combination therapy and the depressed woman. *Depression, 3,* 91–98.

Kaschak, E. (1992). *Engendered lives: A new psychology of women's experience.* New York: Basic Books.

Katz, E. (1994). It's a question of dollars and cents: Prioritizing economic issues in women's treatment. In M. P. Mirkin (Ed.), *Women in context: Toward a feminist reconstruction of psychotherapy* (pp. 541–561). New York: Guilford.

Keller, M. B. (1985). Chronic and recurrent affective disorders: Incidence, course, and influencing factors. In A. Frances & R. Hales (Eds.), *Review of Psychiatry, 7,* Washington, DC: American Psychiatric Press.

Keller, M. B., McCullough, J. P., Klein, D. N., Arnow, B., Dunner, D. L., Gelenber, A. J., Markowitz, J. C., Nemeroff, C. B., Russell, J. M., Thase, M. E., Trivedi, M. H., & Zajecka, J. (2000). A comparison of nefazodone, the cognitive-behavioral analysis of psychotherapy, and their combination for the treatment of chronic depression. *The New England Journal of Medicine, 342* (20), 1462–1471.

Kendler, K. S., Karkowski, L. M., Corey, L. A., & Neale, M. C. (1998). Longitudinal population-based twin study of retrospectively reported premenstrual symptoms and lifetime major depression. *American Journal of Psychiatry, 155* (9), 1234–1240.

Kendler, K. S., Kessler, R. C., Neale, M. C., Heath, A. C., & Eaves, L. J. (1993). The prediction of major depression in women: Toward an integrated etiologic model. *American Journal of Psychiatry, 150* (8), 1139–1148.

Kendler, K. S., Kessler, R. C., Walters, M. S., MacLean, C., Neal, M. S., Heath, A. C., Phil, D., & Eaves, L. J. (1995). Stressful life events, genetic liability, and onset of an episode of major depression in women. *American Journal of Psychiatry, 152,* 833–842.

Kendler, K. S., Thornton, L. M., & Gardner, C. O. (2000). Stressful life events and previous episodes in the etiology of major depression in women: An evaluation of the "kindling" hypothesis. *American Journal of Psychiatry, 157* (8), 1243–1251.

Kerr, S. K., & Emerson, A. M. (in press). Depression, anxiety, and lesbians: A review of the literature. In R. Mathy & S. K. Kerr (Eds.), *Lesbian mental health: A reader for sex educators, counselors, and therapists.* Binghamton, NY: Haworth.

Kessler, R. C., McGonagle, K. A., Nelson, C. B., Hughes, M., Zhao, S., Eshlman, M. A., Wittchen, H. U., & Kendler, K. S. (1994). Sex and depression in the National Comorbidity Survey: II. Cohort effects. *Journal of Affective Disorders, 30,* 15–26.

Kestnbaum, J. D. (1984). Expectations for therapeutic growth: One factor in burn-out. *Social Casework: The Journal of Contemporary Social Work, 65,* 374–377.

Kim, J. E., & Moen, P. (2000). Retirement transitions, gender, and psychological well-being: A life-course, ecological model. Manuscript submitted for publication.

Kirschner, L., Genack, A., & Hauser, S. (1978). Effects of gender on short-term psychotherapy. *Psychotherapy: Theory, Research, and Practice, 15,* 158–167.

Klein, M. H., & Essex, M. J. (1995). Pregnant or depressed? The effect of overlap between symptoms of depression and somatic complaints of pregnancy rates of major depression in the second trimester. *Depression, 2,* 308–314.

Kleinman, A. (1989, May, 19). *Culture, suffering, and psychotherapy.* Paper presented at the conference "Psychotherapy in Diversity: Cross-cultural Treatment Issues," sponsored by the Harvard Medical School, Boston.

Klerman, G. L., Weissman, M. M., Rounsaville, B., & Chevron, E. S. (1984). *Interpersonal psychotherapy for depression.* New York: Basic Books.

Kohut, H. (1977). *The restoration of the self.* New York: International Universities Press.

Kornstein, S. G. (1997). Gender differences in depression: Implications for treatment. *Journal of Clinical Psychiatry, 58,* 12–18.

Kramer, P. D. (2000, October 1). Female troubles. *The New York Times Magazine,* 17–18.

Krupnick, J. L., Sotsky, S. M., Simmens, S., Moyer, J., Elkin, I., Watkins, J., & Pilkonis, P. A. (1996). The role of therapeutic alliance in psychotherapy and pharmacotherapy outcome: Findings in the National Institute of Mental Health Treatment of Depression Collaborative Research Program. *Journal of Consulting and Clinical Psychology, 64,* 532–539.

Kuhn, F. E., & Rackley, C. E. (1993). Coronary artery disease in women: Risk factors, evaluation, treatment, and prevention. *Archives of Internal Medicine, 153,* 2626–2636.

Kupfer, D. J., Frank, E., Perel, J. M., Cornes, C., Mallinger, A. G., Thase, M. E., McEachran, A. B., & Grochincinski, V. J. (1992). Five-year outcome for maintenance in recurrent depression. *Archives of General Psychiatry, 49,* 769–773.

LaFromboise, T. D., Berman, J. S., & Sohi, B. K. (1994). American Indian women. In L. Comas-Diaz & B. Greene (Eds.), *Women of color: Integrating ethnic and gender identities in psychotherapy* (pp. 30–71). New York: Guilford.

Lambert, M. J. (1992). Implications for outcome research for psychotherapy integration. In J. C. Norcross & M. R. Goldstein (Eds.), *Handbook of psychotherapy integration* (pp. 94–129). New York: Basic Books.

Lambert, M. J., & Bergin, A. E. (1994). The effectiveness of psychotherapy. In A. E. Bergin & S. L. Garfield (Eds.), *Handbook of psychotherapy and behavior change* (4th ed., pp. 143–189). New York: Wiley.

Leibenluft, E., Hardin, T. A., & Rosenthal, N. E. (1995). Gender differences in seasonal affective disorder. *Depression, 3,* 13–19.

Lerner, H. G. (1985). *The dance of anger: A woman's guide to changing the patterns of intimate relationships.* New York: Harper & Row.

Lerner, H. G. (1987). Female depression: Self-sacrifice and self-betrayal in relationships. In R. Formanek & A. Gurian (Eds.), *Women and depression: A lifespan perspective* (pp. 200–221). New York: Springer Publishing.

Lerner, H. G. (1988). *Women in therapy.* New York: Jason Aronson.

Levitan, R. D., Parikh, S. V., Lesage, A. D., Hegadoren, K. M., Adams, M., Kennedy, S. H., & Goering, P. N. (1998). Major depression in individuals with a history of childhood physical or sexual abuse: Relationship to neurovegetative features, mania, and gender. *American Journal of Psychiatry, 155,* 1746–1752.

Lewinsohn, P. M., & Gotlib, I. H. (1995). Behavioral theory and treatment of depression. In E. E. Beckham & W. R. Leber (Eds.), *Handbook of depression* (pp. 352–373). New York: Guilford.

Lewinsohn, P. M., Striegel-Moore, R. H., & Seeley, J. H. (2000). Epidemiology and nature course of eating disorders in young women from adolescence to young adulthood. *Journal of the American Academy of Child & Adolescent Psychiatry, 30* (10), 1284–1292.

Lewinsohn, P. M., Youngren, M. A., & Grosscup, S. J. (1979). Reinforcement and depression. In R. A. Depue (Ed.), *The psychobiology of depressive disorders: Implications for the effects of stress* (pp. 291–313). New York: Academic Press.

Lewinsohn, P. M., Zeiss, A. M., & Duncan, E. M. (1989). Probability of relapse after recovery from an episode of depression. *Journal of Abnormal Behavior, 98,* 107–116.

Lewis, S. Y. (1994). Cognitive-behavioral therapy. In L. Comas-Diaz & B. Greene (Eds.), *Women of color: Integrating ethnic and gender identities in psychotherapy* (pp. 223–238). New York: Guilford.

Lin, K-M., Poland, R. E., & Nakasaki, G. (Eds.). (1993). *Psychopharmacology and psychobiology of ethnicity.* Washington, DC: American Psychiatric Press.

Lippert, L. (1997). Women at midlife: Implications for theories of women's adult development. *Journal of Counseling & Development, 76,* 16–22.

Llewellyn, A. M., Stowe, Z. N., & Nemeroff, C. B. (1997). Depression during pregnancy and the puerperium. *Journal of Clinical Psychiatry, 58* (15), 26–32.

Lloyd, C. (1988). *Depression in professional women.* Unpublished manuscript.

Lott, D. A. (1999). *In session: The bond between women and their therapists.* New York: Freeman.

Magaletta, P. R., & Oliver, J. M. (1999). The hope construct, will, and ways: Their relations with self-efficacy, optimism, and general well-being. *Journal of Clinical Psychology, 55* (5), 439–551.

Mahoney, M. J., & Lyddon, W. J. (1988). Recent developments in cognitive approaches to counseling and psychotherapy. *The Counseling Psychologist, 16,* 190–234.

Manning, M. (1994). *Undercurrents: A life beneath the surface.* San Francisco: Harper Collins.

Markowitz, J. C., & Weissman, M. M. (1995). Interpersonal psychotherapy. In E. E. Beckham & W. R. Leber (Eds.), *Handbook of depression* (pp. 376–390). New York: Guilford.

Maslach, C. (1978). The client role in staff burnout. *Journal of Social Issues, 34,* 111–124.

Mazure, C. M. (1998). Life stressors as risk factors in depression. *Clinical psychology: Science and practice, 5,* 291–313.

McCann, I. L., & Pearlman, L. A. (1990). *Psychological trauma and the adult survivor: Theory, therapy, and transformation.* New York: Brunner Mazel.

McCarn, S. R., & Fassinger, R. E. (1996). Revisioning sexual minority identity formation: A new model of lesbian identity and its implications for counseling and research. *The Counseling Psychologist, 24* (3), 508–534.

McCullough, J. P. (2000). *Treatment for chronic depression: Cognitive behavioral analysis system of psychotherapy (CBASP).* New York: Guilford.

McCullough, J. P., Klein, D. N., Shea, M. T., & Miller, I. (1992, September). *Review of DSM–IV mood disorder data in the field trials.* Paper presented at the 100th Meeting of the American Psychological Association, Washington, DC.

McGrath, E., Keita, G. P., Strickland, B. R., & Russo, N. F. (1990). *Women and depression: Risk factors and treatment issues.* Washington, DC: American Psychological Association.

Meichenbaum, D. (1993). Changing conceptions of cognitive behavior modification: Retrospect and prospect. *Journal of Consulting and Clinical Psychology, 61* (2), 202–204.

Meyer, A. (1957). *Psychobiology: A science of man.* Springfield, IL: Charles C. Thomas.

Miller, A. (1981). *The drama of the gifted child.* New York: Basic Books.

Miller, J. B. (1976). *Toward a new psychology of women.* Boston: Beacon Press.

Miller, J. B. (1991a). The construction of anger in women and men. In J. V. Jordan, A. G. Kaplan, J. B. Miller, I. P. Stiver, & J. L. Surrey (Eds.), *Women's growth in connection: Writings from the Stone Center* (pp. 181–196). New York: Guilford.

Miller, J. B. (1991b). The development of women's sense of self. In J. V. Jordan, A. G. Kaplan, J. B. Miller, I. P. Stiver, & J. L. Surrey (Eds.), *Women's growth in connection: Writings from the Stone Center* (pp. 11–26). New York: Guilford.

Miller, J. B., Jordan, J., Stiver, I. P., Walker, M., Surrey, J., & Eldridge, N. S. (1999). Therapists' authenticity. *Work in Progress, 82.* Wellesley, MA: Stone Center.

Miller, J. B., & Stiver, I. P. (1997). *The healing connection: How women form relationships in therapy and in life.* Boston: Beacon.

Misri, S., & Kostaras, X. (2000). Reproductive psychiatry: An overview. *Medscape Psychiatry and Mental Health Treatment Updates.* Retrieved September 11, 2000, from the World Wide Web: http://www.medscape.com/Medscape/psychiatry/TreatmentUpdate/2000/tu02/ public/toc-tu02.html

Mueller, T. I., Leon, A. C., Keller, M. B., Solomon, D. A., Endicott, J., Coryell, W., Warshaw, M., & Maser, J. D. (1999). Recurrence after recovery from major depressive disorder during 15 years of observational follow-up. *American Journal of Psychiatry, 156,* 1000–1006.

Mulder, P. L., Kenkel, M. B., Shellenberger, S., Constantine, M. G., Streiegel, R., Sears, S. F., Jumper-Thurman, P., Kalodner, M., Danda, C. E., & Hager, A. (2000). *The behavioral health care needs of rural women.* [Report]. Washington, DC: American Psychological Association. Retrieved December 15, 2000, from the World Wide Web: http://www.apa.org/rural/ruralwomen.pdf

Mulrow, C. D., Williams, J. W., Trivedi, M., Chiquette, E., Aguilar, C., Cornell, J. E., Badget, R., Noel, P. H., Lawrence, V., Lee, S., Luther, M., Ramirez, G., Richardson, W. S., & Stamm, K. (February, 1999). *Treatment of depression: Newer pharmacotherapies.* Evidence Report/Technology Assessment Number 7. (AHCPR Publication No. 99-E014). Rockwell, MD: Department of Health and Human Services, Public Health Service, Agency for Health Care Policy and Research.

Myers, J. K., Weissman, M. M., Tishler, G. L., Holzer, C. E. III, Leaf, P. J., Orvaschel, H., Anthony, J. C., Boyd, J. H., Burke, J. D., Jr., Kramer, M., & Stoltzman, R. (1984). Six-month prevalence of psychiatric disorders in three communities: 1980 to 1982. *Archives of General Psychiatry, 41,* 959–967.

National Institutes of Health. (2000, April 4). *Hormone Replacement Study* [Fact Sheet]. Bethesda, MD: Author. Retrieved June 20, 2000, from the World Wide Web: http://www.nhlbi.nih.gov/whi/hrt.htm

National Institute of Mental Health. (1986). *Women's mental health: Agenda for research.* Washington, DC: U.S. Department of Health and Human Services.

National Institute of Mental Health. (2000, March 7). *Public alert on St. John's wort.* [Announcement]. Bethesda, MD: Author. Retrieved from the World Wide Web: http://www.nimh.hih.gov/events/stjohnwort.cfm

National Women's Health Network. (2000). *Taking hormones and women's health: Choices, risks, and benefits.* Washington, DC: National Women's Health Network.

Nezu, A. M., Nezu, C. M., Trunzo, J. J., & McClure, K. S. (1998). Treatment maintenance for unipolar depression: Relevant issues, literature review, and recommendations for research and clinical practice. *Clinical Psychology, 5,* 496–512.

Nietzel, M. T., Russell, R. L., Hemmings, K. A., & Gretter, M. L. (1987). Clinical significance of psychotherapy for unipolar depression: A meta-analytic approach to social comparison. *Journal of Consulting and Clinical Psychology, 55,* 156–161.

Nolen-Hoeksema, S. (1987). Sex differences in unipolar depression: Evidence and theory. *Psychological Bulletin, 101,* 259–282.

Nolen-Hoeksema, S. N. (1990). *Sex differences in depression.* Stanford: Stanford University Press.

Nolen-Hoeksema, S. N., & Gingus, J. S. (1994). The emergence of gender differences in depression during adolescence. *Psychological Bulletin, 115,* 424–443.

Nolen-Hoeksema, S. N., Larson, J., & Grayson, C. (1999). Explaining the gender differences in depression. *Journal of Personality and Social Psychology, 77* (5), 1061–1072.

Norcross, J. C. (1999). Collegially validated limitations of empirically validated treatments. *Clinical Psychology: Science and Practice, 6* (4), 472–476.

Norquist, G., Lebowitz, B., & Hyman, S. (1999). Expanding the frontier of treatment research. *Prevention & Treatment, 2,* 1–10.

Orlinsky, D. E., Grawe, K., & Parks, B. K. (1994). Process and outcome in psychotherapy. In A. E. Bergin & S. L. Garfield (Eds.), *Handbook of psychotherapy and behavior change* (pp. 270–378). New York: Wiley.

Ossana, S. M., Helms, J. E., & Leonard, M. M. (1992). Do "womanist" identity attitudes influence college women's self-esteem and perceptions of environmental bias? *Journal of Counseling and Development, 70,* 402–408.

Pallesen, S., Nordhus, I. H., Havik, O. E., & Nielsen, G. H. (2001). Clinical assessment and treatment of insomnia. *Professional Psychology: Research and Practice, 32* (2), 115–124.

Parlee, M. B. (1992). On PMS and psychiatric abnormality. *Feminism & Psychology, 2* (1), 105–108.

Parry, B. L. (1992). Reproductive-related depressions in women: Phenomenon of hormonal kindling. In J. A. Hamilton & P. N. Harberger (Eds.), *Postpartum psychiatric illness: A picture puzzle* (pp. 200–218). Philadelphia: University of Pennsylvania Press.

Paykel, E. S., Myers, J. K., Dienelt, M. N., Klerman, G. L., Lindenthal, J. J., & Pepper, M. P. (1969). Life events and depression: A controlled study. *Archives of General Psychiatry, 21,* 753–760.

Pearlman, L. A., & Saakvitne, K. W. (1995). *Trauma and the therapist: Countertransference and vicarious traumatization in psychotherapy with incest survivors.* New York: Norton.

Pearlstein, T. B., Frank, E., Rivera-Tovar, A., Thoft, J. S., Jacobs, E., & Mieczkowski, T. A. (1990). Prevalence of Axis I and Axis II disorders in women with late luteal phase dysphoric disorder. *Journal of Affective Disorder, 20,* 129–134.

Peden, A. R. (1991). *The process of recovering in women who have been depressed.* Doctoral dissertation. University of Alabama at Birmingham.

Peruzzi, N., & Bongar, B. (1999). Assessing risk for completed suicide in patients with major depression: Psychologists views of critical factors. *Professional Psychology: Research and Practice, 30* (6), 576–580.

Piaget, J. (1971). *Psychology and epistemology: Towards a theory of knowledge.* New York: Viking.

Piotrkowski, C. S. (1998). Gender harassment, job satisfaction, and distress among employed white and minority women. *Journal of Occupational Health and Psychology, 3* (1), 33–43.

Pope, K. S., & Tabachnick, B. G. (1994). Therapists as patients: A national survey of psychologists experiences, problems, and beliefs. *Professional Psychology: Research and Practice, 25,* 247–258.

Pope, K. S., & Vasquez, M. J. T. (1998). *Ethics in counseling: A practical guide* (2nd ed.). San Francisco: Jossey-Bass.

Raquepaw, J. M., & Miller, R. S. (1989). Psychotherapist burnout: A componential analysis. *Professional Psychology: Research and Practice, 20,* 32–36.

Range, L. M., & Knott, E. C. (1997). Twenty suicide assessment instruments: Evaluation and recommendations. *Death Studies, 21* (1), 25–58.

Raskin, V. D. (1997). *When words are not enough: The women's prescription for depression and anxiety.* New York: Broadway.

Rao, U., Hammen, C., & Daley, S. E. (1999). Continuity of depression during the transition to adulthood: A 5-year longitudinal study of young women. *Journal of the American Academy of Child & Adolescent Psychiatry, 38* (7), 908–915.

Reich, R., & Nussbaum, K. (1994). *Working women count! A report to the nation.* Washington, DC: U.S. Department of Labor.

Reynolds, C. F., Frank, E., Perel, J. M., Imber, S. D., Cornes, C., Miller, M. D., Mazumdar, S., Houck, P. R., Dew, M. A., Stack, J. A., Pollock, B. G., & Kupfer, D. J. (1999). Nortriptyline and interpersonal psychotherapy as maintenance for recurrent major depression: A randomized trial in patients older than 59 years. *Journal of the American Medical Association, 281* (1), 39–45.

Ritter, K. Y. (1993). Depression in women. In E. P. Cook (Ed.), *Women, relationships, and power: Implications for counseling* (pp. 139–178). Alexandria, VA: American Counseling Association.

Rivas-Vazquez, R. A., Johnson, S. L., Blais, M. A., & Rey, G. J. (1999). Selective serotonin reuptake inhibitor discontinuation syndrome: Understanding, recognition, and management for psychologists. *Professional Psychology: Research and Practice, 30* (5), 464–469.

Roberts, J. E., Gilboa, E., & Gotlib, I. H. (1998). Ruminative response style and vulnerability to episodes of dysphoria: Gender, neuroticism, and episode duration. *Cognitive Therapy & Research, 22,* 401–423.

Roberts, R. E., Kaplan, G. A., Shema, S. J., & Strawbridge, W. J. (1997). Does growing old increase the risk for depression? *American Journal of Psychiatry, 154* (10), 1384–1390.

Robins, L. N., & Reiger, D. A. (1991). *Psychiatric disorders in American: The Epidemiological Catchment Area Study.* New York: Free Press.

Robinson, L. A., Berman, J. A., & Neimeyer, R. A. (1990). Psychotherapy for the treatment of depression: A comprehensive review of controlled outcome research. *Psychological Bulletin, 108,* 30–49.

Root, M. P. P. (1990). Resolving the "other" status: Identity development of biracial individuals. *Women and Therapy, 9,* 185–205.

Rossello, J., & Bernal, G. (1999). The efficacy of cognitive-behavioral and interpersonal treatments for depression in Puerto Rican adolescents. *Journal of Consulting and Clinical Psychology, 67* (5), 734–745.

Roth, A., & Fonagy, P. (1996). *What works for whom? A critical review of psychotherapy research.* New York: Guilford.

Rothblum, E. D. (1990). Depression among lesbians: An invisible and unresearched phenomenon. *Journal of Gay & Lesbian Psychotherapy, 1,* 67–87.

Russo, N. F., & Dabul, A. J. (1997). The relationship of abortion to well-being: Do race and religion make a difference? *Professional Psychology: Research and Practice, 28* (1), 23–31.

Sacco, W. P., & Beck, A. T. (1995). Cognitive theory and therapy. In E. E. Beckham & W. R. Leber (Eds.), *Handbook of depression* (pp. 329–351). New York: Guilford.

Safran, J. D., & Inck, T. A. (1995). Psychotherapy integration: Implications for the treatment of depression. In E. E. Beckham & W. R. Leber (Eds.), *Handbook of depression* (pp. 425–434). New York: Guilford.

Sanfilipo, M. P. (1994). Masculinity, feminity, and subjective experience of depression. *Journal of Clinical Psychology, 50,* 144–157.

Sato, T. (1997). Seasonal affective disorder: A critical review. *Professional Psychology: Research and Practice, 28,* 164–169.

Sayers, S. L., Baucom, D. H., & Tierney, A. M. (1993). Sex roles, interpersonal control, and depression: Who can get their way. *Journal of Research in Personality, 27,* 377–395.

Schreiber, R. (1996). (Re)defining my self: Women's process of recovery from depression. *Qualitative Health Research, 6,* 469–491.

Schulberg, H. C., Pilkonis, P. A., & Houck, P. (1998). The severity of major depression and choice of treatment in primary care practice. *Journal of Consulting and Clinical Psychology, 66* (6), 932–938.

Schwartz, G. E., Fair, P. L., Salt, P., Mandel, M. R., & Klerman, G. (1979). Facial expression and imagery in depression: An electromyographic study. In S. Weitz (Ed.), *Nonverbal communication* (pp. 54–63). New York: Oxford University Press.

Schwartz, P. J., Brown, C., Wehr, T. A., & Rosenthal, N. E. (1996). Winter seasonal affective disorder: A follow-up study of the first 59 patients in the National Institute of Mental Health Seasonal Studies Program. *American Journal of Psychiatry, 153* (8), 1028–1036.

Schwartzman, J. B., & Glaus, K. D. (2000). Depression and coronary heart disease in women: Implications for clinical practice and research. *Professional Psychology: Research and Practice, 31* (1), 48–57.

Sears, S. F., Danda, C. E., & Evans, G. D. (1999). PRIME-MD and rural primary care: Detecting depression in a low-income rural population. *Professional Psychology: Research and Practice, 30* (4), 357–360.

Seeman, M. V. (1997). Psychopathology in women and men: Focus on female hormones. *American Journal of Psychiatry, 152* (12), 1641–1647.

Seligman, M. E. P. (1975). *Helplessness: On depression, development, and death.* San Francisco: Freeman.

Seligman, M. E. P. (1991). *Learned optimism.* New York: Knopf.

Seligman, M. E. P., & Csikscentmihalyi, M. (2000). Positive psychology: An introduction. *American Psychologist, 55* (1), 5–14.

Seligman, M. E. P., Schulman, P., DeRubeis, R. J., & Hollon, S. D. (1999). The prevention of depression and anxiety. *Prevention & Treatment, 2* (8), 1–23.

Shalev, A. Y., Freedman, S., Peri, T., Brandes, D., Sahar, T., Orr, S. P., & Pitman, R. K. (1998). Prospective study of posttraumatic stress disorder and depression following trauma. *American Journal of Psychiatry, 155,* 630–637.

Shapiro, F. (1995). *Eye movement desensitization and reprocessing: Principles, protocols, and procedures.* New York: Guilford.

Shea, M. T., Elkin, I., Imber, S. D., Sotsky, S. M., Watkins, J. T., Collins, J. F., Pilkonis, P. A., Beckman, E., Glass, D. R., Dolan, R. T., & Parloff, M. B. (1992). Course of depressive symptoms over follow-up: Findings from the Treatment of Depression Collaborative Research Program. *Archives of General Psychiatry, 49,* 782–787.

Sheehy, G. (1998). *The silent passage: Menopause.* New York: Simon & Schuster.

Sichel, D., & Driscoll, J. W. (1999). *Women's moods: What every woman must know about hormones, the brain, and emotional health.* New York: William Morrow.

Silverstein, B. (1999). Gender differences in the prevalence of clinical depression: The role played by depression associated with somatic symptoms. *American Journal of Psychiatry, 156,* 480–482.

Silverstein, B., & Blumenthal, E. (1997). Depression mixed with anxiety, somaticization, and disordered eating: Relationship with gender-role limitation experienced by females. *Sex Roles, 36,* 709–724.

Silverstein, B., & Lynch, A. D. (1998). Gender differences in depression: The role played by paternal attitudes of male superiority and maternal modeling of gender-limited roles. *Sex Roles, 38,* 539–555.

Silverstein, S., & Perlick, D. (1995). *The cost of competence.* New York: Oxford University Press.

Simonds, S. L. (1994). *Bridging the silence: Nonverbal modalities in the treatment of adult survivors of childhood sexual abuse.* New York: Norton.

Simonds, S. L. (1995). *Sleep tips.* Counseling and Testing Services Self-help Website. Washington State University. Pullman, WA. Retrieved April 24, 2000 from the World Wide Web: http://www.counsel.wsu.edu/csweb/sleep.htm.

Simonds, S. L. (1999, March). *Therapy with depressed women: An integrative approach.* Professional training seminar at Washington State University Counseling and Testing Services, Pullman, WA.

Simonds, S. L. (2000a, March). *Therapy with depressed women: An integrative approach.* Continuing education seminar for The 25th Annual Association of Women in Psychology Conference, Salt Lake City, UT.

Simonds, S. L. (2000b, January) *Women and depression: An integrative treatment approach.* Seminar for Palouse Continuing Education Consortium, Moscow, ID.

Simons, A. D., Murphy, G. E., Levine, J. L., & Wetzel, R. D. (1986). Cognitive therapy and pharmacotherapy for depression: Sustained improvement over one year. *Archives of General Psychiatry, 43* (1), 43–48.

Smith, M., & Lin, K. M. (1996). Gender and ethnic differences in the pharmacogenetics of psychotropics. In M. F. Jensvold, U. Halbreich, & J. A. Hamilton (Eds.), *Psychopharmacology and women: Sex, gender, and hormones* (pp. 121–136). Washington, DC: American Psychiatric Press.

Solomon, D. A., Keller, M. B., Leon, A. C., Mueller, T. I., Lavori, P. W., Shea, M. T., Coryell, W., Warshaw, M., Turvey, C., Maser, J. D., & Endicott, J. (2000). Multiple recurrences of major depressive disorder. *American Journal of Psychiatry, 157* (2), 229–233.

Sommers-Flanagan, J., & Sommers-Flanagan, R. (1995). Intake interviewing with suicidal patients: A systematic approach. *Professional Psychology: Research and Practice, 26* (1), 41–47.

Sommers-Flanagan, R., & Sommers-Flanagan, J. (1999.) *Clinical interviewing* (2nd ed.) New York: Wiley.

Sommerville, P. D., Leaf, P. J., Weissman, M. M., Blazer, D. G., & Bruce, M. L. (1989). The prevalence of major depression in black and white adults in five United States communities. *American Journal of Epidemiology, 130,* 725–735.

Sorenson, S. B., Rutter, C. M., & Aneshensel, C. S. (1991). Depression in the community: An investigation into age at onset. *Journal of Consulting and Clinical Psychology, 59,* 541–546.

Sotsky, S. M. (1997, May). Pharmacotherapy and psychotherapy response in atypical depression: Findings from the Treatment for Depression Collaborative Research Program. Paper presented at the American Psychiatric Association Annual Meeting, San Diego, CA.

Sprock, J., & Yoder, C. Y. (1997). Women and depression: An update on the report of the APA Task Force. *Sex Roles, 36,* 269–303.

State of the art on popular supplements. (2000, May). *Consumer Reports,* 19.

Stewart, D. E. (1998). Are there special considerations in the prescription of serotonin reuptake inhibitors for women? *Canadian Journal of Psychiatry, 43* (9), 900–904.

Staats, A. W. (1996). *Behavior and personality: Psychological behaviorism.* New York: Springer-Verlag.

Stice, E., Hayward, D., Cameron, R. P., Killen, J., & Taylor, C. B. (2000). Body-image and eating disturbances predict onset of depression among female adolescents: A longitudinal study. *Journal of Abnormal Psychology, 109* (3), 438–444.

Stiver, I. P. (1994). Women's struggles in the workplace: A relational model. In M. P. Mirkin (Ed.), *Women in context: Toward a feminist reconstruction of psychotherapy* (pp. 433–452). New York: Guilford.

Stiver, I. P., & Miller, J. B. (1997). From depression to sadness in women's psychotherapy. In J. V. Jordan (Ed.), *Women's growth in diversity: More writings from the Stone Center* (pp. 217–238). New York: Guilford.

Stoppard, J. M. (1989). An evaluation of the adequacy of cognitive/behavioral theories for understanding depression in women. *Canadian Psychology, 30,* 39–49.

Stricker, G. (1994). Reflections on psychotherapy integration. *Clinical Psychology: Science & Practice, 1* (1), 3–12.

Sue, D. W., & Sue, D. (1990). *Counseling the culturally different: Theory and practice* (2nd ed.). New York: Wiley.

Sullivan, H. S. (1953). *The interpersonal theory of psychiatry.* New York: Norton.

Sullivan, P. F., Neale, M. C., & Kendler, K. S. (2000). Genetic epidemiology of major depression: Review and meta-analysis. *American Journal of Psychiatry, 157* (10), 1552–1562.

Swanson, N. G. (2000). Working women and stress. *Journal of the American Medical Women's Association, 55* (2), 76–79.

Swendsen, J. D., & Mazure, C. M. (2000). Life stress as a risk factor for postpartum depression: Current research and methodological issues. *Clinical Psychology: Science and Practice, 7* (1), 17–31.

Tallman, K., & Bohart, A. C. (1999). The client as a common factor: Clients as self-healers. In M. A. Hubble, B. L. Duncan, & S. D. Miller (Eds.), *The heart and soul of change: What works in therapy* (pp. 91–131). Washington, DC: American Psychological Association.

Teasdale, J. D., Segal, Z. V., Zindel, V., Williams, J. M. G., Ridgeway, V. A., Soulsby, J. M., & Lau, M. A. (2000). Prevention of relapse/recurrence in major depression by mindfulness-based cognitive therapy. *Journal of Consulting and Clinical Psychology, 68* (4), 615–623.

Tennant, C. (1985). Female vulnerability to depression. *Psychological Medicine, 15,* 733–737.

Thase, M. E., Frank, E., Kornstein, S. G., & Yonkers, K. A. (2000). Gender differences in response to treatments of depression. In E. Frank (Ed.), *Gender and its effect on psychopathology* (pp. 103–129). Washington, DC: American Psychiatric Press.

Thase, M. E., Simons, A. D., McGeary, J., Cahalane, J. F., Huges, C., Harden, T., & Friedman, E. (1992). Relapse after cognitive behavior therapy of depression: Potential implications for longer courses of treatment. *American Journal of Psychiatry, 149,* 1046–1052.

Thornicroft, G., & Sartorius, N. (1993). The course and outcome of depression in different cultures: 10-year follow-up of the WHO Collaborative Study on the Assessment of Depressive Disorders. *Psychological Medicine, 23,* 1023–1032.

Tkachuk, G. A., & Martin, G. I. (1999). Exercise therapy for patients with psychiatric disorders: Research and clinical implications. *Professional Psychology: Research and Practice, 30,* 275–282.

Turvey, C. L., Carney, C., Arndt, S., Wallace, R. B., & Herzog, R. (1999). Conjugal loss and subsyndromal depression in a sample of elders aged 70 years or older. *American Journal of Psychiatry, 156* (10), 1596–1601.

van Roosmalen, E., & McDaniel, S. A. (1998). Sexual harassment in academia: A hazard to women's health. *Women & Health, 28* (2), 33–54.

Veiel, H. O. F. (1993). Detrimental effects of kin support networks on the course of depression. *Journal of Abnormal Psychology, 102,* 419–429.

Walker, L. E. A. (1984). *Battered woman syndrome.* New York: Springer Publishing.

Walrath, J., Li, F. P., Hoar, S. K., Mead, M. W., & Fraumeni, J. F., Jr. (1985). Causes of death among female chemists. *American Journal of Public Health, 75,* 883–885.

Watson, M. F. (2000, November/December). Learning to heal the healer. *Family Therapy Networker,* 23–24.

Weissman, M. M., Leaf, P. J., Tischler, G. L., Blazer, D. G., Karno, M., Bruce, M. L., & Florio, L. P. (1988). Affective disorders in five United States communities. *Psychological Medicine, 18,* 141–153.

Weissman, M. M., & Markowitz, J. C. (1994). Interpersonal psychotherapy: Current status. *Archives of General Psychiatry, 51,* 599–606.

Weissman, M. M., & Markowitz, J. C. (1998). An overview of interpersonal psychotherapy. In J. C. Markowitz (Ed.), *Interpersonal psychotherapy.* Washington, DC: American Psychiatric Press.

Weissman, M. M., & Meyers, J. K. (1978). Affective disorders in a US urban community: The use of Research Diagnostic Criteria in an epidemiologic survey. *Archives of General Psychiatry, 35,* 1304–1311.

White, M., & Epston, D. (1990). *Narrative means to therapeutic ends.* New York: Norton.

White, M. T., Lemkau, J. P., & Clasen, M. E. (2001). Fibromyalgia: A feminist biopsychosocial perspective. *Women & Therapy, 23,* 45–58.

Wilhelm, R. (1977). *The i ching* (Baynes, C. F., Trans.). Princeton, NJ: Princeton University Press. (Original work published 1924).

Winnicott, D. W. (1965). *Maturational processes and the facilitating environment.* New York: International Universities Press.

Wisner, K. L., Perel, J. M., & Findling, R. L. (1996). Antidepressant treatment during breast-feeding. *American Journal of Psychiatry, 153* (9), 1132–1146.

Wolfe, J. L., & Fodor, I. G. (1975). A cognitive/behavioral approach to modifying assertive behavior in women. *Counseling Psychologist, 5* (4), 45–59.

Wolk, S. I., & Weissman, M. M. (1995). Women and depression: An update. *American Psychiatric Press Review of Psychiatry, 14,* 227–259.

Woods, N. F., & Mitchell, E. S. (1996). Patterns of depressed mood in midlife women: Observations from Seattle Midlife Women's Health Study. *Research in Nursing & Health, 19* (2), 111–123.

Worrell, J., & Remer, P. (1992). *Feminist perspectives in therapy: An empowerment model.* New York: Wiley.

Yahne, C. E., & Miller, W. R. (1999). Evoking hope. In W. R. Miller (Ed.), *Integrating spirituality into treatment: Resources for practitioners* (pp. 217–233). Washington, DC: American Psychological Association.

Yalom, I. D. (1975). *The theory and practice of group psychotherapy.* New York: Basic Books, Inc.

Yapko, M. (2000, April). *Understanding depression: A seminar for health professionals.* Clarkston, WA.

Yonkers, K. A., & Bradshaw, K. D. (1999). Hormone replacement and oral contraceptive therapy: Do they induce or treat mood symptoms? In E. Leibenluft, (Ed.), *Gender differences in mood and anxiety disorders: From bench to bedside* (pp. 91–135). Washington, DC: American Psychiatric Press.

Young, E., & Korszun, A. (1998). Psychoneuroendocrinology of depression: Hypothalmic-pituitary-gonadal axis. *Psychiatric Clinics of North America, 21* (2), 309–323.

Zhang, A. Y., & Snowden, L. R. (1999). Ethnic characteristics of mental disorders in five U.S. communities: Cultural diversity and ethnic minority. *Psychology, 5* (2), 134–146.

Zlotnick, C., Elkin, I., & Shea, M. T. (1998). Does the gender of a patient or the gender of a therapist affect the treatment of patients with major depression? *Journal of Consulting and Clinical Psychology, 66,* 655–659.

# Author's Note

The Elements of Therapy logo is a visual-symbolic representation of Integrative Relational Therapy. This image came to me over a period of months as I took walks in the rural area near my house between my many hours of writing at the computer. When I first envisioned the logo, I did not realize that it was a mirror of the Chinese mandala representing the five essential elements as depicted in the oldest book on earth, the *I Ching*.

The design of concentric circles is common to Buddhist mandalas. The smile represents therapy as a holding environment with the therapist's smile being a mirror for the client. This aspect of the logo was also inspired by the research on smiling and depression (Schwartz et al., 1979) with which I became familiar as a graduate student studying nonverbal behavior in a dance/movement therapy curriculum. I am sure my many years as a Chinese scholar embedded these ways of thinking and seeing in my head. However, I believe my experience of developing the Elements of Therapy logo captures the universality of the multidimensional nature of human endeavors. In other words, it simply describes what is.

# Index